Behavior

in Public Places

Behavior in Public Places

NOTES ON THE SOCIAL ORGANIZATION OF GATHERINGS

ERVING GOFFMAN

THE FREE PRESS
A Division of Macmillan Publishing Co., Inc.
New York

Collier Macmillan Publishers
London

THE FREE PRESS
A Division of Macmillan Publishing Co., Inc.
866 Third Avenue, New York, N.Y. 10022

Collier Macmillan Canada, Ltd.

Library of Congress Catalog Card Number: 62-11850

Printed in the United States of America

First Free Press Paperback Edition 1966

printing number
12   13   14   15   16   17   18   19   20

Acknowledgments

MUCH of the material for this report was gathered in 1954-1957 while I was a visiting member of the Laboratory of Socio-environmental Studies of the National Institute of Mental Health. The mental hospital material derives chiefly from a year's participant observation study of the social life of mental patients, done under the auspices of the Laboratory in 1955-1956. I am grateful to the then Laboratory Chief, John A. Clausen, and to Dr. Winfred Overholser, the then Superintendent of Saint Elizabeths Hospital, Washington, D.C., for what turned out to be complete freedom to look at whatever I wanted and to publish records of what I saw. I am grateful also to the Society for the Study of Human Ecology, whose support allowed me to spend the summer of 1959 working on the manuscript, and to the University of California's Center for the Integration of Social Science Theory, through which I obtained time off from teaching during 1958-1960 for further work on the manuscript.

I would like to express my gratitude to David Schneider, Charlotte Green Schwartz, Gregory Stone, and Fred and Marcia Davis for much help in the early organization of this report.

Contents

PART ONE

Introduction

CHAPTER 1

The Problem

IN DIAGNOSING mental disorder and following its hospital course, psychiatrists typically cite aspects of the patient's behavior that are "inappropriate in the situation." Since this special kind of misconduct is believed to provide one obvious sign of "mental sickness," psychiatrists have given much time to these improprieties, developing the orientation and observational skills needed to study them, describing them in detail, seeking to understand their meaning for the patient, and obtaining a mandate to discuss them in the academic press—a mandate required because many of these delicts are petty, embarrassing, or messy. We sociologists should be grateful for this harvest, all the more so because it has been brought in by delicate hands. We can express our gratitude by trying to appropriate the yield for our own market, offering in exchange some observations about social situations that we appropriated long ago from anthropology.

By and large, the psychiatric study of situational improprieties has led to studying the offender rather than the rules and social circles that are offended. Through such studies, however, psychiatrists have inadvertently made us more aware of an important area of social life—that of behavior in public and semipublic places. Although this area has not been recognized as a special domain for sociological inquiry, it perhaps should be, for rules of conduct in streets, parks, restaurants, theaters, shops, dance floors, meeting halls, and other gathering places of any community tell us a great deal about its most diffuse forms of social organization.

Sociology does not provide a ready framework that can order these data, let alone show comparisons and continuities with behavior in private gathering places such as offices, factory floors, living rooms, and kitchens. To be sure, one part of "collective behavior"—riots, crowds, panics—has been established as something to study. But the remaining part of the area, the study of ordinary human traffic and the patterning of ordinary social contacts, has been little considered. It is well recognized, for instance, that mobs can suddenly emerge from the peaceful flow of human traffic, if conditions are right. But little concern seems to have been given to the question of what structure this peaceful intercourse possesses when mob formation is not an issue. It is the object of this report to try to develop such a framework. Some data have been drawn from a study of a mental hospital[1] (hereafter called Central Hospital), some from a study of a Shetland Island community[2] (hereafter called Shetland Isle), some from manuals of etiquette, and some from a file where I keep quotations that have struck me as interesting. Obviously, many of these data are of doubtful worth, and my interpretations— especially of some of them—may certainly be questionable, but I assume that a loose speculative approach to a fundamental area of conduct is better than a rigorous blindness to it.

I will rely on the familiar distinction between acts that are approved and acts that are felt to be improper. This simple dichotomy makes for economy of presentation, allowing me to bypass unresolved issues and to proceed to ones that might be resolved. Before taking this license, however, some matters it covers should be mentioned.

1. Saint Elizabeths Hospital, Washington, D.C. This is a 7000-bed Federal hospital, which functions chiefly as the public mental hospital for the District of Columbia.

2. A community of 300 with a subsistence farming economy studied for a year in 1949-51, reported in part in E. Goffman, "Communication Conduct in an Island Community" (unpublished Ph.D. dissertation, Department of Sociology, University of Chicago, 1953).

Although some specific illustrations used in this report are taken from sources dealing with non-Western society, my own experience has been mainly with middle-class conduct in a few regions of America, and it is to this that most of my comments apply. An act can, of course, be proper or improper only according to the judgment of a specific social group, and even within the confines of the smallest and warmest of groups there is likely to be some dissensus and doubt. The degree of dissensus or consensus in a group concerning the propriety of an act—and even the boundaries of the group itself—cannot be established by my assertions but only by systematic empirical research. This report, however, is full of such unverified assertions. Yet this avowed weakness should not be confused with one that is disavowed: nowhere in this report do I mean to convey that I personally hold some act to be proper or improper, although the method of presentation may occasionally give this impression.

It is in the context of this middle-class point of reference that I want to explain my use of quotations from etiquette manuals. When Mrs. Emily Post makes a pronouncement as to how persons of cultivation act, and how other persons ought therefore to act, sociologists often become offended. Their good reason for snubbing Mrs. Post is that she provides little evidence that the circle about which she speaks has any numerical or social significance, that its members do in fact conduct themselves as she says they do, or even that these persons—or any others—consider that one *ought* so to conduct oneself.

These doubts impute much more creativity to etiquette writers than they possess. Although these writers do not empirically test their claims as to what is regarded as proper, it seems to me they are still describing some of the norms that *influence* the conduct of our middle classes, even though on many occasions other factors will predominate. Moreover, these books are one of the few sources of suggestions about the structure of public conduct in America. It is my feeling that the main drawback to using these books as data for social science is not the unvalidated nature of the statements they contain—for statements can always be checked by research—but rather that these books tend to

provide a mere catalogue of proprieties instead of an analysis of
the system of norms underlying those proprieties.

In America only a few sociologists, such as W. Lloyd Warner,
and a few historians, such as Arthur M. Schlesinger,[3] have given
attention to etiquette manuals; I know of even fewer psychiatrists who consider that they are dealing with the same issues as
do these books. Yet it might be argued that one of the best
guides to a systematic understanding of the observable conduct
of mental patients in and out of hospitals, and of others' response
to this conduct, is to be found in etiquette manuals.

In addition to the question of evidence, there is another problem in using the naive distinction between approved and disap-
proved behavior; namely, that the concept of approval itself is
by no means innocent, covering an array of ill-explored
variables.

One variable has to do with the strength of approval for up-
holding the rule. Some approved acts receive applause upon performance, as when heroism or very great skill is displayed. Some
pass quite unnoticed and do not constitute a felt event, as when
an American high-school girl refrains from wearing nylon hose
with her saddle shoes but wears bobby socks instead.[4]

A second variable has to do with the consequence of failing to
uphold the rule. At one extreme are acts, neither demanded nor
expected, that are rarely performed. Some of these are recorded
in etiquette books as exemplary instances of meticulous courtesy, more to illustrate the ideal forces that it is felt should be at
work in society than to provide a recipe for daily living. At the
other extreme are mandatory acts such as the paying of fines,
where failure to comply may lead to jail. Between these extremes
are "tolerated" acts, which are specifically noted with only an
inhibited frown, constituting offenses that the offended person,
given the setting, is obliged to let pass.

Nor do these two variables, a type of approval and a type of

3. Specifically in his *Learning How to Behave* (New York: The Macmillan Company, 1946).

4. C. W. Gordon, *The Social System of the High School* (New York: The Free
Press of Glencoe, 1957), p. 118.

disapproval, in their various combinations, complete the picture. The whole matter is further complicated by the fact that these two variables often refer not to concrete kinds of acts, such as the raising of one's hat to a lady, but to classes of acts, the members of which are phenomenally different but normatively equivalent and substitutable in the setting. And even these classes are themselves of various sizes. For example, the requirement of "formal dress" may oblige a woman to wear her only evening dress, whereas the requirement "afternoon dress," equally a normative stipulation, is one the individual may satisfy through what she feels is freedom to choose among her three afternoon ensembles. Freedom of choice within a class of required conduct may blind the individual to constraint regarding the class as a whole.

It can be seen, then, how much mischief may be done by equating two situations because the same act is "approved" in each, since approval itself can mean significantly different things. I can only note that in this report one type of approved act will be of central importance—the "negatively eventful" kind, which gives rise to specific negative sanctions if not performed, but which, if it is performed, passes unperceived as an event.

A prefatory conceptual note must be added here. A conceptual model frequently employed these days in the social sciences is the "closed natural system." Such a system of concrete behavior involves a differentiation of activities whose integration, one with another, allows for the emergence of over-all functions maintained through an equilibrium of interaction of the component activities. Presumably, the equilibrium can be of different kinds—self-corrective, moving, and the like.

A less complicated conceptual model is the "game." In the standard "zero-sum" type there is an orderly exchange of moves among a small number of teams, the moves being made in accordance with restricting rules. The moves made by one team add up to a single line of effort directed toward frustrating the design of the other teams' action, the whole game engendering a single unfolding history of mutually oriented, antagonistic lines of action.[5]

In this report I propose to employ a framework that is much simpler than that of the natural system or the game, but more inclusive: the model of "social order." Briefly, a social order may be defined as the consequence of any set of moral norms that regulates the way in which persons pursue objectives. The set of norms does not specify the objectives the participants are to seek, nor the pattern formed by and through the coordination or integration of these ends, but merely the modes of seeking them. Traffic rules and the consequent traffic order provide an obvious example. Any social system or any game may be viewed quite properly as an instance of social order, although the perspective of social order does not allow us to get at what is characteristically systemic about systems or what is gamelike about games.

There appear to be many types of social order, of which the legal order and the economic order are important examples. Within each such order, mere behavior is transformed into a corresponding type of conduct. Particular concrete acts, of course, are likely to be performed in accordance with the regulations of more than one of these orders.

In this study I shall try to be concerned with one type of regulation only, the kind that governs a person's handling of himself and others during, and by virtue of, his immediate physical presence among them; what is called face-to-face or immediate interaction will be involved.

Here a note should be added about the term "public." The norms supporting public order, as public order is traditionally defined, regulate not only face-to-face interaction but also matters that need not entail immediate contact between persons: for example, during medieval times, the obligation (often ill-sustained) to keep one's pigs out of the streets, even though

5. There are "non-zero-sum" games of coordination and collaboration, but the analysis of these games seems to start with zero-sum games.

there was much available there for pigs to eat,[6] and the obligation to extinguish lights and fires by a given hour lest the town be endangered by fire.[7] Nowadays, a householder is obliged to maintain his walks and roads in good repair and to keep his town land free of noxious refuse. In addition, public order traditionally refers more to the regulation of face-to-face interaction among those members of a community who are not well acquainted than it does to interaction occurring in private walled-in places where only familiars meet. Traditionally, "public places" refer to any regions in a community freely accessible to members of that community; "private places" refer to soundproof regions where only members or invitees gather— the traditional concern for public order beginning only at the point where a private gathering begins to obtrude upon the neighbors. Although I will use these terms in these traditional ways, it should be appreciated that no analytical significance is implied. In the study of *groups*, the distinction between primary and secondary and between private and public meeting places may indeed be significant, but in the study of *gatherings*, all occasions when two or more persons are present to one another can be fruitfully treated initially as a single class.

We will deal, then, with the component of behavior that plays a role in the physical traffic among people. Although it may be felt that this involves conduct of little weight, a matter merely of etiquette and manners, there have always been writers, such as Della Casa, who have provided hints that it is important, and why:

For though generosity, loyalty, and moral courage are without doubt nobler and more praiseworthy qualities than charm and courtesy, nevertheless polite habits and a correct manner of speech and behaviour may benefit those who possess them no less than a noble spirit and a stout heart benefit others. For since each one of us is daily obliged to meet other people and converse with them, we

6. G. T. Salusbury, *Street Life in Medieval England* (Oxford: Pen-in-Hand, 1948), pp. 65-69.
7. "Curfew," *Encyclopaedia Britannica* (14th ed., 1947), 6, 873-874.

need to use our manners many times each day. But justice, fortitude, and the other virtues of the higher and nobler sort are needed less frequently. We are not required to practise generosity or mercy at all hours, nor could any man do so very often. Similarly, those who are endowed with courage and strength are seldom called upon to show their valour by their deeds.[8]

Before proceeding, there are some ready answers to the question of proper public conduct that should be mentioned.

There are many social settings that persons of certain status are forbidden to enter. Here an effort to prevent penetration of ego-boundaries, contamination by undesirables, and physical assault seems to be involved.

Rules of trespass, for example, prevent unauthorized individuals from entering a private dwelling place at any time, and a semiprivate one during off hours. Less familiar are the many rulings that restrict the right to be present in open, unwalled public places: in nineteenth-century London, for example, the exclusion of certain categories from some parks, and the informal exclusion of common people from riding promenades such as Rotten Row; in Islamic cities built on a *quartier* basis, the restriction of persons to their own neighborhood after dark; the temporary prohibitions, during periods of martial law, upon being about after dark; evening curfews making it illegal for youths below a certain age to be about without the company of an adult; boarding-school rulings about late-hour presence on town streets; military rulings placing certain areas out of bounds or off limits for categories of personnel; informal police rulings requiring night-time racial segregation on public streets in designated areas of the city.

Where these rules of exclusion exist, it is plain that the individual's mere presence, regardless of his conduct while present, communicates either that he possesses the entrance qualifications or that he is behaving improperly. Here we find one motive for either wanting to enter a particular place or wanting not to be seen in it.

8. G. Della Casa, *Galateo*, trans. R. S. Pine-Coffin (London: Penguin Books, 1958), pp. 21-22.

I have suggested that in many situations certain categories of persons may not be authorized to be present, and that should they be present, this in itself will constitute an improper act. Common sense, however, also has something to say about those who are authorized to be present. The rule of behavior that seems to be common to all situations and exclusive to them is the rule obliging participants to "fit in." The words one applies to a child on his first trip to a restaurant presumably hold for everyone all the time: the individual must be "good" and not cause a scene or a disturbance; he must not attract undue attention to himself, either by thrusting himself on the assembled company or by attempting to withdraw too much from their presence. He must keep within the spirit or ethos of the situation; he must not be *de trop* or out of place. Occasions may even arise when the individual will be called upon to act as if he fitted into the situation when in fact he and some of the others present know this is not the case; out of regard for harmony in the scene he is required to compromise and endanger himself further by putting on an air of one who belongs when it can be shown that he doesn't. A brave instance may be cited from an early American etiquette book:

> If you should happen to be paying an evening visit at a house, where, unknown to you, there is a small party assembled, you should enter and present yourself precisely as you would have done had you been invited. To retire *precipitately* with an apology for the intrusion would create a *scene,* and be extremely awkward. Go in, therefore, converse with ease for a few moments, and then retire. Take care to let it be known the next day, in such a way as that the family shall hear of it, that you were not aware that there was any company there.[9]

No doubt different social groupings vary in the explicitness with which their members think in such terms, as well as in the phrases selected for doing so, but all groupings presumably have some concern for such "fitting in."

9. *The Laws of Etiquette,* by "A Gentleman" (Philadelphia: Carey, Lee and Blanchard, 1836), pp. 77-78.

The notion of "fitting in" relates to another bit of common sense: what is proper in one situation may certainly not be proper in another. The underlying general sentiment possessed by the individual—where in fact he has one—may have to give way to the requirements of the situation. This theme appears in social science literature in the form of "situational determinism," for example, in race relations studies, where it is pointed out that castelike taboos in one sphere of life can exist alongside equalitarianism in other spheres, although the same set of persons is involved.[10]

But here surely is the beginning of inquiry, not the end. Although an individual may conduct himself in a particular way solely because of the felt pressure of propriety, this merely tells us about one possible motive for conforming. We still do not know *why* this particular form of conduct is the one here approved—namely, how the ruling arose historically, and what its current social function is. To approach these issues, I must turn to a more roundabout analysis.

10. See, for example, J. Lohman and D. Reitzes, "Note on Race Relations in Mass Society," *American Journal of Sociology*, 58 (1952), 240-246; C. Rogler, "Some Situational Aspects of Race Relations in Puerto Rico," *Social Forces*, 27 (1949), 72-77.

CHAPTER 2

Introductory

Definitions

THE exchange of words and glances between individuals in each other's presence is a very common social arrangement, yet it is one whose distinctive communication properties are difficult to disentangle. Pedantic definitions seem to be required.

An individual may give information through the linguistic means formally established in society for this purpose, namely, speech or recognized speech substitutes such as writing and pictorial signs or gestures. One speaks here of an individual sending messages to someone who receives them. But the individual may also give information expressively, through the incidental symptomatic significance of events associated with him. In this case one might say that he emits, exudes, or gives off information to someone who gleans it. Linguistic messages can be "about" anything in the world, the sender and the subject matter having no necessary connection, coinciding only when autobiographical statements are being made. Expressive messages are necessarily "about" the same causal physical complex of which the transmitting agency is an intrinsic part. Consensus as to the meaning of linguistic messages seems more firmly established than it is in regard to that of expressive messages. Linguistic messages can be translated, stored, and held up as legal evidence; expressive messages tend to be ones for which the giver cannot be made legally responsible, it being usually possible for him to deny that he meant quite what others claim he meant. Linguistic messages are felt to be voluntary and intended; expressive messages, on the other hand, must often preserve the fiction that they are uncalculated, spontaneous, and involuntary, as in some cases they are.[1] Every linguistic message carries some expressive information, namely, that the sender is sending messages. In any case, most concrete messages combine linguistic and expressive components, the proportion of each differing widely from message to message.

The information that an individual provides, whether he sends it or exudes it, may be *embodied* or *disembodied*.[2] A frown, a spoken word, or a kick is a message that a sender conveys by means of his own *current* bodily activity, the transmission occurring only during the time that his body is present to sustain this activity. Disembodied messages, such as the ones we receive from letters and mailed gifts, or the ones hunters receive from the spoor of a now distant animal, require that the organism do something that traps and holds information long after the organism has stopped informing. This study will be concerned only with embodied information.

No ordinary English verb seems to cover all the senses—sight, hearing, smell, taste, and touch—that restrict the media and provide the receiving equipment through which an individual is able to obtain information. Terms such as "perceive," which have a special visual reference, have had to be used in a wider way, while terms such as "experience" have had to be used more narrowly. Some terms, such as "audit" or "monitor," have had to be manufactured.

In everyday thinking about the receiving senses, it is felt that ordinarily they are used in a "naked" or "direct" way. This apparently implies a restriction on boosting devices—mechanical,

1. The dichotomy "voluntary-involuntary" is one of the least innocent in our trade. Later in this report an effort will be made to suggest some of the problems it raises.

2. Compare the usage by T. S. Szasz, *The Myth of Mental Illness* (New York: Hoeber-Harper, 1961), p. 116 ff.

chemical, or electrical—except as these raise the faulty senses of a particular individual to average unassisted strength: glasses, for example, but not binoculars; hearing aids but not microphones. Electric lighting would have to be allowed as merely raising a room to day-time standards.

When one speaks of experiencing someone else with one's naked senses, one usually implies the reception of embodied messages. This linkage of naked senses on one side and embodied transmission on the other provides one of the crucial communication conditions of face-to-face interaction. Under this condition any message that an individual sends is likely to be qualified and modified by much additional information that others glean from him simultaneously, often unbeknownst to him; further, a very large number of brief messages may be sent.

Now the individual can, of course, receive embodied messages by means of his naked senses without much chance of these communication roles being reversed, as when he spies on persons through a crack in the wall or overhears them through a thin partition.[3] Such asymmetrical arrangements may even be established as part of an occupational setting, as in the procedure by which psychoanalysts or priests observe their clients without being as easily observed in return. Ordinarily, however, in using the naked senses to receive embodied messages from others, the individual also makes himself available as a source of embodied information for them (although there is always likely to be some differential exploitation of these monitoring possibilities). Here, then, is a second crucial communication condition of face-to-face interaction: not only are the receiving and conveying of

---

3. An asymmetrical communication relation of this kind, Polonius notwithstanding, is of course more practical when boosting devices, such as concealed microphones, are employed. In Shetland Isle pocket telescopes were commonly used for the purpose of observing one's neighbors without being observed in the act of observing. In this way it was possible to check constantly what phase of the annual cycle of work one's neighbors were engaged in, and who was visiting whom. This use of the telescope was apparently related to the physical distance between crofts, the absence of trees and other blocks to long-distance perception, and the strong maritime tradition of the Islands. It may be added that every community and even every work place would seem to have some special communication arrangements of its own.

the naked and embodied kind, but each giver is himself a receiver, and each receiver is a giver.

The implications of this second feature are fundamental. First, sight begins to take on an added and special role. Each individual can *see* that he is being experienced in some way, and he will guide at least some of his conduct according to the perceived identity and initial response of his audience.[4] Further, he can be seen to be seeing this, and can see that he has been seen seeing this. Ordinarily, then, to use our naked senses is to use them nakedly and to be made naked by their use. We are clearly seen as the agents of our acts, there being very little chance of disavowing having committed them; neither having given nor having received messages can be easily denied, at least among those immediately involved.[5]

The factor emerges, then, that was much considered by Adam Smith, Charles Cooley, and G. H. Mead; namely, the special mutuality of immediate social interaction. That is, when two persons are together, at least some of their world will be made up out of the fact (and consideration for the fact) that an adaptive line of action attempted by one will be either insightfully facilitated by the other or insightfully countered, or both, and that such a line of action must always be pursued in this intelligently helpful and hindering world. Individuals sympathetically take the attitude of others present, regardless of the end to which they put the information thus acquired.[6]

4. In the asymmetrical case, where a person is being spied upon by direct or indirect means, he may greatly modify his conduct if he suspects he is being observed, even though he does not know the identity of the particular audience that might be observing him. This is one of the possibilities celebrated in Orwell's *1984*, and its possibility is one of the forces operative in socially controlling persons who are alone.

5. When two-way television is added to telephones, the unique contingencies of direct interaction will finally be available for those who are widely separated. In any case these mediated "point-to-point" forms of communication can be characterized by the degree to which they restrict or attenuate the communicative possibilities discussed here.

6. As R. E. Park suggested in "Human Nature and Collective Behavior," *American Journal of Sociology*, 32 (1927), 738:

In human society every act of every individual tends to become a gesture, since what one does is always an indication of what one intends to do. The conse-

I have cited two distinctive features of face-to-face interaction: richness of information flow and facilitation of feedback. I suggest that these features have enough structuring significance to provide one analytical rationale for the separate treatment this report gives to the social norms regulating behavior of persons immediately present to one another.

The physical distance over which one person can experience another with the naked senses—thereby finding that the other is "within range"—varies according to many factors: the sense medium involved, the presence of obstructions, even the temperature of the air. On Shetland Isle, during cold nights, mainland visitors walking together along the bay in apparent isolation who laughed loudly by the strict local standards could cause Shetlanders an eighth of a mile away to raise their eyebrows. Conversely, when an individual whispers or uses eye expressions, his body acts as a focusing barrier, effectively restricting the usual sphere of propagation of sense stimuli, so that reception is limited to those very close to him or directly in front of him.

The full conditions of *copresence*, however, are found in less variable circumstances: persons must sense that they are close enough to be perceived in whatever they are doing, including their experiencing of others, and close enough to be perceived in this sensing of being perceived. In our walled-in Western society, these conditions are ordinarily expected to obtain throughout the space contained in a room, and to obtain for any and all persons present in the room. On public streets (and in other relatively unobstructed places) the region of space in which mutual presence can be said to prevail cannot be clearly drawn, since persons who are present at different points along the street may be able to observe, and be observed by, a slightly

---

quence is that the individual in society lives a more or less public existence, in which all his acts are anticipated, checked, inhibited, or modified by the gestures and the intentions of his fellows. It is in this social conflict, in which every individual lives more or less in the mind of every other individual, that human nature and the individual may acquire their most characteristic and human traits.

different set of others. This qualification aside, I shall use the term *gathering* to refer to any set of two or more individuals whose members include all and only those who are at the moment in one another's immediate presence. By the term *situation* I shall refer to the full spatial environment anywhere within which an entering person becomes a member of the gathering that is (or does then become) present. Situations begin when mutual monitoring occurs, and lapse when the second-last person has left. In order to stress the full extent of any such unit, I will sometimes employ the term *situation at large.*

Along with "gathering" and "situation," another basic concept must be tentatively defined. When persons come into each other's immediate presence they tend to do so as participants of what I shall call a *social occasion.* This is a wider social affair, undertaking, or event, bounded in regard to place and time and typically facilitated by fixed equipment; a social occasion provides the structuring social context in which many situations and their gatherings are likely to form, dissolve, and re-form, while a pattern of conduct tends to be recognized as the appropriate and (often) official or intended one—a "standing behavior pattern," to use Barker's term.[7] Examples of social occasions are a social party, a workday in an office, a picnic, or a night at the opera.

For the course of a social occasion, one or more participants may be defined as responsible for getting the affair under way, guiding the main activity, terminating the event, and sustaining order. Also, a differentiation is sometimes found among full-fledged participants and various grades of onlookers. Further, between beginning and end there is often an "involvement contour," a line tracing the rise and fall of general engrossment in the occasion's main activity.[8]

Some social occasions, a funeral, for example, have a fairly sharp beginning and end, and fairly strict limits on attendance

7. R. Barker and H. Wright, *Midwest and Its Children* (Evanston, Ill.: Row, Peterson, n.d.), p. 7 and pp. 45-46.
8. An illustration of social occasion analysis may be found in D. Riesman, R. Potter, and J. Watson, "The Vanishing Host," *Human Organization,* 19 (1960), 17-27.

and tolerated activities. Each class of such occasions possesses a distinctive ethos, a spirit, an emotional structure, that must be properly created, sustained, and laid to rest, the participant finding that he is obliged to become caught up in the occasion, whatever his personal feelings. These occasions, which are commonly programmed in advance, possess an agenda of activity, an allocation of management function, a specification of negative sanctions for improper conduct, and a preestablished unfolding of phases and a highpoint. Other occasions, like Tuesday afternoon downtown, are very diffuse indeed, and may not be seen by participants as entities with any appreciable development and structure of their own that can be looked forward to and looked back upon as a whole. (Here the individual may see a line of development in his own period of participation but not in the occasion as a whole.) In these cases the very useful term employed by Barker and his associates, *behavior setting,* might be sufficient.[9] Diffuse social occasions can, of course, develop a structure and direction as they go along.

Some social occasions, often called "unserious" or "recreational," are felt to be ends in themselves, and the individual avowedly participates for the consummate pleasure of doing so. Other occasions, called "serious," are officially seen as merely means to other ends. Finally, some occasions are seen as "regular" ones—instances that form part of a series of like occasions, the series being seen as a unit, and developing as such, in terms of a daily, weekly, or annual cycle, often with the same participants. Other occasions, such as spur-of-the-moment parties, are one-shot affairs, or their series-like character is not perceived as such.

There are many complications associated with the concept of social occasion,[10] but some such term must be used, for when a gathering occurs it does so under the auspices of a wider entity

9. Barker and Wright, *op. cit.,* pp. 7-10 and 45-50. The authors provide a very useful review of the conceptual problems involved in the use of such a term.

10. A description of the general characteristics of social occasions is attempted in "Communication Conduct," Chap. 9. A very good presentation of the complexities involved can be found in K. L. Pike, *Language in Relation to a Unified Theory of the Structure of Human Behavior* (Glendale, California: Summer Institute of Linguistics, 1954), Part 1.

of this kind. I hope it will become apparent that the regulations of conduct characteristic in situations and their gatherings are largely traceable to the social occasion in which they occur.

Since different participants in a social occasion may perform quite different roles, it might be argued that what is an occasion of play for one individual may be an occasion of work for another, as in the case of the guest and the servant at a party. Nevertheless, too much relativity is not justified. However differently participants may feel about a past social occasion, they can presumably agree as to which occasion they are talking about. Further, he who must work during and at an occasion defined for play still knows that his job locates him in a play occasion, not in a serious one, the fact that it does being an important job-contingency for him.

There is another sense, however, in which multiple social realities can occur in the same place. Once a social situation is referred back to the social occasion that sets the tone for the gathering in it, we must admit the possibility that the same physical space may be caught within the domain of two different social occasions. The social situation then may be the scene of potential or actual conflict between the sets of regulations that ought to govern. Note the famous conflict of definitions in the situation between summer tourists, who would like to extend summer-resort informality to the stores in the local town, and the natives, who would like to preserve proper business decorum in such places. Even within the same social establishment it is possible to find these overlapping definitions in the situation. Thus, in an office building or library where a rather strict decorum may obtain, the maintenance crews may see the occasion quite differently: they may work in profane clothing, run down the hallway when a quick repair is required, enter rooms at will, shout easily down the hall, plug a portable radio into the outlet nearest to their work, and maintain a level of conversational loudness quite prohibited to the office staff. Here we find something more than different roles in the same occasion, for no single main activity may be accorded precedence, at least in the short run. The social situations that occur in these overlapping behavior settings support gatherings that possess a special type of normative disorganization.

The possibility that the same physical space can come to be used as a setting for more than one social occasion, and hence as a locus for more than one set of expectations, is regularly recognized in society and typically restricted. Thus, in the important case of public streets, there is a tendency in Western society to define these places as the scene of an overriding social occasion to which other occasions ought to be subordinated. Potentially competing definitions in the situation then give way to a kind of public decorum. This decorum itself, of course, is typically subverted momentarily by parades, convention antics, marriage and funeral processions, ambulances, and fire trucks, all of which impress their special tone upon the public ear for a brief time.

It is situations and their gatherings, not social occasions, that we will mainly consider here, but for this a few terms must be introduced to help us distinguish between what is and what is not relevant in situations.

The term *situated* may be used to refer to any event occurring within the physical boundaries of a situation. Accordingly, the second person upon a scene transforms everything done by himself and by the one already there into situated activity, even though there may be no apparent change in the way the person already present continues with what he had been doing. The newcomer, in effect, transforms a solitary individual and himself into a gathering.

When we look at situated activity we often find that one component of it could just as well have occurred outside of situations, with no persons, or only one person, present. Thus, *some* of the loss an individual sustains when he is robbed at gunpoint in his house he could lose if his house were ransacked while he was away on vacation. Likewise, some of what is conveyed in a conversation could be conveyed through correspondence. Work tasks that an individual performs while others are present he can sometimes perform equally well when alone. This aspect of ac-

tivity may occur *in* situations but is not *of* situations, characteristically occurring at other times outside situations. This un-
blushing part of reality I will refer to as the *merely-situated*
aspect of situated activity. This component of activity comes
under normative regulation, allowing us to speak of obligations
and offenses that are merely-situated. But my only interest in
such matters will be to be able to segregate them analytically
from the component of situated activity that will concern us
here; namely, the part that could not occur outside situations,
being intrinsically dependent on the conditions that prevail
therein. This part will be referred to as the *situational* aspect of
situated activity. The risk to one's body when one is being
robbed at gunpoint of household effects is situational; the loss of
effects, as was previously suggested, is merely-situated. Some of
the meaning of words conveyed in conversation is merely-situated; the coloration given these words by bodily expressed
emotion, however, is distinctly situational. Similarly, for example, a member of the public in a reference library is expected
to draw out and use a book, and not to spend his time in other
pursuits, as adolescents learn from the librarian if they noisily
employ the library as a place of assignation. Here we have the
situational aspect of conduct. Within certain limits, however,
the individual's choice of particular books to read, his skill at
reading, and the profit to which he puts what he has learned
from reading are his own business, or that of the persons who
may have assigned him a reading task. This is the merely-situated
aspect of his library activity.

Once we distinguish clearly between the merely-situated and
the situational, we can return to consider the idea of public
order. Copresence renders persons uniquely accessible, available, and subject to one another. Public order, in its face-to-face
aspects, has to do with the normative regulation of this accessibility.

Perhaps the best explored face-to-face aspect of public order
as traditionally defined is what is sometimes called "public
safety." Its basic rules are few and clear, and, in Western society

today, heavily reinforced by police authority. Here the focus of regulation is upon the use that an individual can make of his body as a physical object or of instruments he can manipulate with his body. In going about their separate businesses, individuals—especially strangers—are not allowed to do any physical injury to one another, to block the way of one another, to assault one another sexually, or to constitute a source of disease contagion. While this kind of "King's Peace" currently prevails at most hours in most of our streets in most of our cities and towns, there are still neighborhoods where this order is not well guaranteed, and certainly in our past there have been times and places where such a guarantee was the exception rather than the rule.[11] A version of this safety problem can be found today on back wards of mental hospitals, where some patients understandably acquire the reputation of being "food throwers," bringing to ward mealtime a special kind of disorder. And, of course, in the lay notion that mental patients cannot be trusted not to strike out at others unexpectedly, there is an active reminder of ingredients of public order that might otherwise be taken for granted.

The harm produced by physical interference in any of its forms is partly due to the social humiliation of being seen as helpless by the offender and possibly by others, and so has distinctly social-psychological components. Other important ways in which the regulations ensuring physical safety impinge upon nonphysical matters will be considered later.

For our present purposes, the aspect of public order having to do with personal safety will be passed by. I will be concerned with the fact that when persons are present to one another they can function not merely as physical instruments but also as communicative ones. This possibility, no less than the physical one, is fateful for everyone concerned and in every society ap-

11. For medieval England see, for example, L. O. Pike, *A History of Crime in England* (2 vols.; London: Smith, Elder, 1873), esp. 1, 242-254. A view of public order in the East End of London near the turn of the century may be found in Arthur Morrison's novel *A Child of the Jago* (first published 1896; London: Penguin Books, 1946).

pears to come under strict normative regulation, giving rise to a kind of communication traffic order. It is this aspect of order that is mainly to be considered in this report. (Incidentally, it is in this aspect of public order that most symptoms of mental disorder seem to make themselves felt initially.) The rules pertaining to this area of conduct I shall call *situational proprieties.* The code derived therefrom is to be distinguished from other moral codes regulating other aspects of life (even if these sometimes apply at the same time as the situational code): for example, codes of honor, regulating relationships; codes of law, regulating economic and political matters; and codes of ethics, regulating professional life.[12]

The communicative behavior of those immediately present to one another can be considered in two steps. The first deals with *unfocused interaction,* that is, the kind of communication that occurs when one gleans information about another person present by glancing at him, if only momentarily, as he passes into and then out of one's view. Unfocused interaction has to do largely with the management of sheer and mere copresence. The second step deals with *focused interaction,* the kind of interaction that occurs when persons gather close together and openly cooperate to sustain a single focus of attention, typically by taking turns at talking. Where no focused interaction occurs, the term *unfocused gathering* can be used. Where focused interaction occurs, clumsier terms will be needed.

Given the definitions at which we have now arrived, it is possible to take another tentative step in the analysis of situational proprieties and to suggest one general element of proper conduct. In American society, it appears that the individual is expected to exert a kind of discipline or tension in regard to his body, showing that he has his faculties in readiness for any face-to-face interaction that might come his way in the situation. Often this kind of controlled alertness in the situation will

12. See the interesting comments by G. Simmel, "Morality, Honor and Law," from his *Soziologie* (3rd. ed.; Munich: Duncker & Humblot, 1923), pp. 403-405, trans. E. C. Hughes (mimeographed, University of Chicago).

mean suppressing or concealing many of the capacities and roles the individual might be expected to display in other settings. Whatever his other concerns, then, whatever his merely-situated interests, the individual is obliged to "come into play" upon entering the situation and to stay "in play" while in the situation, sustaining this diffuse orientation at least until he can officially take himself beyond range of the situation. In short, a kind of "interaction tonus" must be maintained. I would like to add that in considering the conduct through which this aliveness to the situation is demonstrated it is difficult to avoid the conclusion that an attachment to, and respectful regard for, the situation's participants and the encompassing social occasion is being avowed. And in considering the marked infractions of these rules in mental hospital wards, it is difficult to escape the conclusion, as we shall see later, that failure to exhibit "presence" is a normal, understandable expression of alienation from, and hostility to, the gathering itself and the officials in it.

One of the most evident means by which the individual shows himself to be situationally present is through the disciplined management of personal appearance or "personal front," that is, the complex of clothing, make-up, hairdo, and other surface decorations he carries about on his person. In public places in Western society, the male of certain classes is expected to present himself in the situation neatly attired, shaven, his hair combed, hands and face clean; female adults have similar and further obligations. It should be noted that with these matters of personal appearance the obligation is not merely to possess the equipment but also to exert the kind of sustained control that will keep it properly arranged. (And yet, in spite of these rulings, we may expect to find, in such places as the New York subway during the evening rush hour, that some persons, between scenes, as it were, may let expression fall from their faces in a kind of temporary uncaring and righteous exhaustion, even while being clothed and made up to fit a much more disciplined stance.)

I have already suggested that a failure to present oneself to a gathering in situational harness is likely to be taken as a sign of some kind of disregard for the setting and its participants; gross cultural distance from the social world of those present may also be expressed. These expressive implications of well or badly ordered personal appearance are often discussed in etiquette books, sometimes quite aptly:

> But even in a casual encounter, and upon occasions when your habit can have no connexion with the feelings and sentiments which you have towards those whom you meet, neat and careful dressing will bring great advantage to you. A negligent guise shows a man to be satisfied with his own resources, engrossed with his own notions and schemes, indifferent to the opinion of others, and not looking abroad for entertainment: to such a man no one feels encouraged to make any advances. A finished dress indicates a man of the world, one who looks for and habitually finds, pleasure in society and conversation, and who is at all times ready to mingle in intercourse with those whom he meets with; it is a kind of general offer of acquaintance, and provides a willingness to be spoken to.[13]

An interesting expression of the kind of interaction tonus that lies behind the proper management of personal appearance is found in the constant care exerted by men in our society to see that their trousers are buttoned and that an erection bulge is not showing.[14] Before entering a social situation, they often run through a quick visual inspection of the relevant parts of their personal front, and once in the situation they may take the extra precaution of employing a protective cover, by either crossing the legs or covering the crotch with a newspaper or book, especially if self-control is to be relaxed through comfortable sitting. A parallel to this concern is found in the care that women take to

13. Anon., *The Canons of Good Breeding* (Philadelphia: Lee and Blanchard, 1839), pp. 14-15.

14. The difficulty of engaging in this kind of protective concealment is one of the contingencies apparently faced by men with leg paralysis. See E. Henrich and L. Kriegel, eds., *Experiments in Survival* (New York: Association for the Aid of Crippled Children, 1961), p. 192.

see that their legs are not apart, exposing their upper thighs and underclothing. The universality in our society of this kind of limb discipline can be deeply appreciated on a chronic female ward where, for whatever reason, women indulge in zestful scratching of their private parts and in sitting with legs quite spread, causing the student to become conscious of the vast amount of limb discipline that is ordinarily taken for granted. A similar reminder of one's expectations concerning limb discipline can be obtained from the limb movements required of elderly obese women in getting out of the front seat of a car. Just as a Balinese would seem ever to be concerned about the direction and height of his seat, so the individual in our society, while "in situation," is constantly oriented to keeping "physical" signs of sexual capacities concealed. And it is suggested here that these parts of the body when exposed are not a symbol of sexuality merely, but of a laxity of control over the self—evidence of an insufficient harnessing of the self for the gathering.

As has been suggested, the importance of a disciplined management of personal front is demonstrated in many ways by the mentally sick. A typical sign of an oncoming psychosis is the individual's "neglect" of his appearance and personal hygiene. The classic home for these improprieties is "regressed" wards in mental hospitals, where those with a tendency in this direction are collected, at the very same time that conditions remarkably facilitate this sort of disorientation. (Here, dropping of personal front will be tolerated, and sometimes even subtly approved, because it can reduce problems of ward management.) Similarly, when a mental patient starts "taking an interest in his appearance," and makes an effort at personal grooming, he is often credited with having somehow given up his fight against society and having begun his way back to "reality."

One of the most delicate components of personal appearance seems to be the composition of the face. A very evident means by which the individual shows himself to be situationally present is by appropriately controlling through facial muscles the shape and expression of the various parts of this instrument.

Although this control may not be conscious to any extent, it is none the less exerted. We have party faces, funeral faces, and various kinds of institutional faces, as the following comments on life in prison suggest:

> Every new inmate learns to dog-face, that is to assume an apathetic, *characterless* facial expression and posture when viewed by authority. The dog-face is acquired easily when everyone freezes or relaxes into immobility. The face is that typical of streets, of social occasions, of all concealment. Relaxation comes when inmates are alone: there is an exaggeration of the smiling effervescence of the "friendly" party. The face that is protective by day is aggressively hardened and hate-filled by night, against the stationed or pacing guard. Tensity and dislike follow assumption of the face, guards react with scrupulous relaxedness, holding the face "soft" with an effort often accompanied by slight trembling of hands.[15]

An interesting fact about proper composition of the face is that the ease of maintaining it in our society would seem to decline with age, so that, especially in the social class groupings whose women long retain an accent on sexual attractiveness, there comes to be an increasingly long period of time after awakening that is required to get the face into shape, during which the individual in her own eyes is not "presentable." A point in age is also reached when, given these youthful standards of what a face in play should look like, there will be viewing angles from which an otherwise properly composed face looks to have insufficient tonus.

The disciplined ordering of personal front is one way, then, in which the individual is obliged to express his aliveness to those about him. Another means is the readiness with which he attends to new stimuli in the situation and the alacrity with which he responds to them with body movements. I think that the individual so generally maintains a proper motor level in

15. B. Phillips, "Notes on the Prison Community," in H. Cantine and D. Rainer, eds., *Prison Etiquette* (Bearsville, New York: Retort Press, 1950), pp. 105-106.

situations that this is one type of propriety that is very difficult indeed to become aware of. Here again mental wards help us. For example, a common symptom displayed by persons diagnosed as schizophrenic consists of very slow body movements as shown, say, during hallway pacing. While thus engaged, the patient may respond to a question from an attendant by turning his head slowly in the direction of the voice, and this only by moving his whole trunk, as if his neck were completely stiff, while keeping his face immobile. (This kind of conduct is somewhat similar to the kind that is popularly thought to occur in sleepwalking, and calls forth a similar response; namely, the feeling of someone being in the situation physically but not fully present for purposes of interaction.) Bleuler has given us fine descriptions of the extremes of this deadness to the situation, as he has with so many schizophrenic symptoms, pointing to the inward emigration that presumably occurs at these times:

> Autism is also manifested by many patients externally. (Naturally, this is, as a rule, unintentional.) Not only do they not concern themselves with anything around them, but they sit around with faces constantly averted, looking at a blank wall; or they shut off their sensory portals by drawing a skirt or bed clothes over their heads. Indeed, formerly, when the patients were mostly abandoned to their own devices, they could often be found in bent-over, squatting positions, an indication that they were trying to restrict as much as possible of the sensory surface area of their skin.[16]

It should be added that this lack of presence may be nicely demonstrated in establishments that are not medical but are none the less similar in many ways to mental hospitals:

> About the prison yard and the shops one sees inmates for whom smiles, small talk, alertness, and attention to the environment come easily. One also sees about half as many men who seldom smile, who seldom talk, who stumble as they walk in lines, whose errors in

16. E. Bleuler, *Dementia Praecox or the Group of Schizophrenias*, trans. J. Zinkin (New York: International Universities Press, 1950), pp. 65-66.

their tasks cause small concern, and who respond normally to social stimuli only when a stimulus is strong or different. Status or social approbation is as nothing. It is reverie-plus that controls them.[17]

In general, then, if the individual is to be in the situation in full social capacity, he will be required to maintain a certain level of alertness as evidence of his availability for potential stimuli, and some orderliness and organization of his personal appearance as evidence that he is alive to the gathering he is in. A problem for analysis, of course, is to go on to isolate analytically the various ways in which insufficient presence may be manifested.

17. D. Clemmer, *The Prison Community* (reissue; New York: Holt, Rinehart, and Winston, 1958) , p. 244.

PART TWO

Unfocused Interaction

CHAPTER 3

Involvement

1. Body Idiom

As ALREADY suggested, when individuals come into one another's immediate presence in circumstances where no spoken communication is called for, they none the less inevitably engage one another in communication of a sort, for in all situations, significance is ascribed to certain matters that are not necessarily connected with particular verbal communications. These comprise bodily appearance and personal acts: dress, bearing, movement and position, sound level, physical gestures such as waving or saluting, facial decorations, and broad emotional expression.

In every society these communication possibilities are institutionalized. While many such usable events may be neglected, at least some are likely to be regularized and accorded a common meaning. Half-aware that a certain aspect of his activity is available for all present to perceive, the individual tends to modify this activity, employing it with its public character in mind. Sometimes, in fact, he may employ these signs solely because they can be witnessed. And even if those in his presence are not quite conscious of the communication they are receiving, they will none the less sense something sharply amiss should the uncustomary be conveyed. There is, then, a body symbolism, an idiom of individual appearances and gestures that tends to call forth in the actor what it calls forth in the others, the others drawn from those, and only those, who are immediately present.[1]

Now these embodied expressive signs can function to qualify whatever an individual may mean by a statement he makes to others and thus play a role in the focused interaction of, say, a conversational gathering. However, it is the special character of many of these events, when seen as communications, that they cannot be easily focused or shielded, tending, in the extreme, to be accessible to everyone in the situation at large. Further, while these signs seem ill suited for extended discursive messages, in contrast to speech, they do seem well designed to convey information about the actor's social attributes and about his conception of himself, of the others present, and of the setting. These signs, then, form the basis of unfocused interaction, even though they can also play a role in the focused kind.

In this realm of unfocused interaction, no one participant can be officially "given the floor"; there is no official center of attention. Although the individual may exert special care over this kind of conduct in order to make a good impression on a particular person in the setting—as when a girl wears a perfume she knows her boyfriend likes—such a performance tends to be presented as if it were primarily for the benefit of everyone in the vicinity.

Body idiom, then, is a conventionalized discourse.[2] We must

1. Bodily action as a basis for social interaction is touched on in social science literature under the heading "nonverbal communication." The postural aspects of this behavior have been systematically diagrammed by G. W. Hewes, "World Distribution of Certain Postural Habits," *American Anthropologist*, 57 (1955), 231-244. A very acute general treatment may be found in R. Birdwhistell, *Introduction to Kinesics* (Washington, D.C.: Department of State, Foreign Service Institute, 1952). See also J. Ruesch and W. Kees, *Nonverbal Communication: Notes on the Visual Perception of Human Relations* (Berkeley: University of California Press, 1956); T. S. Szasz, *The Myth of Mental Illness* (New York: Hoeber-Harper, 1961); S. Feldman, *Mannerisms of Speech and Gestures in Everyday Life* (New York: International Universities Press, 1959), Part 2; D. Efron, *Gesture and Environment* (New York: King's Crown Press, 1941); M. Critchley, *The Language of Gesture* (London: Edward Arnold, 1939); and E. T. Hall, *The Silent Language* (New York: Doubleday, 1959).

2. G. H. Mead's distinction between "significant" and "nonsignificant" gestures is not entirely satisfactory here. Body idiom involves something more than a nonsignificant "conversation of gestures," because this idiom tends to evoke the same meaning for the actor as for the witness, and tends to be employed by the actor

see that it is, in addition, a normative one. That is, there is typically an obligation to convey certain information when in the presence of others and an obligation not to convey other impressions, just as there is an expectation that others will present themselves in certain ways. There tends to be agreement not only about the meaning of the behaviors that are seen but also about the behaviors that ought to be shown.

Although an individual can stop talking, he cannot stop communicating through body idiom; he must say either the right thing or the wrong thing. He cannot say nothing. Paradoxically, the way in which he can give the least amount of information about himself—although this is still appreciable—is to fit in and act as persons of his kind are expected to act. (The fact that information about self can be held back in this way is one motive for maintaining the proprieties.) Finally, it should be noted that while no one in a society is likely to be in a position to employ the whole expressive idiom, or even a major part of it, nevertheless everyone will possess some knowledge of the same vocabulary of body symbols. Indeed, the understanding of a common body idiom is one reason for calling an aggregate of individuals a society.

2. Involvement

Granted that the individual makes information available through body idiom, the question then arises as to what this information is about. We can begin to answer this question by looking at one of the most obvious types of propriety—"occasioned activity."

During any social occasion we can expect to find some activities that are intrinsically part of the occasion in the sense, for

---

because of its meaning for the witness. Something less than significant symbolism seems to be involved, however: an extended exchange of meaningful acts is not characteristic; an impression must be maintained that a margin of uncalculating spontaneous involvement has been retained in the act; the actor will usually be in a position to deny the meaning of his act if he is challenged for performing it.

example, that a political speech is an expected part of a political rally. Such "occasioned activity" is likely to be legitimated as appropriate in social situations that form under the aegis of the corresponding social occasion, providing one basis for the common-sense notion that "there is a time and place for everything." But we must then ask why a particular activity is defined as appropriate for the social occasion in the first place. More important, the display of properly occasioned activity seems to be only one of the general forms of propriety, only one of the ways of fitting in.

There is, however, one promising point about these considerations. To be engaged in an occasioned activity means to sustain some kind of cognitive and affective engrossment in it, some mobilization of one's psychobiological resources; in short, it means to be *involved* in it.[3] Further, by asking of any piece of obligatory situational behavior what it conveys about the allocation of involvement of the actor, we find that a limited number of themes occurs, and that each theme is expressed through many different aspects of behavior. In brief, by translating concrete obligatory acts into terms of expressed involvement, we have a way of showing the functional equivalence of aspects of such diverse phenomena as dress, stance, facial expression, and task activity. Underneath apparent differences, we shall be able to glimpse a common structure. To analyze situational proprieties, then, it will be necessary to turn to an analysis of the social regulations that determine the individual's conceptions and allocations of involvement.[4]

The first thing to be noted about "involvement in situations"

3. The term "involved" is used in two other additional senses in everyday speech: that of "commitment," in the sense of having made oneself liable and responsible for certain actions; and that of "attachment," in the sense of vesting one's feelings and identification in something. Because of this ambiguity I have elsewhere used the term "engagement" as I shall in this book use "involvement." See "Role Distance," *Encounters* (Indianapolis: Bobbs-Merrill, 1961).

4. Involvement as a variable is considered in E. F. Borgatta and L. S. Cottrell, Jr., "On the Classification of Groups," *Sociometry*, 18 (1955), 416-417. One aspect of involvement, that of intensity, has been considered by T. R. Sarbin in "Role Theory," section "Organismic Dimension," pp. 233-235 in G. Lindzey, ed., *Handbook of Social Psychology* (Cambridge, Mass.: Addison-Wesley, 1954). My own orientation to involvement derives from G. Bateson and M. Mead, *Balinese Character* (New York: New York Academy of Sciences, 1942).

is the terminological ambiguity of this phrase. I mean to speak now only of situated involvements, those sustained *within* the situation, whereas the phrase "involvement in the situation" has this meaning and also a more circumscribed one, referring to ways in which the individual may have somehow given himself up to the situation as a whole and its gathering, possessing thus a *situational* involvement. I propose to use the term "involvement *within* the situation" to refer to the way the individual handles his situated activities, and will refrain for the moment from using the phrase "involvement *in* the situation" at all.

The involvement that an individual sustains within a particular situation is a matter of inward feeling. Assessment of involvement must and does rely on some kind of outward expression. It is here that we can begin to analyze the effect of the body idiom, for it is an interesting fact that just as bodily activities seem to be particularly well designed to spread their information throughout a whole social situation, so also these signs seem well designed to provide information about the individual's involvement. Just as the individual finds that he must convey something through body idiom, and is required to convey the right thing, so also he finds that while present to others he will inevitably convey information about the allocation of his involvement, and that expression of a particular allocation is obligatory. Instead of speaking of a body idiom, we can now be a little more specific and speak instead of an "involvement idiom" and of rules regarding the allocation of involvement.

Since the involvement idiom of a group appears to be a learned conventional thing, we must anticipate one real difficulty in cross-cultural or even cross-subcultural studies. The same general type of gathering in different cultures may be organized on the basis of different involvement obligations. The audience of a dramatic production in many Far Eastern societies, for example, is required to exhibit less sustained attentiveness and single-mindedness than the audience of many dramatic productions in American society. But entirely apart from this kind of difference, it is the case that the same behavioral cue in one society may by convention carry different involvement implications in another. Thus the members of one religious group may show reverent orientation to the House of the Lord by baring the head and the members of another by taking care to cover it. When a difference in situational conduct is found between two cultures, or in the same culture over time, it becomes a complicated matter to determine what part of this discrepancy reflects a difference in the conventional idiom for expressing the underlying involvement, and what part reflects a difference in this involvement itself.

3. Involvement Shields

Since involvement is not directly visible but can only be inferred through its conventional signs, actual involvement may be of little significance. What we want to know about is "effective" involvement, that is, the involvement that the actor and the others sense he is maintaining, or sense he is (or might be) sensed to be maintaining.

A demand regarding engrossment is a demand on the inner spirit of the engrossed person. Naturally, at times his heart may not lie where the social occasion requires it to. In such cases a solution is to conceal improper involvement and to affect appropriate involvement. Another solution, of course, is for the disaffected individual to realize in advance that he will not be able or willing to comply with the involvement rulings and to refrain from entering the situation in the first place. A similar separation from the situation is sometimes provided by sympathetic others. Thus, if an individual must be given bad news that is likely to "break him up," the giver may wait for a suitable moment when the recipient is off by himself, and there is not likely to be an immediate call for his situational presence.[5] The

5. An extreme example of how sympathetic others can help shelter an individual is found in the protective patterns of the male lower class, where someone who has become drunk, evincing in every inch of his manner that he is incapable of appropriate involvement, may be concealed bodily from the authorities by his friends and "buddies."

recipient can then respond emotionally to the news he receives without doing damage in a wider social situation, where his plight might be appreciated but his response hardly permitted to everyone present.

Given the fact that involvement signs must be signified and witnessed before the appropriateness of involvement allocation can be inferred, we may expect to find a variety of barriers to perception used as *involvement shields,* behind which individuals can safely do the kind of things that ordinarily result in negative sanctions. Because one perceives the individual's involvement in reference to the whole context of his activity, involvement can be shielded by blocking perception of either bodily signs of involvement or objects of involvement, or both. Bedrooms and bathrooms are perhaps the main shielding places in Anglo-American society,[6] bathrooms having special interest here because in many households these are the only rooms in which the solitary person can properly lock himself. And it may be only under these guaranteed conditions that some individuals will feel safe in manifesting certain situationally improper involvements.[7]

Every social establishment, in fact, has some crevices that provide this kind of shelter. At Central Hospital, for example, it was considered "unprofessional" for nurses to smoke outdoors on the grounds, for it seemed that smoking was felt to portray a self that was somehow insufficiently dedicated to the needy world of the patients. Student nurses walking through the tunnel that joined the two halves of the grounds would sometimes slow up and spitefully light a cigarette during their very brief

6. These places and other "backstage" regions are considered at length in *The Presentation of Self in Everyday Life* (New York: Doubleday Anchor, 1959), Chap. 3.

7. Situational proprieties have, of course, pursued some categories of persons even here. There are convents where modesty is said to be maintained even when alone in the bathtub, apparently on the assumption that a deity is present. And during the sixteenth century, when travelers were obliged to share inn beds with strangers of the same sex, it was hoped, in theory at least, that the sleeper would conduct himself decorously during the night so as not unduly to disturb others in the situation. See H. Nicolson, *Good Behaviour* (London: Constable, 1955), p. 134, and N. Elias, *Über den Prozess der Zivilisation* (2 vols.; Basel: Falken, 1939), "Über das Verhalten im Schlafraum," 1, 219-230.

period of low visibility. The horseplay they engaged in at this time was a further expression of "breaking role," of enjoying what Everett C. Hughes has called "role release."

There are involvement shields that have the useful attribute of being portable. Thus, while women in European society no longer employ fans, let alone masks, to conceal a blush or a failure to blush,[8] hands are now used to cover closed eyes that are obliged to be open,[9] and newspapers to cover mouths that should not be open in a yawn. Similarly, in coercive institutions such as prisons, involvement in smoking may be concealed by cupping the cigarette in one's hand.[10]

A question to ask about involvement shields is whether or not it is really felt to be legitimate to employ them, whether—to take the extreme case—it is permissible to go "out of play" when entirely alone. Thus, when a fully relaxed person is unexpectedly intruded upon by a visitor, both are likely to feel embarrassment. The discovered person does not quite have the right, apparently, to have been undressed interactionally, and the intruder does not quite have the right to have caught the other in his impropriety. The exception here, it should be added, has its own significance for us: given the status of the discovered person, there may be categories of discoverers, such as servants, courtiers, and young children, who do not have the social power to cause merely-situated acts to be performed with much of a situational covering. As a functional concomitant of this incapacity, these "nonpersons" often have the privilege of entering a room unannounced, without the preliminary warnings, such as a telephone call or a knock, that full persons are

8. E. S. Turner, *A History of Courting* (New York: Ballantine Books, 1954), p. 73.

9. Closed eyes, of course, do not always express the fact that the individual has departed from the gathering by dozing off. There are moments of love-making or chamber music listening when closed eyes may be a respectful sign of deep emotional involvement in the proceedings. In these cases, however, the eyes are shut in a special way to show that the person behind the eyelids is still present in a properly occasioned capacity.

10. See, for example, G. Dendrickson and F. Thomas, *The Truth About Dartmoor* (London: Gollancz, 1954), p. 171.

often obliged to give.[11] Incidentally, it is just when an individual feels he is sheltered from others' view, and suddenly discovers he is not, that we obtain the clearest picture of what he owes to the gathering, for at such moments of discovery the discovered individual is likely to assemble himself hurriedly, inadvertently demonstrating what he lays aside and what he puts on solely by virtue of the mere presence of others. In order to guard against these embarrassments, and in order to generate within himself other persons' view of him, the individual may maintain presentability even when alone—thus forcing us to allow that situational behavior may occur even in the absence of an actual social situation.

Ordinarily we think of involvement shields as one means by which the individual can maintain the impression of proper involvement while he is actually delinquent in his situational obligations. Interestingly enough, while the quite extensive forms of situational withdrawal that a psychotic patient sometimes employs may provide him with a needed way of defending himself against the past or the present, the consistent maintenance of this withdrawal may become at times a taxing necessity and a discipline all of its own. Hence some of these patients can be observed using involvement shields to conceal not a momentary lack of orientation in the situation but a momentary occurrence of it. The television screen, the Sunday funnies, and new visitors to the ward seem to provide special temptations, leading patients to show a lively interest when they think no one is observing them. The following modes of conduct have been recorded:

> the patient reveals that she is able to focus on others when she is not involved herself and when she feels unobserved in the process. In situations in which this occurs and she discovers she is being observed, she quickly turns her attention inward.[12]

11. See "Communication Conduct," Chap. 16, and *The Presentation of Self,* pp. 151-153.
12. M. Schwartz, "Social Interaction of a Disturbed Ward of a Hospital" (unpublished Ph.D. dissertation, Department of Sociology, University of Chicago, 1951), p. 94.

Even in the more usual case, however, where the shelter is employed to conceal withdrawal in the situation, we must not misunderstand the significance of using these devices. The use of a shelter says just as much for the power of situational obligations as it does for the tendency of persons to seek some means of squirming out of them. It is only when it is glaringly apparent that a shield is being used for such concealment, or when a shield could easily be used and is not, that instances of situational insolence occur. An example may be cited from my hospital field notes:

> Crowded ward for regressed females. A patient notices that her sanitary napkin is askew. She gets up from the bench and in an open methodical way starts fishing for the napkin by running her hand up her leg and under her skirt. However, even when she bends down, her hand cannot quite reach far enough. She stands up and nonchalantly drops her dress down off her shoulders, letting it fall to the floor. She then calmly fixes the napkin in place, and afterward pulls the dress back up again, all the while showing not unawareness but regal unconcern for the need of guile or subterfuge. The manner of her action, not the aim of the action itself, expresses contempt for the situation.

The idea of involvement shields has been stressed because it points out a very characteristic attribute of situated conduct. Since the domain of situational proprieties is wholly made up of what individuals can experience of each other while mutually present, and since channels of experience can be interfered with in so many ways, we deal not so much with a network of rules that must be followed as with rules that must be taken into consideration, whether as something to follow or carefully to circumvent.

CHAPTER 4

Some Rules About
the Allocation of Involvement

INVOLVEMENT refers to the capacity of an individual to give, or withhold from giving, his concerted attention to some activity at hand—a solitary task, a conversation, a collaborative work effort. It implies a certain admitted closeness between the individual and the object of involvement, a certain overt engrossment on the part of the one who is involved. Involvement in an activity is taken to express the purpose or aim of the actor. To discuss involvement, we can begin with common-sense distinctions institutionalized in our American society and presumably in others.

Men and animals have a capacity to divide their attention into *main* and *side* involvements. A main involvement is one that absorbs the major part of an individual's attention and interest, visibly forming the principal current determinant of his actions. A side involvement is an activity that an individual can carry on in an abstracted fashion without threatening or confusing simultaneous maintenance of a main involvement. Whether momentary or continuous, simple or complicated, these side activities appear to constitute a kind of fuguelike dissociation of minor muscular activity from the main line of an individual's action. Humming while working and knitting while listening are examples.

Along with the distinction between main and side involvements, we must make another that can easily be confused with the first. We must distinguish between *dominant* and *subordinate* involvements. A dominating involvement is one whose claims upon an individual the social occasion obliges him to be ready to recognize; a subordinate involvement is one he is allowed to sustain only to the degree, and during the time, that his attention is patently not required by the involvement that dominates him. Subordinate involvements are sustained in a muted, modulated, and intermittent fashion, expressing in their style a continuous regard and deference for the official, dominating activity at hand. Thus, while waiting to see an official, an individual may converse with a friend, read a magazine, or doodle with a pencil, sustaining these engrossing claims on attention only until his turn is called, when he is obliged to put aside his time-passing activity even though it is unfinished.

Typically, it is expected that a main involvement will be a dominating one and a side involvement a subordinate one, as when a worker smokes a cigarette unthinkingly but only when and where the job allows. This relationship, however, is by no means invariable. Many dominating involvements, such as work tasks, can be sustained automatically and unthinkingly for long periods, allowing the individual to devote his main focus of attention to pursuits such as idle gossip, which, however involving, will be put aside when the task requires attention. A telegrapher, for example, can tap out messages while sustaining a conversational byplay with a fellow worker.

Once we see that an undemanding but socially dominating activity can be sustained while the individual's main focus of attention is temporarily drawn to another issue, we can go on to see that while thus engaged he can sustain additional side involvements, like smoking, which are themselves subordinated to the temporary and unofficial main involvement. We should also see that claims upon the individual can suddenly change, and that what had been a dominant involvement can suddenly be demoted in status and become subordinated to a new source of involvement now considered properly to be the one of first priority.

In our society, it is recognized that certain activities are to be carried on only as main and dominating involvements; many social ceremonies are instances. It is also recognized that certain other activities are to be carried on only as side involvements and subordinate ones, as, for example, chewing gum. (These slight involvements are not to be accorded main attention even when no main involvement is required.) Within these limits, however, what is defined as a dominating involvement at one time be defined as subordinate at another. Thus, on the job, the drinking of a cup of coffee may be a subordinate involvement; during official coffee breaks, it may be the dominating activity.

1. The Management of Subordinate Involvements

I have suggested that subordinate involvements—side and main—express, by definition, at least a surface respect for what is agreed should be the controlling business at hand, however demanding they may be in fact. It is implied that such subordinate involvements ought to catch only the individual's lesser and unimportant self. It is understandable, then, that when an individual wishes to give weight to these subordinate activities he will conceal and cover them with a show of their being merely distractions. It is also understandable that these involvements will be a constant threat to obligatory behavior, ever ready to absorb more of the individual's concern that is felt proper. This is especially the case with involvements well established as subordinate side ones, since these involvements, defined and described as "minor" in everyday terms, will never be entirely prohibited in the situation, and hence a few will always be available as beginning points for defection.

The idiom of subordinate involvements differs widely from one cultural group to another. Even between the English and

American pattern we find a difference, as Dickens reminds us in his British response to an American custom:

> As Washington may be called the headquarters of tobacco-tinctured saliva, the time is come when I must confess, without any disguise, that the prevalence of those two odious practices of chewing and expectorating began about this time to be anything but agreeable, and soon became most offensive and sickening. In all the public places of America this filthy custom is recognized. In the courts of law the judge has his spittoon, the crier his, the witness his, and the prisoner his; while the jurymen and spectators are provided for, as so many men who in the course of nature must desire to spit incessantly. In the hospitals the students of medicine are requested, by notices upon the wall, to eject their tobacco juice into the boxes provided for that purpose, and not to discolor the stairs. In public buildings visitors are implored, through the same agency, to squirt the essence of their quids, or "plugs," as I have heard them called by gentlemen learned in this kind of sweetmeat, into the national spittoons, and not about the bases of the marble columns. But in some parts this custom is inseparably mixed up with every meal and morning call, and with all the transactions of social life.[1]

Dickens said in 1842, of course, what many Americans would say now, so it should be apparent that involvement idiom can change through time within the same nation. Thus, some signs, such as whittling, taking snuff, or toying with one's key chain, are largely passing out of currency as part of the available vocabulary; others, such as spinning, have disappeared altogether in our American society; others, such as keeping an ear cocked to the radio or phonograph, have come into being within living memory; still others, such as smoking, have changed their meaning and have ceased to connote the degree of situational license they once did.

Different social groupings, too, will have different subordinate involvements available to them. At Central Hospital, for example, during breaks in the rehearsal for the patient stage

1. Charles Dickens, *American Notes* (Greenwich, Conn.: Premier Americana, Fawcett Publications, 1961) , pp. 134-135.

production, a few of the middle-class female patients would "doodle" with the entire body by means of practice ballet movements; this idiom was not available to the lower-class females present. In our society, knitting is a subordinate involvement ordinarily prohibited to men, just as pipe smoking is to women. And, as in all matters of involvement allocation, age-grade differences in permissible subordinate involvements are very marked. In many American movie houses, for example, there is a daily and weekly cycle of civic order, the day, and especially Saturday and Sunday afternoons, being defined as a time when a wide range of subordinate involvement is tolerated, while the other times are defined as occasions when few subordinate involvements are allowed. In Chicago, there are, in fact, movie houses that specialize in the kind of social order maintained by children:

> The theater is characterized as showing old films. Only little kids can be enthralled by dated pictures. Therefore the theater is classified as for little kids. Since it is not a place to be taken seriously, it can serve as a kind of indoor recreation hall for the older children, a place where they can devote more attention to each other than to the screen.[2]

Similarly, it may be permissible for a child on the street to suck his thumb, or lick a sucker, or inflate chewing-gum bubbles until they burst, or draw a stick along a fence, or fully interrupt his main line of activity to take a stone from his shoe. But the adult mental patients in Central Hospital who were observed conducting themselves in some of these ways were felt by staff to be acting "symptomatically."

For any specific class of social gatherings, we may expect to find regulations concerning the kinds of subordinate involvement that will be tolerated. As has been suggested, this selection seems to be based on an assessment of the amount of one's attention and self that would be absorbed through these activities and the amount, therefore, that would be left over for the domi-

2. E. Freidson, "An Audience and Its Taste" (unpublished Ph.D. dissertation, Department of Sociology, University of Chicago, 1952), p. 216.

nating involvement. For example, it is reported that, during a group therapy session conducted by and for the staff of a child residential treatment center, it was considered acceptable for a participating member of the staff to hold a cat on her lap; to give the animal more than occasional pats, however, was felt to be a sign of withdrawal from the session.[3]

As with other aspects of involvement structure, there is an ecology regarding subordinate involvement. It has been said, for example, that between the wars in London there were districts such as Bond Street where a lady did not walk while holding anything more than gloves, a leash, or a walking umbrella, and where similar restrictions applied to gentlemen. A small parcel carried under the arm was not *comme il faut,* for such an involvement in visible muscular activity apparently implied a threat to the kind of finished poised appearance deemed proper. From this extreme, a continuum could be traced in the same city to places where people properly went about struggling under shoulder harnesses or heavy objects such as boxes or large tools.[4]

Prohibitionary rules about subordinate involvements, unlike many other kinds of involvement regulation, are frequently made quite explicit. The settings of many gatherings present posted rules, for example, about not smoking or not chewing gum. In disciplinary settings such as jails, these rules can extend to the prohibition of talk during meals. In some convents these rules may even govern the "conduct of the eyes" during meditation and prayers, so that the act of merely looking around the

3. Hannah Meara, "The Group Therapy Session as a Social Situation," unpublished paper.

4. In those peasant societies where persons are used to working all through the waking hours, instead of during a special time of day as in our society, a very great amount of side involvement seems to be tolerated and even enjoined, at least from the point of view of our own involvement idiom. For example, we are told of South American Indians:

It is held to be typical of Indian women to be occupied with spinning while walking along the road, while selling in the market, and while gossiping with each other, and men are similarly seen engaged in some braiding or cording work, or even spinning, as they walk.

(B. R. Salz, "The Human Element in Industrialization," *American Anthropological Association Memoir No. 85,* 1955, p. 101.)

room may constitute an unacceptable subordinate involvement.[5]

There are interesting historical changes in regard to permissible and impermissible subordinate involvements in particular situations. In many university classrooms in the last two decades, for example, knitting and smoking have become permissible, signifying, perhaps, a downgrading of the dignity of the occasion and an upgrading of the status of the students relative to the faculty. A somewhat similar change in idiom and in involvement rulings can be found among American adolescents. This group seems to have greater license in regard to informal conduct in public places than it had a generation ago. At the same time, the vogue of the portable transistor radio has guaranteed a source of absorbing subordinate involvement that can be carried into a multitude of different situations.[6]

Given the fact that a subordinate involvement provides a diversion of self from a dominant involvement, even if this diversion is felt to be a minor kind, we may expect that when a dominant involvement seems to threaten the security of an individual and his self-control within the situation, he may initiate or affect a subordinate involvement in order to show that he is

5. Nuns are apparently trained to maintain greater withdrawal from the situation at large than laity, this being an important part of their socialization into their calling and a brake upon quick adaptation to the secular world should they leave the sisterhood. See Kathryn Hulme, *The Nun's Story* (London: Muller, 1956) , p. 67, and Sister Mary Francis, *A Right to be Merry* (New York: Sheed and Ward, 1956) , p. 18:

> To return to the train ride, when a cloistered nun is out of her cloister, she is still a cloistered nun. She observes the spirit of her vow of enclosure wherever she is, and as many of its practical regulations as she can when she is outside. Thus, no contemplative nun would wander about the train "making friends" or striking up chance conversations. Neither would she stare about curiously at everything and everybody within her visual or aural focus.

6. Portable radios have not come into use without resistance, at least in some countries. A Reuters news release from Dijon, France *(San Francisco Chronicle,* May 28, 1961) reports:

> Canon Felix Kir, 85, left-wing mayor of Dijon, banned the playing of portable radios in public here today.
> The cleric, who is also dean of the French National Assembly, where he is a deputy, issued the order after receiving dozens of complaints and after making a personal visit to the local swimming pool.
> "I had to leave," he said. "I could not bear the cacophony of noise from all the radios—it was like a fairground."

in command of his circumstances. Tactful persons who are sources of threat may initiate this defense for him; their offering him a cigarette is an example.[7]

2. Obligations Regarding Main Involvements

In many social situations, a particular main involvement will be seen as an intrinsic part of the social occasion in which the situation occurs, and will be defined as preferential if not obligatory. At a card party, for example, participants may be expected to focus their attention on cards, justifying this allocation of involvement by reference to the nature of the social occasion. As suggested, we can therefore speak of occasioned main involvements.

The significance of maintaining an occasioned main involvement can be seen, in relief, by examining what happens when an individual is insufficiently knowing to "catch" the meaning of what is going on. At such times he will have great difficulty in sustaining attention and hence proper involvement within the situation. This is the problem faced by foreign students in a classroom lecture or by persons not British at a cricket match. Similarly, when an amateur examining his car engine to determine why his car has stalled feels uncomfortable under the gaze of the other passengers, this discomfort may arise not only because he has caused them an inconvenience and is demonstrating incompetence, but also because he must act involved in his task and may not know enough about motors to become sincerely caught up in examining one for failings.[8] Interestingly

7. The easiness expressed by smoking can be balanced by the tremor an individual may display in obtaining a light and holding the cigarette. Thinking ahead, he may not know whether smoking or not smoking is the safer course.

8. Insufficient experience is not the only cause of such a predicament. When guests at a small occasion of sociability are momentarily left by their host to their own devices, a similar problem occurs: expecting to be guaranteed sociable interaction, they may find nothing available as a legitimate main involvement and hence no means of being at ease.

enough, if an individual is insufficiently schooled in a subject matter to participate in it from within, as it were, and attempts to compensate for his alienation by wearing exactly the right clothes, employing exactly the right equipment, or assuming exactly the right stance, those around him may say that he is "overinvolved in the situation." In fact, however, it might be more accurate to say that he is insufficiently involved in the occasioned main involvement and overdependent on selected signs of being at one with this activity. In this way we might try to account for the slight uneasiness caused others by a woman not closely related to the deceased who appears at the funeral in a very modish, very complete, black ensemble.

The main involvement sustained by an individual within a social situation can express his apparent purpose in being present; an obligation to have an appropriate main involvement is an obligation to have a particular purpose. As suggested, however, there are social situations in which those present do have a purpose, even an obligatory one, that does not in itself require or even allow a main involvement, for example, when an individual in a vehicle of public transportation sits or stands while awaiting his destination. At such times the individual may sustain quite absorbing main involvements which are patently subordinated to a dominant involvement that cannot yet occur.

Whether an occasioned main involvement is prescribed or not, the participant in a social gathering—at least in a middle-class gathering—may be obliged to sustain at least a certain *minimal main involvement* to avoid the appearance of being utterly disengaged. This is one reason why waiting rooms, club cars, and passenger airplanes in our society often are supplied by management with emergency supplies such as magazines and newspapers, which serve as minimal involvements that can be given weight (when there is nothing but waiting to do) yet can be immediately discarded when one's turn or destination arrives. Newspapers, in particular, play an important role here, providing a portable source of involvement, which can be brought

forth whenever an individual feels he ought to have an involvement but does not.[9]

In our society meals provide an interesting problem in involvement allocation. In public restaurants eating is defined as
the dominating involvement, and yet it is also seen as something
that perhaps ought not to engage very much of the individual's
attention. Often, therefore, subordinate involvements will be
sought out to drain off some unusable involvement capacity.
Thus, when an individual finds he must eat alone without the
cover of conversation with an eating partner, he may bring
along a newspaper or a magazine as a substitute companion.[10]
And should he have nothing to read, he may elect to sit at the
counter and, by having a quick and simple meal, exhibit that
some of his involvement is lodged in other affairs to which he is
rushing. Facing away from the gathering and toward the counter, he can correct for his exposure in the situation by being
located at its edges if not outside it.[11]

Interestingly enough, there are situations in which certain
minor involvements are explicitly demanded, the implication
being that the occasion is not important enough to justify a complete absorption in the occasioned main involvement. In Shetland Isle, young women participating in evening family conversation were sometimes obliged to knit at the same time, this side
involvement being an important sourse of household income.
Similarly, in one convent we learn that nuns understood that:

9. Apparently one deprivation caused by the 1954 newspaper strike in Britain
was that commuters on the Underground had nothing to hide behind—nothing
into which they could properly withdraw. This meant they had to appear to do
nothing, and for a middle-class Briton this could have implied a slight disorientation in the situation, a kind of self-exposure and "over-presence."

10. Interestingly enough, should the individual read from a scholarly tome in
these situations, he may be considered too absorbed for public propriety, too distracted from the dominating activity, and incidentally too little available in the
situation at large should he suddenly be called upon to direct his attention to
something. It may be added that pocket books, serious though they may be in content, tend to scout this ruling because of their appearance and cost; this may be
one reason for their popularity.

11. In some European restaurants a large table is set aside for solitary arrivals
who do not want to eat alone; why this is not done in America suggests interesting differences between American and Continental regulations concerning social
contact and eating.

You came to the recreation with your workbag. . . . In the bag you carried the work your hands must do while you sat in the circle, for no hands might lie idly folded in the lap. The work, moreover, had to be something manual like darning or knitting. It could not be anything self-absorbing like letter-writing, sketching or reading which would take your attention from the sisters sitting around you.[12]

These illustrations of the balance required between main and side involvements may seem to touch on trivial aspects of behavior, but there are circumstances in which the seriousness of the issue becomes very evident. For example, a constant complaint of patients on the admission wards of mental hospitals is that there is literally nothing to do. Not only does the medical treatment that would seem to constitute the occasioned involvement fail to materialize, but all the usual safety devices for providing subordinate involvements, previously mentioned, may be unavailable, or, if available, may have to be relied upon for a greater period of time than they were apparently designed to manage. Here, improper management of involvement within the situation must be displayed in just those circumstances where its observation by others may be very threatening. The patient, in short, is forced to act oddly just at a time and in a place where the one thing uppermost in his mind may be to demonstrate that he is normal. Should the patient take strong exception to his circumstances, he may be shifted to a "seclusion room," where, quite literally, there may be nothing at all available to provide an acceptable main focus of attention. Alone in a stripped room, it will be nearly impossible for him to act suitably engaged and hence nearly impossible to act sane, and so the patient may try to cover up the judas-hole in the cell door in order to prevent passers-by from transforming a private predicament into a social situation.

Failure to sustain a required degree and kind of main involvement does not occur merely because of a lack of appreciative understanding of what is going on or because of an im-

12. K. Hulme, *The Nun's Story, op. cit.,* p. 59.

poverished environment. While present in a gathering, the individual may find that his concerns and interest lie outside it, being the kind that can be satisfied within an actual social situation but not the current one.[13] The expressed impatience that may result, the sense of straining at the situation's bonds, is something everyone has witnessed and displayed. Common, too, are those conditions that lead an individual to say he is bored and to feel too phlegmatic and affectless to engage in a suitable main involvement. It is worth commenting on another possibility, namely, that an individual can apparently feel too anxious and excited to participate properly. Whatever the acceptable main involvements available in the situation, the individual may find himself too agitated to give the required part of himself up to any of them.[14] Persons who fidget and pace approach this condition; and in mental hospitals, manic patients realize it. One of the most poignant mental hospital scenes is that of a patient too excited or distraught to settle into what is available in the situation, yet desperately attempting to do so. Thus, one famous ex-patient, describing his efforts to control himself during periods of excitement, records:

> I have often felt this ["unhealthy mental excitement"] and felt also that it could be often controlled by a determined exercise of the will. Often I have risen and walked firmly through the room or field, holding myself in as I would rein in a horse which was striving to break away in spite of curb-chain, bridle, or bit.[15]

Sometimes the patient gives the impression that he knows he cannot hope to contain himself in the situation and is now concerned merely with giving others some impression of being properly present. In Central Hospital I observed one patient who would walk from one end of the day-room to the other,

13. The parallel phenomenon in conversations is considered in E. Goffman, "Alienation from Interaction," *Human Relations*, 10 (1957), 47-60.
14. This kind of preoccupation has been memorialized for us in the expectant father cartoon.
15. *The Philosophy of Insanity*, by a Late Inmate of the Glasgow Royal Asylum for Lunatics at Gartnavel (New York: Greenberg, 1947), p. 23.

where there was a doorway leading out to the porch, bravely attempting to give the impression that there was something on the porch he had to see to, and then, without entering the porch, retrace his steps and repeat the cycle. Another patient, a young psychotic woman, with the incredibly rapid tempo of a patient with motor excitement, seemed to attempt to squeeze herself back into the situation by dumping one ashtray into another, one bowl of water into another, one plate of food into another, apparently in the vain hope that it would look as though she were doing something acceptable and meaningful. Another, in repeatedly leaving her cafeteria seat, going to the doorway, and then coming back, would try to cover this anxious action by keeping on her face the studied look of someone who had to be somewhere at a particular time.

There are many social situations where individuals can be found who affect to be caught up in the occasioned proceedings but who in fact have their own special business to pursue and hence their own allocation of involvement. The phrase "to mix with the crowd" tends to be reserved for criminals, detectives, reporters, and other heroes of dissimulation, but the process is in actuality quite a common one.[16] Thus, in some urban public libraries, the staff and the local bums may reach a tacit understanding that dozing is permissible as long as the dozer first draws out a book and props it up in front of his head. In Central Hospital an interesting example of this dissimulation occurred in regard to well-liked attendants who would participate in the organized recreational activity of the parole patients and be quite fully accepted by the patients while doing so. Yet when a fight occurred among the patients at these times, or an attempted escape, the attendant often seemed to be on the scene even before some of the patients present realized anything untoward had happened. At such moments some patients became a little disillusioned, realizing that the attendant's participation was in part merely a show, that his spirit had not been caught up by the occasion, and that all along he had been alertly stand-

16. *The Presentation of Self*, pp. 145-149.

ing guard. It is in cases such as these, when the show of proper involvement is given away, that we obtain a clear outline of the constraints that are usually unfelt and invisible.

Within the walls of a social establishment, formal rules about occasioned main involvements are commonly found. Thus, an important status line in industry can be drawn at the point where employees can be explicitly enjoined to "get to work." (An extreme is seen, apparently, in some Alabama work camps, where "indifference to work" may be punished by the lash or by "cuffing up.") It is well known that "make-work" occurs in these circumstances; namely, an outward show of task activity, an affectation of occasioned main involvement performed at moments of inspection. This activity can be purely situational since it often accomplishes nothing but show.

The problem of maintaining an appropriate main involvement has special bearing on street behavior. The act of purposefully going about one's business, of looking ". . . as though [one] is coming from some place or going to some place,"[17] involves a dominating objective that leaves the actual focus of attention free for other things; one's destination, and therefore one's dominant involvement, lie outside the situation. Where the subordinate main involvements that can result become intense, as in a heated quarrel or a warm caress, the individual may be seen by others as delinquent in the regard that he owes the gathering at large.

In addition to giving the impression of having been diverted from what ought to be the business in mind, individuals may give the impression of having no business at all to get to. Being present in a public place without an orientation to apparent goals outside the situation is sometimes called lolling, when position is fixed, and loitering, when some movement is entailed. Either can be deemed sufficiently improper to merit legal action. On many of our city streets, especially at certain hours, the police will question anyone who appears to be doing nothing and ask him to "move along." (In London, a recent

17. E. G. Love, *Subways Are for Sleeping* (New York: Harcourt, Brace & World, 1957) , p. 28.

court ruling established that an individual has a right to walk on the street but no legal right merely to stand on it.) In Chicago, an individual in the uniform of a hobo can loll on "the stem," but once off this preserve he is required to look as if he were intent on getting to some business destination. Similarly, some mental patients owe their commitment to the fact that the police found them wandering on the streets at off hours without any apparent destination or purpose in mind. An illustration of these street regulations is found in Samuel Beckett's description of the plight of his fictional crippled hero, Molloy, who tries to manage his bicycle, his crutches, and his tiredness all at the same time:

> Thus we cleared these difficult straits, my bicycle and I, together. But a little further on I heard myself hailed. I raised my head and saw a policeman. Elliptically speaking, for it was only later, by way of induction, or deduction, I forget which, that I knew what it was. What are you doing there? he said. I'm used to that question, I understood it immediately. Resting, I said. Resting, he said. Resting, I said. Will you answer my question? he cried. So it always is when I'm reduced to confabulation, I honestly believe I have answered the question I am asked and in reality I do nothing of the kind. I won't reconstruct the conversation in all its meanderings. It ended in my understanding that my way of resting, my attitude when at rest, astride my bicycle, my arms on the handlebars, my head on my arms, was a violation of I don't know what, public order, public decency.[18]

> [Molloy is then taken to jail, questioned, and released.]

> What is certain is this, that I never rested in that way again, my feet obscenely resting on the earth, my arms on the handlebars and on my arms my head, rocking and abandoned. It is indeed a deplorable sight, a deplorable example, for the people, who so need to be encouraged, in their bitter toil, and to have before their eyes manifestations of strength only, of courage and of joy, without which they might collapse, at the end of the day, and roll on the ground.[19]

18. Samuel Beckett, *Molloy* (New York: Grove Press, 1955), pp. 25-26.
19. *Ibid.,* pp. 31-32.

Lolling and loitering are often, but not always, prohibited. In societies in which café life is institutionalized, much permitted lolling seems to exist. Even in our own society, some toleration is given to "lolling groups," in which participants open themselves up to any passing momentary focus of attention and decline to maintain a running conversation unless disposed to do so. These clusters of persons passing the time of day may be found on slum corners, outside small-town stores and barber shops,[20] on the streets during clement weather in some metropolitan wholesale clothing districts, and, paradoxically, on the courthouse lawns of some small towns.[21]

The rule against "having no purpose," or being disengaged, is evident in the exploitation of untaxing involvements to rationalize or mask desired lolling—a way of covering one's physical presence in a situation with a veneer of acceptable visible activity. Thus, when individuals want a "break" in their work routine, they may remove themselves to a place where it is acceptable to smoke and there smoke in a pointed fashion. Certain minimal "recreational" activities are also used as covers for disengagement, as in the case of "fishing" off river banks where it is guaranteed that no fish will disturb one's reverie, or "getting a tan" on the beach—activity that shields reverie or sleep, although, as with hoboes' lolling, a special uniform may have to be worn, which proclaims and institutionalizes this relative inactivity. As might be expected, when the context firmly provides a dominant involvement that is outside the situation, as when riding in a train or airplane, then gazing out the window, or reverie, or sleeping may be quite permissible. In short, the more the setting guarantees that the participant has not withdrawn

20. See, for example, J. West, *Plainville, U.S.A.* (New York: Columbia University Press, 1945), pp. 99-103, and H. Lewis, *Blackways of Kent* (Chapel Hill: University of North Carolina Press, 1955), "The Idling Complex," pp. 68-72.

21. See the papers on "petty offenders" by I. Deutscher: "The White Petty Offender in the Small City," *Social Problems*, 1 (1953), 70-73; "The Petty Offender: A Sociological Alien," *Journal of Criminal Law, Criminology and Police Science*, 44 (1954), 592-595; "The Petty Offender: Society's Orphan," *Federal Probation*, 19 (1955), 12-18.

from what he ought to be involved in, the more liberty it seems
he will have to manifest what would otherwise be considered
withdrawal in the situation.

Here it is useful to reintroduce a consideration of subordinate
involvements such as reading newspapers and looking in shop
windows. Because these involvements in our society represent
legitimate momentary diversions from the legitimate object of
going about one's business, they tend to be employed as covers
when one's objective is not legitimate, as the arts of "tailing"
suspects have made famous. When Sam Spade affects to be examining a suit in a store window, his deeper purpose is not to
try to suggest that he is interested in suits but that he has the
same set of purposes as a person in a public street who diverts
himself for a moment in going about his business to gaze in a
window. Similarly, as an ex-bum tells us, when one's appearance
and real purpose put one outside of the current behavior setting, then a pointedly correct subordinate involvement may be
essential to convince others that one's dominant involvement is
of the kind that is associated with these subordinate involvements:

> One idiosyncrasy that he [a friend] has discovered but cannot ac-
> count for is the attitude of station policemen toward book readers.
> After seven-thirty in the evening, in order to read a book in Grand
> Central or Penn Station, a person either has to wear horn-rimmed
> glasses or look exceptionally prosperous. Anyone else is apt to come
> under surveillance. On the other hand, newspaper readers never
> seem to attract attention and even the seediest vagrant can sit in
> Grand Central all night without being molested if he continues to
> read a paper.[22]

3. Margins of Disinvolvement

The deviations that have been considered all deny in some
way the domination of the individual by the social occasion in

22. E. G. Love, *Subways Are for Sleeping, op. cit.,* p. 28.

which he finds himself. From this, however, it should not be assumed that propriety in situations can be guaranteed by a complete investment of self in an occasioned main involvement. Whatever the prescribed main involvements, and whatever their approved intensity, we usually find, at least in our middle-class society, that the individual is required to give visible evidence that he has not wholly given himself up to this main focus of attention. Some slight margin of self-command and self-possession will typically be required and exhibited. This is the case even though this obligation often must be balanced against the previously mentioned obligation to maintain a minimum of an acceptable main involvement.

Ordinarily the individual can so successfully maintain an impression of due disinvolvement that we tend to overlook this requirement. When a real crisis comes, which induces his complete absorption in a situated task, the crisis itself, as a new social occasion, may conceal, exonerate, and even oblige what would otherwise be a situational delict. During minor crises, however, when the individual has cause to withdraw from general orientation to the gathering but has no license to do so, we may witness wonderfully earnest attempts to demonstrate proper disinvolvement in spite of difficulties. Thus, when a man fully invests himself in running to catch a bus, or finds himself slipping on an icy pavement, he may hold his body optimistically stiff and erect, wearing a painful little smile on his face, as if to say that he is really not much involved in his scramble and has remained in situationally appropriate possession of himself.

There are, apparently, different kinds of overinvolvement in situated activities, as when the individual loudly overinvests himself in cheering at an amateur boxing match or silently overimmerses himself in a chess problem. Again one sees how activities which differ so very much on the surface can have the same expressive significance. Interestingly enough, evidence of the quieter kind of overinvolvement often comes to us through a special class of fuguelike side involvements, these repetitive acts implying that the individual is very deeply involved in a task, often an occasioned one.[23] There seem to be few situations defined to allow such withdrawal into an activity. Therefore, when an intensely involved individual is caught out in one of these dissociated side involvements, he typically reacts with embarrassment, hastily reallocating his involvement in a more acceptable and more accepting way. Only in those situations, such as examinations and competitive sports, where intensive situated involvement is firmly tied to the purpose of the occasion, are deep task involvements likely to be tolerated.

A very common form of involvement control occurs at mealtimes, where, in many sections of Anglo-American society, the individual is expected to eat relatively slowly, not to take food from his neighbor's plate, and in general to conduct himself as if getting his fill were not the most important thing in the world —as if, in fact, eating required very little attention itself. (In Shetland Isle, for example, a community in which most persons were always a little hungry, it was difficult to find an instance where an individual accepting a second helping of food did not first avow that he had had enough and next proclaim that he had been given too much.) In mental hospitals, staff pay tribute to these rulings by constructing social types to epitomize patients who flagrantly break them. There is, for example, the "stuffer," who presses food into his mouth until his cheeks bulge and he turns red and gasps for want of air; there is also the "food grabber," who, not being trusted to respect his neighbor's plate, will either be served alone or tied to his chair during mealtime by means of a sash looped through his shirt collar, like a dog on a leash, to keep him out of other people's territory. Other, less extreme instances found in the hospital form a bridge to behavior

23. Along with these fuguelike signs we are likely to find disarray of posture (and by implication some evidence of rules regarding posture) . One of the early —and one of the few—students of ordinary social gatherings comments:

> When a student in the class-room becomes really absorbed in the problem in hand, he is likely to slip down on his shoulder blades, spread his feet, ruffle his hair, and do any number of other unconventional deeds. Let the spell be broken, and up he sits, rearranges his clothes, and again becomes socially proper.

(C. H. Woolbert, "The Audience," *Psychological Monographs*, 21 [1916], 48-49.)

found in free society. At Central Hospital, for example, it was characteristic of some of the "sicker" adult patients to eat their dessert first, thus suggesting too little control of their desire for sweets and too much involvement in eating. This, of course, is a delict often found in small children, who must be taught to conceal both "overeagerness" for oral indulgences and "oversatisfaction" while consuming them.[24]

In our society, one interesting sign that is taken as evidence of overinvolvement is perspiration; another is a "shaky" voice. More important than these is the phenomenon of shaky hands, a problem for the aged. Individuals with chronic tremors of this kind become "faulty persons," burdening all ordinary interaction with a display of what can be taken as insufficient control over the self. Certain strategies, perhaps independently hit upon, are employed to conceal this sign and to prevent it from giving the lie to the front of proper involvement maintained by the rest of the individual's body. One technique is for the individual to put his hands in his pockets; another, to hold them fast on the table; a third, to hold one shaky hand with the other, while resting one elbow on the table for support.

It may be suggested that the tendency to hold something of himself in reserve may so color an individual's activity that, in those special situations where relatively complete abandonment to a main involvement is required, he may find that he is unable to let himself go. Perhaps the incidence of middle-class frigidity can be understood partly in these terms. In any case, sexual intercourse in our society is preferably carried on under the involvement shield of darkness, for darkness can allow participants to enjoy some of the liberty of not being in a situation at all. This problem, but not this solution, is found, of course, in other settings. Thus, the sharing of an office with another often

24. Appetitive self-control and other involvement rulings are an important part of what parents must teach their children. One basis for the often-stated similarity between mental patients and children is that both groupings must be pressed into compliance with involvement rulings by those in charge. It can be claimed, then, that "regression" is not a return to an infantile state of libidinal organization but rather a manifestation of those problems of situational discipline that incidentally are found among children.

means a limit on work, because extreme concentration and immersion in a task will become an improper handling of oneself in the situation. Some co-workers apparently resolve the issue by gradually according each other the status of nonperson, thus allowing a relaxation of situational proprieties and an increase in situated concentration. This may even be carried to the point where one individual allows himself half-audible "progress grunts" such as, "What do you know!" "Hm hm," "Let's see," without excusing himself to his co-worker.[25] Other dissociated side involvements such as hair twisting may also be indulged in and tolerated in such circumstances.

---

25. Edgar Schein has suggested that if an individual feels obliged to affect deep immersion in some focus of attention, he may of course affect these expressions.

CHAPTER 5

Some Rules About
the Objects of Involvement

I HAVE suggested that in social situations the individual appor-
tions his involvement among main and side involvements, dominating and subordinate ones, and that in each situation a particular apportionment will be defined as proper. In addition,
some general deviations from involvement propriety were described: overdemanding subordinate involvement; lack of occasioned main involvement; insufficient main involvement; and
overinvolvement. In this chapter the specific *objects* or *directions* of involvement will be considered—ones that seem to be a
central concern of involvement regulations and infractions. I
shall be returning to the same behavior, therefore, but from a
slightly different perspective.

1. Auto-involvements

The individual's own body, or an object directly associated
with his body, provides a very common object for his own
involvement. And while such activity may have a technical
instrumental rationale, as when an individual attempts to remove a splinter with a needle, usually a self-decorative or self-
indulgent element is seen to be at work. In any case, as instances
of auto-involvements, of self-directed, self-absorbing physical

acts, we have: eating, dressing, picking one's teeth, cleaning one's fingernails, dozing, and sleeping.[1] These activities will be referred to as "auto-involvements"; the easier term "self-involvements" would seem also to include absorption in less distinctively somatic matters, such as discussion and fantasies concerning the self.

There are marked regional differences regarding permissible auto-involvements while present before others. On business streets in American cities it is permissible for adults to chew gum and even pop small candies into their mouths. But the eating practices found on beach boardwalks would be considered a little out of place—too self-involving not to be a slight affront to others in the situation.

By and large, these "own body" concerns are perceived as subordinate side involvements. An interesting group of examples is quoted by Saul Bellow, with some indignation and wonderment, in an essay dealing with distractions:

While doing housework: You can keep your face creamed, your hair in pin curls; you can practice good standing and walking posture; when you're sitting at the kitchen counter peeling potatoes you can do your ankle exercises and foot strengtheners, and also practice good sitting posture. . . . *While telephoning* (at home, of course) : You can do neck exercises; brush your hair; do ankle exercises, eye exercises, foot strengtheners, and chin-and-neck exercises; practice good standing or sitting posture; even massage your gums (while listening to the other person) . . . . *While reading or watching TV:* You can brush your hair; massage your gums; do your ankle and hand exercises and foot strengtheners; do some bust and back exercises; massage your scalp; use the abrasive treatment for removing superfluous hair.[2]

When others are present, however, these auto-involvements are often seen as improperly distracting from dominating involve-

1. Many examples are provided in M. H. Krout, *Autistic Gestures,* Psychological Monographs, 46 (1935) .
2. Saul Bellow, "Distractions of a Fiction Writer," in *New World Writing No. 12* (New York: New American Library, 1957) , p. 231, quoting from a popular booklet by Constance Hart, *The Handbook of Beauty.*

ments; in any case, situational restrictions are commonly placed upon them. Etiquette books, of course, give warnings against these involvements while in the presence of others:

> Men should never look in the mirror nor comb their hair in public. At most, a man may straighten his necktie and smooth his hair with his hand. It is probably unnecessary to add that it is most unattractive to scratch one's head, to rub one's face or touch one's teeth, or to clean one's fingernails in public. All these things should be done privately. Even a mannerism such as passing one's finger over the cheek or behind the ear can be most unattractive, particularly if it is done in an abstracted, searching way.[3]

As the beginning of this quotation suggests, one type of auto-involvement occurs when the individual checks up on or corrects the state of his personal appearance. One sign that some situations are becoming more laxly defined in our society is that apparently it has become less and less improper for a woman to attend to her personal front in public places without retiring to a special room to do so, as in putting on lipstick or adjusting her hat while at a restaurant table. In any case, this reparative work is felt to be so strategically necessary that provision is often made for appropriate involvement shelters in which these activities can safely occur. In many business offices, for example, one can find half-shielded washstands where a secretary can look into a mirror to apply make-up, comb her hair, examine the effect her face is creating, and the like, being able here to indulge in a degree of auto-involvement not elsewhere permitted.

Mirrors are important objects to study when considering the problem of managing auto-involvements. In American society, apparently, the temptation to make use of nearby mirrors is very difficult to resist; here a level of self-control that ordinarily prevents unacceptable auto-involvement sometimes fails. Often adults can be caught out in fugitive involvements of this kind, reminding us that as children they went through a period of

3. Millicent Fenwick, *Vogue's Book of Etiquette* (New York: Simon and Schuster, 1948) , p. 11.

explicit training to stop them from looking at themselves in mirrors (or in reflecting windows) while in the presence of others.

Attention to personal appearance often entails some pleasurable self-stimulation, providing additional reason for appropriating the terms "preening gesture" and "grooming behavior" from animal sociology for use in describing human social behavior.[4] An extreme instance of this kind of self-absorbing involvement can be seen in the license accorded on beaches to apply suntan oil to one's own skin, slowly and assiduously. But, of course, even in quite formally defined occasions the individual may exercise some liberty to caress fleetingly an exposed part of his own body.

Perhaps the most extreme form of auto-involvement in our middle-class society is masturbation. We appreciate that masturbation may be defined as tolerable on some mental wards, but we tend to overlook the implications of this for normal lower-class, one-sexed settings. Thus, at Central Hospital there were chronic male wards on which two kinds of masturbation occurred: that done by persons felt to be psychotically lax or undisciplined; and "normal" masturbation, that done, typically in a half-concealed fashion, by those patients recognized by their fellows and the attendants as being on the ward not so much because of mental disorder as because they had gotten into some kind of "trouble." Here is an instance where the act is somewhat the same but where the psychodynamic implications are quite different.[5] The "normal" form of masturbation, and the lax social definitions associated with it, are reported, of course, in other all-male, predominantly lower-class settings, such as prisons.[6] Female settings, too, provide instances of this kind of

4. I draw here on suggestions by Ray Birdwhistell.

5. A useful statement of some of the psychodynamic implications of undue auto-involvement may be found in T. S. Szasz, "The Psychology of Bodily Feelings in Schizophrenia," *Psychosomatic Medicine,* 19 (1957), 11-16.

6. See, for example, A. Hassler, *Diary of a Self-Made Convict* (Chicago: Regnery, 1954), p. 63: ". . . it is commonplace to walk into the washroom and find one or more men masturbating into the urinals."

auto-involvement, and similarly within what would appear to be the framework of normal psychology:

"During a visit which I once paid to a manufactory of military clothing," Pouillet writes, "I witnessed the following scene. In the midst of the uniform sound produced by some thirty sewing-machines, I suddenly heard one of the machines working with much more velocity than the others. I looked at the person who was working it, a brunette of 18 or 20. While she was automatically occupied with the trousers she was making on the machine, her face became animated, her mouth opened slightly, her nostrils dilated, her feet moved the pedals with constantly increasing rapidity. Soon I saw a convulsive look in her eyes, her eyelids were lowered, her face turned pale and was thrown backward; hands and legs stopped and became extended; a suffocated cry, followed by a long sigh, was lost in the noise of the workroom. The girl remained motionless a few seconds, drew out her handkerchief to wipe away the pearls of sweat from her forehead, and, after casting a timid and ashamed glance at her companions, resumed her work. The forewoman, who acted as my guide, having observed the direction of my gaze, took me up to the girl, who blushed, lowered her face, and murmured some incoherent words before the forewoman had opened her mouth, to advise her to sit fully on the chair, and not on its edge.

"As I was leaving I heard another machine at another part of the room in accelerated movement. The forewoman smiled at me, and remarked that this was so frequent that it attracted no notice. It was specially observed, she told me, in the case of young workgirls, apprentices, and those who sat on the edge of their seats, thus much facilitating friction of the labia."[7]

There is one further class of auto-involvements that should be examined, what might be called "creature releases." These consist of fleeting acts that slip through the individual's self-control and momentarily assert his "animal nature." They appear to provide a brief release from the tension experienced by the individual in keeping himself steadily and entirely draped in

7. Havelock Ellis, *Studies in the Psychology of Sex* (2 vols.; New York: Random House, 1936), 1, 176-177, citing Pouillet, *L'Onanisme chez la Femme*, Paris, 1880.

social clothing—momentary capitulations to the itches that plague a performer who does not want to sneeze in his role. Loss of control of these creature releases is an important means by which individuals demonstrate that they are sustaining little situational presence.

A continuum or hierarchy of these creature releases seems to be recognized, varying according to the degree to which they discredit one's readiness for what the situation is likely to bring. At one extreme are the minor releases such as scratching, momentary coughing, rubbing one's eyes, sighing, yawning, and so forth; at the other extreme are such acts as flatulence, incontinence, and the like; in the middle ranges of the continuum are dozing off, belching, spitting, nose picking, or loosening one's belt. Extending from one end of the continuum to the other are various depths of sudden so-called emotional expressions, such as an outright laugh, a shout or cry, an unsuppressed curse; these acts can suggest a momentary loss of control over affect theretofore held in acceptable check. It may be added that since these creature releases tend by nature to be brief, they are well suited to furtive or shielded expression, as when a man hides a yawn behind his hand, or scratches his private parts from within his pants pocket, or circumspectly wipes his itchy nose on a shielding handkerchief.

2. *Away*

While outwardly participating in an activity within a social situation, an individual can allow his attention to turn from what he and everyone else considers the real or serious world, and give himself up for a time to a playlike world in which he alone participates. This kind of inward emigration from the gathering may be called "away," and we find that strict situational regulations obtain regarding it.[8]

8. The term "away" is taken from G. Bateson and M. Mead, *Balinese Character* (New York: New York Academy of Sciences, 1942) , pp. 68-69. See also "Communication Conduct in an Island Community," Chap. 17.

Perhaps the most important kind of away is that through which the individual relives some past experiences or rehearses some future ones, this taking the form of what is variously called reverie, brown study, woolgathering, daydreaming, or autistic thinking.[9] At such times the individual may demonstrate his absence from the current situation by a preoccupied, faraway look in his eyes, or by a sleeplike stillness of his limbs, or by that special class of side involvements that can be sustained in an utterly "unconscious" abstracted manner—humming, doodling, drumming the fingers on a table, hair twisting, nose picking, scratching. (Incidentally, these fuguelike side involvements, as suggested previously, are also the ones that can convey that the individual has become carried far away by a meditative task he is performing.) In any case, reverie constitutes an eloquent sign of departure from all public concrete matters within the situation.

The degree to which individuals ordinarily go away in situations in which they are participants, whether concealing this disaffection from the others or not, is little known. It can be assumed, however, that every round of life provides at least a few places for getting away with going away. Some occupations are especially rich in this regard. In the tourist hotel on Shetland Isle, for example, dishwashers could keep pace with the work while allowing their minds to wander completely, and would sometimes end up in abstracted singing that was so patently away as to be cut short by the manager. So, too, at the community gatherings, local musicians on the stage were able to play while allowing themselves to drift quite far away; they would come out of their several reveries together at the end of a number with a little wave of joking that showed how far from the dancers they had actually been. Certain jobs, of course, such as that of night watchman, may be chosen with these away possibilities in mind.

Some social establishments seem particularly plagued by the

9. A psychiatric version of autism is presented by E. Bleuler. See his *Dementia Praecox*, also "Autistic Thinking," in D. Rapaport, trans., *Organization and Pathology of Thought* (New York: Columbia University Press, 1951), Chap. 20.

fact that members find too many opportunities for reverie. The biographer of an ex-nun, for example, writes as follows about a group of newly professed nuns in a convent:

> Her companions came as usual with their little black bags, but some of them, she observed, had the look of sleepwalkers. Their wide-open eyes seemed to be focused on a distant glory as they made their bows to the presiding Mistress and took the nearest unoccupied chair without, as formerly, looking about to choose a place in the circle where their presence might do the most good. . . .
>
> "The tendency toward mysticism is always a problem in a mixed Order such as ours where work and contemplation must go hand in hand. One sees this often in the newly professed and while it is a very beautiful thing to see a young nun apparently communing directly with God, she is nevertheless lost to the community when in that rapture and someone's else mind, hands and feet must do her work meanwhile. One can never know, of course, if it is the real thing or simply one of those unconscious singularizations to which we all fall prey from time to time."
>
> The silence of the preoccupied ones did not escape the attention of the presiding Mistress. She drew the dreamers back into the sewing circle with direct questions about their assignments. . . .[10]

On some mental hospital wards, aways are not directly penalized and patients may spend years walking up and down the hallways ruminating on the relations they left behind them, coming out of their away only when hospital administration forcibly impinges on them.[11] In such settings, awayness may be not only tolerated but also engendered, as when a patient in seclusion finds nothing tangible in the cell to put his mind on, or when all the patients on a ninety-bed ward are herded into one of the two dayrooms in order that the other can be mopped or waxed, and thus find themselves bunched so closely together that a useful defense is to withdraw into oneself and suppress orientation to the others. In these contexts the participant-observer can

10. K. Hulme, *The Nun's Story* (London: Muller, 1956) , pp. 69-70.
11. A good description of this state in terms of what he calls "chronic demoralization" and "despair" is provided by H. S. Sullivan, "Psychiatric Aspects of Morale," *American Journal of Sociology,* 47 (1941) , 281.

soon learn to disattend to incontinence and hallucinations occurring eighteen inches away. And in such settings we know
something about how hard it may be for the individual to bring
himself out of his away in order to participate in talk with
others present.[12] Perhaps these facts can help one to understand
the classic back-ward phenomenon of the patient who is sufficiently "present" to ask courteously for a cigarette but who is
sufficiently preoccupied to let the cigarette burn short enough
to char his fingers.

As was suggested in connection with lolling, individuals develop many untaxing activities as covers behind which to go
into a reverie. The coffee-and-cigarette break when taken by
oneself is an instance of this. Public eateries have underwritten
this practice by placing seats for lone eaters in front of a running mirror, thus enabling the patron to facilitate the away
process by covertly looking at himself. Persons who find themselves disenchanted with the whole system of situational obligations in society may seek out those places where reverie is likely
to be tolerated. As one very literate patient in Central Hospital
is recorded to have said:

> To avoid gossip I began to frequent dives of every type, where I
> thought no one would see me. I merely sat there for hours thinking
> and looking off into space, entertaining a confused set of ideas.

While the silent or brown study kind of awayness is perhaps
the main type, other kinds are also observable. First, there is
what is usually called "talking to oneself," which can be narrowly defined as holding a vocal or gestural conversation where
the person with whom one is conversing is oneself. On the stage
these actions are termed soliloquies and have been institutionalized as permissible dramaturgical devices. In real life in our
society, however, there tends to be the understanding that only
the mentally ill, the not yet taught, and the foolish engage in

12. See, for example, M. L. Hayward and J. E. Taylor, "A Schizophrenic Patient Describes the Action of Intensive Psychotherapy," *Psychiatric Quarterly*, 30
(1956) , 1-38.

this activity. Actually, there are many circumstances in which persons will talk to themselves and find that this is tolerated. For example, if an individual acts ineptly he may carefully curse himself audibly to show that he, too, finds such ineptness unacceptable and, in addition, uncharacteristic of him, apparently preferring to be someone who talks to himself rather than someone who characteristically errs as he has just done. Similarly, in what we call "muttering," the individual seems willing to be known as someone who talks to himself rather than as someone who accepts affronts without taking action. Except when this kind of face-saving is occurring, however, persons who talk to themselves typically take care to do so only when they are certain of not being confronted with someone and hence with a social situation. Self-talkers who are particularly wary of being suddenly come upon may shield their potential impropriety by leaving their mouths open a little, so that signs of vocalization can be less readily detected by suddenly appearing witnesses.

Another variety of away occurs when the individual audibly engages in rehearsing or reliving a conversation with a real person other than himself who happens not to be there. Individuals, of course, frequently converse this way "in their minds," as when practicing what they will say to their boss or to an audience. But rarely, it would seem, do they audibly give the show away.

There is a final type of away that should be mentioned. When an individual finds himself in a gathering from whose activities he wishes to insulate himself, he may give up his attention to an activity that is of a fanciful, fantasy kind (and in this sense similar to the imagined world of the reverie), and yet use materials for the construction of this alienated world that are visible to others. A component of disinterested intellectual pursuit will be present. This type of activity is illustrated by the individual who constructs elaborate doodles, or piles matches on the top of a bottle, or works jigsaw puzzles, and by the child who walks in such a way as to avoid the cracks in the pavement, or hops for a distance on one foot, or holds a stick against fence posts as he passes by, or kicks a can along his route.[13] In American society another instance is provided by the mother who takes interactional leave of the situation in which she is physically fixed by playing for a moment with her infant, even while another adult may be directing statements to the conversational cluster of which the parent is a ratified member. The positive sanction behind mother-love, and the notion that, ceremonially speaking, children are not complete persons and hence not complete distractions, help to give impunity to those who employ this strategy. In Shetland Isle the ubiquitous household cat was similarly significant: a Shetlander caught in a social gathering he found undesirable sometimes turned to teasing the cat, repeating half-aloud the responses his teasings would presumably call forth could the cat talk. Thus, a man who was drawn to the kitchen by the warmth and tea available there, but repelled by the circle of women present, could have his comfort in safety by using the cat as a means of removing himself from the women's circle.

Chronic patients in Central Hospital frequently employed these "toy-involvements" as a means of going away. Walking up the steps in a line of patients coming back from lunch, one person would suddenly stoop and take delight in examining a small fleck of color in the concrete. Other patients, especially ones felt to be extremely regressed and deteriorated, would for long periods of time focus their total attention on little bits of grime adhering to the ends of their fingers, sometimes licking the specks, or, on little mounds of dust on the floor, or they would slowly and carefully trace with their fingertips the grain and other markings on the floor next to where they were crouched. In these ways they effectively pulled the whole world in on them until the circle of reality was not more than a foot in diameter around their noses. Of course, some of the toy-involvements used by the patients were not far from civil practices. For example, when a delivery truck would park outside the patient

13. These kinds of contained diversions are nicely illustrated in H. Wright and R. Barker, *Methods in Psychological Ecology* (Topeka, Kansas: Ray's Printing Service, 1950), esp. p. 166.

canteen building, one patient would draw finger patterns on the dust of the panel body; another, on the ward, would while away the time by cutting chains out of newspapers.

A final comment should be added. A brief spate of behavior can, of course, exhibit more than one type of improper involvement, showing in several different ways how the individual has insufficient situational presence. Improper creature releases, for example, are often associated with the state of being away. Thus, at Central Hospital it was possible to observe a patient ejecting chewed chicken from her overstuffed mouth and carefully examining it with both hands in a bemused way, or doing the same with the mucus she had removed from her nose. Another female patient would spit, but not far enough out to clear her dress, and would then show concentrated interest in watching the spittle slowly spread and disappear into the cloth. An angry elderly male patient would cough up phlegm and then play with it abstractedly on the table before eventually wiping it off.

3. Occult Involvements

Soliloquies and audible internal dialogues are characterized by the individual's knowing that the person he is talking to is either himself or is not there in real conversation with him. Reveries have the same character: the individual knows he really is not in the world he is allowing himself to drift into, or at least he can be easily reminded of the fact. However, there is a kind of awayness where the individual gives others the impression, whether warranted or not, that he is not aware that he is "away." This is the area of what psychiatry terms "hallucinations" and "delusionary states." Corresponding to these "unnatural" verbal activities, there are unnatural bodily ones, where the individual's activity is patently tasklike but not "understandable" or "meaningful." The unnatural action may even involve the holding or grasping of something, as when an adult mental patient retains a tight hold on a doll or a fetish-like piece of cloth. Here the terms "mannerism," "ritual act," or "posturing" are applied, which, like the term "unnatural," are clear enough in their way but hardly tell us with any specificity what it is that characterizes "natural" acts. I shall refer to these somehow unnatural conversational and bodily activities as "occult involvements."

Occult involvements are characteristically distinguished from aways by the difference in consequence following discovery. A person who is in a reverie, and is discovered or discovers himself in it, typically snaps back to interactional attention and reorients himself to the situation at large; those with occult involvements characteristically do not. A four-year-old child may tell you not to interrupt him when he is talking roles to himself, but an adult who assumes this right is felt to be involved in an occult way.

One of the disturbing and characteristic things about occult involvements, both verbal and bodily, is that the others present cannot "get at" the general intention by which the individual is apparently governed, and cannot credit the offender's account should he offer one. This suggests that in ordinary life there is an expectation that all situated activity, if not obviously "occasioned," will have a degree of transparency, a degree of immediate understandability, for all persons present. It is not that the specific actions of the actor must be fully understood—they certainly are not, for example, when the family watches the repairman fix the TV set—but merely that they be given a situational coating through being in a context of known ends or generally recognized techniques. If the others present have no such guarantee that the actor's mind is in a known and natural place for minds to be, they may sense that his mind may be too far away to allow for appropriate concern for the gathering. Occult involvements, of course, are among the classic psychiatric symptoms that lead to commitment proceedings. A person who weeps or is acutely apprehensive without apparent cause, or who burns his personal belongings, or who tears up his postal-savings certificates, or who dips his Bible in a bowl of water, gives the impression of not being present in the situation in the sense that his coparticipants presumably are. As one female patient suggested in group therapy:

> It seems patients are always getting in trouble walking. I walked for two days and the cops picked me up; I was going, I thought, to a little island to get away. I had a loaf of bread and some fishing hooks.

Perhaps it is this quality of not being present and not being readily recallable to the gathering, rather than the specificities of the improper conduct itself, that creates the disturbing impressions. Certainly the tendency to evoke this impression of alienation from activity within the situation is one of the few things that all of these quite diverse behaviors share.

Impressions of occult involvement often occur not because of any direct orientation of the individual to something not there but as a by-product of the way he handles something recognized by others to be there. For example, the psychiatric notion of affect that is improper, inappropriate, or shallow can refer to the patient responding in a light-hearted, mirthful way to something that concerns him seriously. It may be felt that, if the patient allocates this kind of involvement to such matters, he has fixed his serious concern upon something that is not natural and is not present. A similar impression is given by the patient who is on the grounds when it begins to rain and who, unlike others caught outside, does not walk faster or pull his clothes more tightly about him. Since he does not have a fitting concern for his own physical welfare, it is an open question as to just what it is he is concerned with. Bordering on this form of occult involvement, incidentally, is the absent-minded professor theme —a person too much immersed in faraway abstruse thought to show proper mindfulness of some of the petty situated details that confront ordinary walkers. But here, of course, it is just the presence of professorial matters of intellectual interest that gives these figures the claim of natural distraction and the right to be absent-minded professors.[14]

When an individual is perceived in an occult involvement, observers may not only sense that they are not able to claim him at the moment but also feel that the offender's complete activity up till then has been falsely taken as a sign of his participation with them, that all along he has been alienated from their world. (This seems to be especially so in those wakeful occult involvements where the offender can supply a lively statement of the object of his special engrossment, which, however, persons present cannot possibly credit.) This retrospective aspect of the offense is often followed by the feeling that all of the offender's oncoming conduct is suspect.[15] The kind of trust-in-the-other that is necessary if persons are to be in each other's presence and get on with their separate affairs can then be lost, and the offender ruined as a candidate for social intercourse. In a sense, then, a paranoid person is someone who has acted in such a way as to cause others to be suspicious and watchful of everything that he does; the persecutory feelings that result may be quite justified.[16]

While the taboo against occult involvement becomes of special significance for persons who are, or who become, mental patients, it has a controlling diffuse effect throughout our society, and it is here, perhaps, among nonpatients, that its most revealing significance lies. Although an individual may never in fact sustain an occult involvement, he is sure to find himself, in some situation or other, acting in a way that others might construe, at least for a moment, as occult. In such cases, he must modify his act to protect his reputation. Thus, when a man goes

14. Here a wonderfully limiting case was provided by Albert Einstein, whose clothing pattern seemed to provide a unique illustration of the permissibly unconventional. Although his attire suggested that he was entirely off in his own world, his particular exclusive world could be recognized as a real or meaningful one. The one person who could best get away with dressing like an Einstein was Einstein.

15. Here I am grateful to the unpublished work of Harold Garfinkel.

16. In this connection see the suggestive paper by E. Lemert, "Paranoia and the Dynamics of Exclusion," *Sociometry*, 25 (1962), 2-20.

down on all-fours to find a cufflink in the grass, and a passer-by suddenly obtrudes upon the lonely search, the seeker is likely to break the rule against audibly talking to himself in order to make it perfectly clear that his pursuit is a natural one. Similarly, when one person comes upon another who is waiting at an entrance for a third, the waiting person may glance at his watch and look up and down the street to give a visible familiar shape to his intention, ensuring the protection of a proper dominating activity that now requires him to be inactive.

Two qualifications should now be appended to what has been said about occult involvements. First, the fact that others regularly interpret the activity of an individual as "meaningless" or "crazy" is not proof that it is, nor even proof that meaning will have to be sought by reverting to the kind of extended symbolic interpretation sometimes attempted in psychoanalysis.[17] Second, the occultness of an act is not intrinsic to it, and, of course, must be related to some group that so defines it. There are societies in which conversation with a spirit not present is as acceptable when sustained by properly authorized persons as is conversation over a telephone in American society. And even in American society, those who attend a séance would not consider it inappropriate for the medium to interact with "someone on the other side," whether they believed this to be a staged or a genuine interaction. And certainly we define praying as acceptable when done at proper occasions. But in all of these cases, the observers either believe that the actor is in fact communicating to someone or something, or they are tactfully aware that an appreciable number of other participants may believe this. To the degree that such beliefs and tactful concerns are shared, these involvements, of course, cease to be occult in the sociological sense, whatever their scientific status.

---

17. A good example of this kind of analysis in depth may be found in M. A. Sechehaye, *Symbolic Realization*, trans. B. and H. Wursten (New York: International Universities Press, 1951).

PART THREE

Focused
Interaction

CHAPTER 6

Face Engagements

EARLIER it was suggested that a consideration of situational proprieties can be divided into two analytical parts—unfocused interaction, concerned with what can be communicated between persons merely by virtue of their presence together in the same social situation; and focused interaction, concerned with clusters of individuals who extend one another a special communication license and sustain a special type of mutual activity that can exclude others who are present in the situation. It is this focused interaction that will now be considered.

1. Civil Inattention

When persons are mutually present and not involved together in conversation or other focused interaction, it is possible for one person to stare openly and fixedly at others, gleaning what he can about them while frankly expressing on his face his response to what he sees—for example, the "hate stare" that a Southern white sometimes gratuitously gives to Negroes walking past him.[1] It is also possible for one person to treat others as if they were not there at all, as objects not worthy of a glance, let

1. J. H. Griffin, *Black Like Me* (Boston: Houghton Mifflin, 1961), pp. 54, 128.

alone close scrutiny. Moreover, it is possible for the individual, by his staring or his "not seeing," to alter his own appearance hardly at all in consequence of the presence of the others. Here we have "nonperson" treatment; it may be seen in our society in the way we sometimes treat children, servants, Negroes, and mental patients.[2]

Currently, in our society, this kind of treatment is to be contrasted with the kind generally felt to be more proper in most situations, which will here be called "civil inattention." What seems to be involved is that one gives to another enough visual notice to demonstrate that one appreciates that the other is present (and that one admits openly to having seen him), while at the next moment withdrawing one's attention from him so as to express that he does not constitute a target of special curiosity or design.

In performing this courtesy the eyes of the looker may pass over the eyes of the other, but no "recognition" is typically allowed. Where the courtesy is performed between two persons passing on the street, civil inattention may take the special form of eyeing the other up to approximately eight feet, during which time sides of the street are apportioned by gesture, and then casting the eyes down as the other passes—a kind of dimming of lights. In any case, we have here what is perhaps the slightest of interpersonal rituals, yet one that constantly regulates the social intercourse of persons in our society.

By according civil inattention, the individual implies that he has no reason to suspect the intentions of the others present and no reason to fear the others, be hostile to them, or wish to avoid them. (At the same time, in extending this courtesy he automatically opens himself up to a like treatment from others present.) This demonstrates that he has nothing to fear or avoid in being seen and being seen seeing, and that he is not ashamed of himself or of the place and company in which he finds himself. It will therefore be necessary for him to have a certain "directness" of eye expression. As one student suggests, the individual's

2. *The Presentation of Self,* pp. 151-153.

gaze ought not to be guarded or averted or absent or defensively dramatic, as if "something were going on." Indeed, the exhibition of such deflected eye expressions may be taken as a symptom of some kind of mental disturbance.[3]

Civil inattention is so delicate an adjustment that we may expect constant evasion of the rules regarding it. Dark glasses, for example, allow the wearer to stare at another person without that other being sure that he is being stared at.[4] One person can look at another out of the corner of his eyes. The fan and parasol once served as similar aids in stealing glances, and in polite Western society the decline in use of these instruments in the last fifty years has lessened the elasticity of communication arrangements.[5] It should be added, too, that the closer the onlookers are to the individual who interests them, the more exposed his position (and theirs), and the more obligation they will feel to ensure him civil inattention. The further they are from him, the more license they will feel to stare at him a little.

3. M. D. Riemer, "Abnormalities of the Gaze—A Classification," *Psychiatric Quarterly*, 29 (1955), 659-672.

4. A notable observer of face-to-face conduct, the novelist William Sansom, disputes this point in "Happy Holiday Abroad," in *A Contest of Ladies* (London: Hogarth Press, 1956), p. 228:

> Slowly he walked the length of the beach, pretending to saunter, studying each bather sideways from behind his black spectacles. One would think such dark glasses might conceal the inquisitive eye: but Preedy knew better, *he* knew they do the opposite, as soon as they are swivelled anywhere near the object it looks like a direct hit. You cannot appear to glance just beyond with your dark guns on.

5. See P. Binder, *Muffs and Morals* (New York: Morrow, n.d.), Chap. 9, "Umbrellas, Walking-Sticks, and Fans," pp. 178-196. The author suggests, p. 193:

> Another quizzing fan [in eighteenth-century England] had an inset of mica or gauze, so that a lady might cunningly use her fan as a lorgnette while her face appeared to be screened from view. This type of fan was intended for use at a risqué play, where modesty required some equivalent to the earlier facemask.

Successful devices of this kind must incorporate three features: the user must be able to look at the other, be able to give the appearance of not being ashamed of being seen by the other, and be able to conceal that he is in fact spying. Children in Shetland Isle primary schools handle visiting strangers with something like a fan—but one that fails in the last two counts—by shyly hiding their faces behind their two hands while peeking out at the visitor from a crack between two fingers.

In addition to these evasions of rules we also may expect frequent infractions of them. Here, of course, social class subculture and ethnic subculture introduce differences in patterns, and differences, too, in the age at which patterns are first employed.

The morale of a group in regard to this minimal courtesy of civil inattention—a courtesy that tends to treat those present merely as participants in the gathering and not in terms of other social characteristics—is tested whenever someone of very divergent social status or very divergent physical appearance is present. English middle-class society, for example, prides itself in giving famous and infamous persons the privilege of being civilly disattended in public, as when the Royal children manage to walk through a park with few persons turning around to stare. And in our own American society, currently, we know that one of the great trials of the physically handicapped is that in public places they will be openly stared at, thereby having their privacy invaded, while, at the same time, the invasion exposes their undesirable attributes.[6]

> The act of staring is a thing which one does not ordinarily do to another human being; it seems to put the object stared at in a class apart. One does not talk to a monkey in a zoo, or to a freak in a sideshow—one only stares.[7]

An injury, as a characteristic and inseparable part tof the body, may be felt to be a personal matter which the man would like to keep private. However, the fact of its visibility makes it known to anyone whom the injured man meets, including the stranger. A visible injury differs from most other personal matters in that anyone can deal with it regardless of the wish of the injured person; anyone can stare at the injury or ask questions about it, and in both cases communicate to and impose upon the injured person his feelings and evaluations. His action is then felt as an intrusion into

6. See the very useful paper by R. K. White, B. A. Wright, and T. Dembo, "Studies in Adjustment to Visible Injuries: Evaluation of Curiosity by the Injured," *Journal of Abnormal and Social Psychology*, 43 (1948) , 13-28.
7. *Ibid.*, p. 22.

privacy. It is the visibility of the injury which makes intrusion into privacy so easy. The men are likely to feel that they have to meet again and again people who will question and stare, and to feel powerless because they cannot change the general state of affairs . . .[8]

Perhaps the clearest illustration both of civil inattention and of the infraction of this ruling occurs when a person takes advantage of another's not looking to look at him, and then finds that the object of his gaze has suddenly turned and caught the illicit looker looking. The individual caught out may then shift his gaze, often with embarrassment and a little shame, or he may carefully act as if he had merely been seen in the moment of observation that is permissible; in either case we see evidence of the propriety that should have been maintained.

To behave properly and to have the *right* to civil inattention are related: propriety on the individual's part tends to ensure his being accorded civil inattention; extreme impropriety on his part is likely to result in his being stared at or studiously not seen. Improper conduct, however, does not automatically release others from the obligation of extending civil inattention to the offender, although it often weakens it. In any case, civil inattention may be extended in the face of offensiveness simply as an act of tactfulness, to keep an orderly appearance in the situation in spite of what is happening.

Ordinarily, in middle-class society, failure to extend civil inattention to others is not negatively sanctioned in a direct and open fashion, except in the social training of servants and children, the latter especially in connection with according civil inattention to the physically handicapped and deformed. For examples of such direct sanctions among adults one must turn to despotic societies where glancing at the emperor or his agents may be a punishable offense,[9] or to the rather refined rules prevailing in some of our Southern states concerning how much of a look a colored male can give to a white female, over how

8. *Ibid.*, pp. 16-17.
9. R. K. Douglas, *Society in China* (London: Innes, 1894), p. 11.

much distance, before it is interpreted as a punishable sexual advance.[10]

Given the pain of being stared at, it is understandable that staring itself is widely used as a means of negative sanction, socially controlling all kinds of improper public conduct. Indeed it often constitutes the first warning an individual receives that he is "out of line" and the last warning that it is necessary to give him. In fact, in the case of those whose appearance tests to the limit the capacity of a gathering to proffer civil inattention, staring itself may become a sanction against staring. The autobiography of an ex-dwarf provides an illustration:

> There were the thick-skinned ones, who stared like hill people come down to see a traveling show. There were the paper-peekers, the furtive kind who would withdraw blushing if you caught them at it. There were the pitying ones, whose tongue clickings could almost be heard after they had passed you. But even worse, there were the chatterers, whose every remark might as well have been "How do you do, poor boy?" They said it with their eyes and their manners and their tone of voice.
>
> I had a standard defense—a cold stare. Thus anesthetized against my fellow man, I could contend with the basic problem—getting in and out of the subway alive.[11]

2. The Structure of Face Engagements

When two persons are mutually present and hence engaged together in some degree of unfocused interaction, the mutual proffering of civil inattention—a significant form of unfocused interaction—is not the only way they can relate to one another. They can proceed from there to engage one another in focused

10. See, for example, the notable Webster-Ingram case reported November 12-13, 1952 (AP). In many societies in Africa and Asia, a similar taboo exists regarding glances that males cast females.

11. H. Viscardi, Jr., *A Man's Stature* (New York: John Day, 1952), p. 70, as cited in B. A. Wright, *Physical Disability—A Psychological Approach* (New York: Harper & Bros., 1960), p. 214.

interaction, the unit of which I shall refer to as a *face engage-ment* or an *encounter*.[12] Face engagements comprise all those instances of two or more participants in a situation joining each other openly in maintaining a single focus of cognitive and visual attention—what is sensed as a single *mutual activity*, entailing preferential communication rights. As a simple example —and one of the most common—when persons are present together in the same situation they may engage each other in a talk. This accreditation for mutual activity is one of the broadest of all statuses. Even persons of extremely disparate social positions can find themselves in circumstances where it is fitting to impute it to one another. Ordinarily the status does not have a "latent phase" but obliges the incumbents to be engaged at that very moment in exercising their status.

Mutual activities and the face engagements in which they are embedded comprise instances of small talk, commensalism, love-making, gaming, formal discussion, and personal servicing (treating, selling, waitressing, and so forth). In some cases, as with sociable chats, the coming together does not seem to have a ready instrumental rationale. In other cases, as when a teacher pauses at a pupil's desk to help him for a moment with a problem he is involved in, and will be involved in after she moves on, the encounter is clearly a setting for a mutual instrumental activity, and this joint work is merely a phase of what is primarily an individual task.[13] It should be noted that while many face engagements seem to be made up largely of the exchange of verbal statements, so that conversational encounters can in

12. The term "encounter," which is much the easier of the two to use, has some common-sense connotations that ought here to be ruled out. First, the term is sometimes used to refer to mediated, as well as to direct, contact between two persons, as when persons have correspondence with each other. Secondly, the term is sometimes used with an implication of there having been difficulty or trouble during the interaction, as in the phrase "a run-in." Finally, the term is sometimes used to cover occasions which bring two persons into easy access to each other, regardless of how many times they may come together in a joint conversation during this time, as in the phrase, "I next encountered him at the Jones's party." I have attempted to consider the internal dynamics of encounters in "Fun in Games" in *Encounters*, pp. 17-81.

13. Suggested by Arthur Stinchcombe.

fact be used as the model, there are still other kinds of encounters where no word is spoken. This becomes very apparent, of course, in the study of engagements among children who have not yet mastered talk, and where, incidentally, it is possible to see the gradual transformation of a mere physical contacting of another into an act that establishes the social relationship of jointly accrediting a face-to-face encounter.[14] Among adults, too, however, nonverbal encounters can be observed: the significant acts exchanged can be gestures[15] or even, as in board and card games, moves. Also, there are certain close comings-together over work tasks which give rise to a single focus of visual and cognitive attention and to intimately coordinated contributions, the order and kind of contribution being determined by shared appreciation of what the task-at-the-moment requires as the next act. Here, while no word of direction or sociability may be spoken, it will be understood that lack of attention or coordinated response constitutes a breach in the mutual commitment of the participants.[16]

14. See, for example, the early study by A. Beaver, *The Initiation of Social Contacts by Preschool Children* (New York: Bureau of Publications, Teachers College, Columbia University, Child Development Monographs, No. 7, 1932), pp. 1-14.

15. D. Efron, *Gesture and Environment* (New York: King's Crown Press, 1941), p. 38.

16. The kind of intimate coordination consequent on involvement in the same task is nicely described in F. B. Miller, " 'Situational' Interactions—A Worthwhile Concept?" *Human Organization*, 17 (Winter, 1958-59), 37-47. After pointing out the differences between this kind of focused interaction and the kind necessarily involving speech or gestures, the writer does not, however, go on to consider the similarities, such as the fact that withdrawal of attention, or ineptness, can give rise to the same kind of corrective social control in both cases. A well-described illustration of a task activity as an engagement may be found in T. Burling, *Essays on Human Aspects of Administration* (New York State School of Industrial and Labor Relations, Cornell University, Bulletin 25, August, 1953), pp. 10-11:

What is actually happening is that the changing needs of the patient, as they develop in the course of the operation, determine what everybody does. When a surgical team has worked long enough together to have developed true teamwork, each member has such a grasp of the total situation and of his role in it that the needs of the patient give unequivocal orders. A small artery is cut and begins to spurt. In a chain-of-command organization the surgeon would note this and say to the assistant, "Stop that bleeder." The assistant, in turn, would say to the surgical nurse, "Give me a hemostat," and thus, coordinated effort would be achieved. What actually happens is that the bleeder gives a simultane-

Where there are only two participants in a situation, an encounter, if there is to be one, will *exhaust* the situation, giving us a *fully-focused gathering*. With more than two participants, there may be persons officially present in the situation who are officially excluded from the encounter and not themselves so engaged. These unengaged[17] participants change the gathering into a *partly-focused* one. If more than three persons are present, there may be more than one encounter carried on in the same situation—a *multifocused* gathering. I will use the term *participation unit* to refer both to encounters and to unengaged participants; the term *bystander* will be used to refer to any individual present who is not a ratified member of the particular encounter in question, whether or not he is currently a member of some other encounter.

In our society, face engagements seem to share a complex of properties, so that this class of social unit can be defined analytically, as well as by example.

An encounter is initiated by someone making an opening move, typically by means of a special expression of the eyes but sometimes by a statement or a special tone of voice at the beginning of a statement.[18] The engagement proper begins when this

---

ous command to all three members of the team, all of whom have been watching the progress of the operation with equal attention. It says to the surgeon, "Get your hand out of the way until this is controlled." It says to the instrument nurse, "Get a hemostat ready," and it says to the assistant, "Clamp that off." This is the highest and most efficient type of cooperation known. It is so efficient that it looks simple and even primitive. It is possible only where every member of the team knows not only his own job thoroughly, but enough about the total job and that of each of the other members to see the relationship of what he does to everything else that goes on.

17. An "unengaged" participant may of course be involved in a task or other main focus of attention and hence not be "disengaged" in the situation.
18. When the individual is socially subordinated to the one to whom he is about to initiate an encounter overture, he may be required to use a minimal sign so that the superior can easily continue to overlook it, or can respond to it at his own convenience. For example, *Esquire Etiquette* (New York: Lippincott, 1953), p. 24, in listing the habits of a good secretary, includes "waiting to be recognized, when she has stepped in to speak to you, before interrupting whatever you are doing." In such cases the fiction is maintained that the superordinate alone can initiate an engagement. The classic case here is the mythical butler who coughs discreetly so that his master will take note of his presence and allow him to deliver a message.

overture is acknowledged by the other, who signals back with his eyes, voice, or stance that he has placed himself at the disposal of the other for purposes of a mutual eye-to-eye activity—even if only to ask the initiator to postpone his request for an audience.

There is a tendency for the initial move and the responding "clearance" sign to be exchanged almost simultaneously, with all participants employing both signs, perhaps in order to prevent an initiator from placing himself in a position of being denied by others. Glances, in particular, make possible this effective simultaneity. In fact, when eyes are joined, the initiator's first glance can be sufficiently tentative and ambiguous to allow him to act as if no initiation has been intended, if it appears that his overture is not desired.

Eye-to-eye looks, then, play a special role in the communication life of the community, ritually establishing an avowed openness to verbal statements and a rightfully heightened mutual relevance of acts.[19] In Simmel's words:

19. In face engagements embodying a formal sports activity, opening moves may take other forms, as when boxers touch gloves, or swordsmen touch foils, in order to establish a sporting bracket or frame, as it were, around the oncoming encounter. Where participants know each other well, clearance signs may be taken for granted, and the initiator may pause slightly or in other ways slightly modify his opening action, as a courtesy, and then proceed as if clearance had been granted.

Interestingly enough, some face engagements are of the kind in which coordination of activity is typically embodied in the usual ritual brackets of eye-recognition and exchange of words, but which, under special circumstances, are carefully initiated, maintained, and terminated *without* usual verbal or gestural overlay. Thus, in many mental hospitals, patients expect to be able to call on *any* patient who is smoking for a light, regardless of how withdrawn or regressed the smoker may appear to be. The gestured request for a light seems to be invariably complied with, but very often the complier addresses himself to the technical task alone, declining any other kind of negotiation or business. A similar kind of deritualized encounter is found where a man holds a door open for a woman he does not know, under circumstances that could imply an overture or could bring home undesirable facts about the woman for being in the region; under such circumstances the male may be careful to proffer civil inattention even while nicely adjusting his physical behavior to the movements of the woman. Emily Post, *Etiquette* (New York: Funk and Wagnalls, 1937), p. 26, suggests a similar courtesy:

Lifting the hat is a conventional gesture of politeness shown to strangers only, not to be confused with bowing, which is a gesture used to acquaintances and friends. In lifting his hat, a gentleman merely lifts it slightly off his forehead—

Of the special sense-organs, the eye has a uniquely sociological function. The union and interaction of individuals is based upon mutual glances. This is perhaps the most direct and purest reciprocity which exists anywhere. This highest psychic reaction, however, in which the glances of eye to eye unite men, crystallizes into no objective structure; the unity which momentarily arises between two persons is present in the occasion and is dissolved in the function. So tenacious and subtle is this union that it can only be maintained by the shortest and straightest line between the eyes, and the smallest deviation from it, the slightest glance aside, completely destroys the unique character of this union. No objective trace of this relationship is left behind, as is universally found, directly or indirectly, in all other types of associations between men, as, for example, in interchange of words. The interaction of eye and eye dies in the moment in which directness of the function is lost. But the totality of social relations of human beings, their self-assertion and self-abnegation, their intimacies and estrangements, would be changed in unpredictable ways if there occurred no glance of eye to eye. This mutual glance between persons, in distinction from the simple sight or observation of the other, signifies a wholly new and unique union between them.[20]

It is understandable, then, that an individual who feels he has cause to be alienated from those around him will express this through some "abnormality of the gaze," especially averting of the eyes.[21] And it is understandable, too, that an individual who wants to control others' access to him and the infor-

by the brim of a stiff hat or by the crown of a soft one—and replaces it; he does not smile or bow, nor does he even look at the object of his courtesy. No gentleman ever subjects a lady to his scrutiny or his apparent observation if she is a stranger.

20. From his *Soziologie*, cited in R. E. Park and E. W. Burgess, *Introduction to the Science of Sociology* (2nd. ed.; Chicago: University of Chicago Press, 1924), p. 358. An interesting statement of some of the things that can be conveyed through eye-to-eye contact alone is given by Ortega y Gasset in his *Man and People* (New York: Norton, 1957), pp. 115-117. He implies that there is a whole vocabulary of glances, describing several of them.

21. M. D. Riemer, "The Averted Gaze," *Psychiatric Quarterly*, 23 (1949), 108-115. It would be very interesting to examine techniques employed by the blind and the dumb to provide functional substitutes for clearance cues and other eye contributions to the structure of face-to-face communication.

mation he receives may avoid looking toward the person who is
seeking him out. A waitress, for example, may prevent a waiting
customer from "catching her eye" to prevent his initiating an
order. Similarly, if a pedestrian wants to ensure a particular
allocation of the street relative to a fellow pedestrian, or if a
motorist wants to ensure priority of his line of proposed action
over that of a fellow motorist or a pedestrian, one strategy is to
avoid meeting the other's eyes and thus avoid cooperative
claims.[22] And where the initiator is in a social position requiring him to give the other the formal right to initiate all encounters, hostile and teasing possibilities may occur, of which
Melville's *White Jacket* gives us an example:

> But sometimes the captain feels out of sorts, or in ill-humour, or is
> pleased to be somewhat capricious, or has a fancy to show a touch
> of his omnipotent supremacy; or, peradventure, it has so hap-
> pened that the first lieutenant has, in some way, piqued or offended
> him, and he is not unwilling to show a slight specimen of his do-
> minion over him, even before the eyes of all hands; at all events,
> only by some one of these suppositions can the singular circum-
> stance be accounted for, that frequently Captain Claret would per-
> tinaciously promenade up and down the poop, purposely averting
> his eye from the first lieutenant, who would stand below in the
> most awkward suspense, waiting the first wink from his superior's
> eye.
>
> "Now I have him!" he must have said to himself, as the captain
> would turn toward him in his walk; "now's my time!" and up
> would go his hand to his cap; but, alas! the captain was off again;
> and the men at the guns would cast sly winks at each other as the
> embarrassed lieutenant would bite his lips with suppressed vexa-
> tion.
>
> Upon some occasions this scene would be repeated several times,
> till at last Captain Claret, thinking that in the eyes of all hands his
> dignity must by this time be pretty well bolstered, would stalk to-

---

22. The general point behind this example has been made by T. C. Schelling in
his analysis of the bargaining power of the individual who can convincingly commit himself to a line of action, in this case by communicating his inability to receive demands and threats through messages. See Schelling's "An Essay on Bargaining," *The American Economic Review*, 46 (1956), 281-306, esp. pp. 294-295.

ward his subordinate, looking him full in the eyes; whereupon up goes his hand to the cap front, and the captain, nodding his acceptance of the report, descends from his perch to the quarter-deck.[23]

As these various examples suggest, mutual glances ordinarily must be withheld if an encounter is to be avoided, for eye contact opens one up for face engagement. I would like to add, finally, that there is a relationship between the use of eye-to-eye glances as a means of communicating a request for initiation of an encounter, and other communication practices. The more clearly individuals are obliged to refrain from staring directly at others, the more effectively will they be able to attach special significance to a stare, in this case, a request for an encounter. The rule of civil inattention thus makes possible, and "fits" with, the clearance function given to looks into others' eyes. The rule similarly makes possible the giving of a special function to "prolonged" holding of a stranger's glance, as when unacquainted persons who had arranged to meet each other manage to discover one another in this way.[24]

Once a set of participants have avowedly opened themselves up to one another for an engagement, an eye-to-eye ecological huddle tends to be carefully maintained, maximizing the opportunity for participants to monitor one another's mutual perceivings.[25] The participants turn their minds to the same

23. Herman Melville, *White Jacket* (New York: Grove Press, n.d.) , p. 276.

24. Evelyn Hooker, in an unpublished Copenhagen address, August 14, 1961, titled "The Homosexual Community," suggests: "It is said by homosexuals that if another catches and holds the glance, one need know nothing more about him to know that he is one of them."

25. This may not be a universal practice. According to an early report on the Northwest Coast Amazons:

> When an Indian talks he sits down, no conversation is ever carried on when the speakers are standing unless it be a serious difference of opinion under discussion; nor, when he speaks, does the Indian look at the person addressed, any more than the latter watches the speaker. Both look at some outside objects. This is the attitude also of the Indian when addressing more than one listener, so that he appears to be talking to some one not visibly present.

(T. Whiffen, *The North-West Amazons* [London: Constable, 1915], p. 254.) In our own society, however, we can readily understand that when convicts are forbidden

subject matter and (in the case of talk) their eyes to the same
speaker, although of course this single *focus* of attention can
shift within limits from one topic to another and from one
speaker or target to another.[26] A shared definition of the situation comes to prevail. This includes agreement concerning per-
ceptual relevancies and irrelevancies, and a "working consensus," involving a degree of mutual considerateness, sympathy,
and a muting of opinion differences.[27] Often a group atmos-

---

to talk to one another but desire to do so, they can effectively shield their joint
involvement by talking without moving their lips and without looking at each
other. See, for example, J. Phelan, *The Underworld* (London: Harrap, 1953), pp.
7-8 and 13. We can also understand that when technical considerations prevent
eye-to-eye accessibility (as in the case of a surgical nurse receiving orders from a
surgeon who must not take his eyes from the surgical field), considerable discipline will be required of the recipient if communication is to be maintained.
Finally, we can appreciate that the blind will have to learn to act as if the
speaker is being watched, even though in fact the blind recipient could as well
direct his sightless gaze anywhere. In the latter connection see H. Chevigny, *My
Eyes Have a Cold Nose* (New Haven: Yale University Press, 1962), p. 51.

26. Cf. R. F. Bales *et al.*, "Channels of Communication in Small Groups,"
American Sociological Review, 16 (1951), 461-468, p. 461:

The conversation generally proceeded so that one person talked at a time, and
all members in the particular group were attending the same conversation. In
this sense, these groups might be said to have a "single focus," that is, they did
not involve a number of conversations proceeding at the same time, as one finds
at a cocktail party or in a hotel lobby. The single focus is probably a limiting
condition of fundamental importance in the generalizations reported here.

To this the caution should be added that the multiple focuses found in places like
hotel lobbies would occur simultaneously with unfocused interaction.

27. Hence, as Oswald Hall has suggested to me, when closeness and sympathy
are to be held to a minimum, as when a butler talks to a house guest, or an en-
listed man is disciplined by an officer, eye-to-eye communion may be avoided by
the subordinate holding his eyes stiffly to the front. An echo of the same factor is
to be found even in mediated conversation, where servants are obliged to answer
the telephone by saying "Mrs. So-and-So's residence" instead of "Hello."
This tendency for eye-to-eye looks to involve sympathetic accommodation is
nicely suggested in Trotsky's description of street disturbances during the "five
days" in *The History of the Russian Revolution*, trans. Max Eastman (New
York: Simon and Schuster, 1936), 1, 109:

In spite of the auspicious rumors about the Cossacks, perhaps slightly exagger-
ated, the crowd's attitude toward the mounted men remains cautious. A horse-
man sits high above the crowd; his soul is separated from the soul of the dem-
onstrator by the four legs of his beast. A figure at which one must gaze from
below always seems more significant, more threatening. The infantry are beside
one on the pavement—closer, more accessible. The masses try to get near them,

phere develops—what Bateson has called ethos.[28] At the same

look into their eyes, surround them with their hot breath. A great rôle is played by women workers in the relation between workers and soldiers. They go up to the cordons more boldly than men, take hold of the rifles, beseech, almost command: "Put down your bayonets—join us." The soldiers are excited, ashamed, exchange anxious glances, waver; someone makes up his mind first, and the bayonets rise guiltily above the shoulders of the advancing crowd. The barrier is opened, a joyous and grateful "Hurrah!" shakes the air.

A more formalized version of the same tendency is described as obtaining among the Bedouins. See A. Musil, *The Manners and Customs of the Rwala Bedouins* (New York: American Geographical Society, Oriental Explorations and Studies No. 6, 1928), p. 455:

A salutation, if returned, is a guarantee of safety in the desert, *as-salâm salâme.* If a stranger travels unaccompanied by a *ḥawi* through the territory of a tribe unknown to him and salutes someone—be it only a little girl—and is saluted in return, he may be reasonably certain that he will be neither attacked nor robbed, for even a little girl with all her kin will protect him. Should the fellow tribesmen of the girl attack and rob him, *mâḥûd*, he has only to ask the help of her kinsfolk, who must take his part. The girl is the best witness: "A traveler saluted me at such and such a place, of about such and such an age, dressed thus and so, riding on a she-camel," of which she also gives a description. Frequently even an enemy saves himself in this manner when hotly pursued. Realizing that he cannot escape, he suddenly changes his course, returns by a roundabout way to the camp of his pursuers, salutes a child, and, taking its hand, allows himself to be led to the tent of the parents. The adult Bedouins, being more cautious, do not answer at once when saluted by a man they do not know. Especially if two or three are riding together and approach a camp at night, the guard replies to their salute thus:
"Ye are outlawed; I shall not return your salutation; *tarâkom mwaṣṣedîn w-lâ 'alejkom radd as-salâm."* For an outlawed one, *mwaṣṣed,* is treated like an enemy to whom a salutation is of no use whatever.

Because of the obligation of considerateness among members of an engagement, and especially between a speaker and the particular member to whom he addresses his remarks, individuals sometimes "talk into the air" or mutter, pointedly addressing their remarks to no one, or to a child or pet. The person for whose benefit the remarks are intended may thus be half forced into the role of overhearer, allowing greater liberties to be taken with him than could be comfortably managed in direct address.

28. G. Bateson, *Naven* (Cambridge: Cambridge University Press, 1936), pp. 119-120:

When a group of young intellectual English men or women are talking and joking together wittily and with a touch of light cynicism, there is established among them for the time being a definite tone of appropriate behavior. Such specific tones of behavior are in all cases indicative of an ethos. They are expressions of a standardised system of emotional attitudes. In this case the men have temporarily adopted a definite set of sentiments towards the rest of the world, a definite attitude towards reality, and they will joke about subjects which at another time they would treat with seriousness. If one of the men

time, a heightened sense of moral responsibility for one's acts also seems to develop.[29] A "we-rationale" develops, being a sense of the single thing that we the participants are avowedly doing together at the time. Further, minor ceremonies are likely to be employed to mark the termination of the engagement and the entrance and departure of particular participants (should the encounter have more than two members). These ceremonies, along with the social control exerted during the encounter to keep participants "in line," give a kind of ritual closure to the mutual activity sustained in the encounter. An individual will therefore tend to be brought all the way into an ongoing encounter or kept altogether out of it.[30]

Engagements of the conversational kind appear to have, at least in our society, some spatial conventions. A set of individuals caused to sit more than a few feet apart because of furniture arrangements will find difficulty in maintaining in-

---

suddenly intrudes a sincere or realist remark it will be received with no enthusiasm—perhaps with a moment's silence and a slight feeling that the sincere person has committed a solecism. On another occasion the same group of persons may adopt a different ethos; they may talk realistically and sincerely. Then if the blunderer makes a flippant joke it will fall flat and feel like a solecism.

29. And so we find that bringing someone into a face engagement can be used by the initiator as a form of social control, as when a teacher stops a student's *sotto voce* comments by looking him in the eye and saying, "What did you say?" or when failure to accord civil inattention is handled as Norman Mailer describes in his novel *The Deer Park* (New York: Signet Books, 1957) p. 212:

Beda [a celebrity] looked at a woman who had been staring at him curiously, and when he winked, she turned away in embarrassment. "Oh God, the tourists," he said.

Interestingly enough, since joint participation in an encounter allows participants to look fully at each other—in fact, enjoins this to a degree—we find that one strategy employed by an individual when he is caught out by the person he is staring at is to act as if this staring were the first move in an overture to engagement, thereby ratifying and legitimating the failure to accord civil inattention.

30. One well-established way of confirming and consolidating a leave-taking is for the leave-taker to move away physically from the other or others. In places like Shetland Isle this can cause a problem when two persons pause for a moment's sociability and then find that their directions of movement do not diverge sharply. If the two persons walk at a normal pace, they find themselves attempting to close out the encounter while still having easy physical access to each other. Sometimes one individual offers an excuse to break into a run; sometimes, even if it takes him out of his way, he may take a path diverging sharply from that taken by his erstwhile coparticipant.

formal talk;[31] those brought within less than a foot and a half of each other will find difficulty in speaking directly to each other, and may talk at an off angle to compensate for the closeness.[32]

In brief, then, encounters are organized by means of a special set of acts and gestures comprising communication about communicating. As a linguist suggests:

> There are messages primarily serving to establish, to prolong, or to discontinue communication, to check whether the channel works ("Hello, do you hear me?"), to attract the attention of the interlocutor or to confirm his continued attention ("Are you listening?" or in Shakespearean diction, "Lend me your ears!"—and on the other end of the wire "Um-hum!").[33]

31. R. Sommer, "The Distance for Comfortable Conversation: A Further Study," *Sociometry*, 25 (1962), 111-116. See also his "Studies in Personal Space," *Sociometry*, 22 (1959), 247-260.

32. See E. T. Hall, *The Silent Language* (New York: Doubleday, 1959), pp. 204-206. In B. Schaffner, ed., *Group Processes*, Transactions of the Fourth (1957) Conference (New York: Josiah Macy, Jr. Foundation, 1959), p. 184, R. Birdwhistell comments as follows in a symposium discussion:

> It appears that Americans, when standing face to face, stand about arm's length from each other. When they stand side by side, the distance demanded is much less. When "middle majority Americans" stand closer than this in a face-to-face position they will either gradually separate or come toward each other and begin to emit signs of irritation. However, if they are put in a situation in which they are not required to interact—say on a streetcar—they can stand quite close, even to the point of making complete contact.
>
> The amount of this territory seems to vary culturally. So, there can be a situation where two or three ethnic groups occupy different territories, that is, varying amounts of personal space. For example, put together a Southeastern European Jew (who occupies about half the area of personal space) and a middle class American and a high degree of irritation results, particularly if the middle class American keeps drifting around to the side, in order not to be insulting, and the Southeastern European Jewish man tries to move around to get face-to-face relationship. You get an actual dance, which very often turns into what is practically a fight.

From all of this it follows that among persons arranged in a discussion circle, persons adjacent to each other may tend not to address remarks to each other, except to pass side comments, since a voice full enough to embrace the circle would be too full for the distance between them. For experimental evidence, see B. Steinzor, "The Spatial Factor in Face to Face Discussion Groups," *Journal of Abnormal and Social Psychology*, 45 (1950), 552-555.

33. R. Jakobson, "Closing Statement: Linguistics and Poetics," in T. A. Sebeok, ed., *Style in Language* (New York: Wiley, 1960), p. 355. Cf. the concept of metacommunication in J. Ruesch and G. Bateson, *Communication* (New York: Norton, 1951).

Everyday terms refer to different aspects of encounters. "Cluster," "knot," "conversational circle"—all highlight the physical aspects, namely, a set of persons physically close together and facially oriented to one another, their backs toward those who are not participants. "Personal encounter" refers to the unit in terms of the opportunity it provides or enforces for some kind of social intimacy. In the literature, the term "the interaction" is sometimes used to designate either the activity occurring within the cluster at any one moment or the total activity occurring from the moment the cluster forms to the moment at which it officially disbands. And, of course, where spoken messages are exchanged, especially under informal circumstances, the terms "chat," "a conversation," or "a talk" are employed.

It may be noted that while all participants share equally in the rights and obligations described, there are some rights that may be differentially distributed within an encounter. Thus, in spoken encounters, the right to listen is one shared by all, but the right to be a speaker may be narrowly restricted, as, for example, in stage performances and large public meetings. Similarly, children at the dinner table are sometimes allowed to listen but forbidden to talk;[34] if not forbidden to talk, they may be "helped out" and in this way denied the communication courtesy of being allowed to finish a message for themselves.[35] And in other engagements, one category of participant may be allowed to say only "Yes, sir," or "No, sir," or restricted to the limited signalling that a modulation of applause allows. The differential rights of players vis-à-vis kibitzers in games provide another example.

When the communion of a face engagement has been established between two or more individuals, the resulting state of ratified mutual participation can last for varying periods. When a clearly defined task is involved, the engagement may last for

34. J. H. S. Bossard, "Family Modes of Expression," *American Sociological Review*, 10 (1945), 226-237, p. 229.
35. *Ibid.*

hours. When no apparent work or recreational task is involved, and what is perceived as sociability alone holds the participants, certain durations seem to be favored. The contact may be very brief, as brief, in fact, as the opening meeting of eyes itself. In our own middle-class society there are "chats," where two individuals pause in their separate lines of action for what both recognize to be a necessarily brief period of time; there are greetings, whereby communion is established and maintained long enough for the participants to exchange brief interpersonal rituals; and, briefest of all, there are recognitional or "friendly" glances. (Of course, a recognitional glance may be merely the first interchange in an extended greeting, and a greeting merely the opening phase of a chat, but these extensions of coparticipation are not always found.) Except for the ritual of civil inattention, the mere exchange of friendly glances is perhaps the most frequent of our interpersonal rituals.

Encounters of an obligatory kind are linked to the world of domestic convivial occasions. In some social circles, a guest entering a party has a right to be greeted by the host or hostess and convoyed into the proceedings in visible contact with the authorizing person, this encounter thereby legitimating and celebrating the newcomer's participation in the occasion. His departure may be marked with the same kind of ceremony, officially bringing his participation to an end.[36] The occasion then closes in and over the place he has left, and if he should have to return for something he has forgotten, embarrassment is likely to be felt, especially if the ethos of the occasion has changed, and especially if marked ceremonial attention had been given his leave-taking.[37]

36. Here there is an interesting difference between Anglo-American and French custom; in France, the entering or departing person ratifies his entrance or departure not only through contact with the person managing the occasion but often also by a hand-shaking engagement with some or all of the other guests present.

37. The same sort of embarrassment occurs when a member of an organization, who has been given a farewell party and gift to mark a termination of his membership and to set the stage for the group's developing a new relation to a substitute, then finds that he must remain with or return to the organization. He finds that the group has "worked through" his membership, leaving him present but socially not there.

Encounters, of course, tend to be taken as an expression of the state of a social relationship. And, as will be considered later, to the degree that contact is practical, it may have to be made so as not to deny the relationship.[38] Further, each engagement tends to be initiated with an amount of fuss appropriate to the period of lapsed contact, and terminated with the amount appropriate to the assumed period of separation. There results a kind of tiding over, and a compensation for the diminishing effects of separation.[39] At a party, then, a version of Mrs. Post's ruling is likely to prevail:

> In meeting the same person many times within an hour or so, one does not continue to bow after the second, or at most third meeting. After that one either looks away or merely smiles.[40]

The same mere smile between the same two persons newly coming withing range of each other in a foreign country may constitute a grievous affront to their relationship.

I have suggested that a face engagement is a sufficiently clear-cut unit that an individual typically must either be entirely within it or entirely outside it. This is nicely borne out by the trouble caused when a person attempts to be half-in and half-out. None the less, there are communication arrangements that seem to lie halfway between mere copresence and full scale coparticipation, one of which should be mentioned here. When two persons walk silently together down the street or doze next to each other at the beach, they may be treated by others as "being together," and are likely to have the right to break

38. Face engagements, of course, are not the only kinds of contact carrying ceremonial functions. Gifts, greeting cards, and salutatory telegrams and telephone calls also serve in this way. Each social circle seems to develop norms as to how frequently and extensively these ought to be employed to affirm relationships among geographically separated people, depending on the costs faced by each group in using these several devices. Just as friends at the same social party are obliged to spend at least a few moments chatting together, so a husband out of town on business may be considered "in range" and be obliged to telephone home in the evening.

39. E. Goffman, "On Face-Work," *Psychiatry*, 18 (1955) , 229.

40. Emily Post, *Etiquette, op. cit.*, p. 29.

rather abruptly into spoken or gestured communication, although they can hardly be said to sustain continuously a mutual activity. This sense of being together constitutes a kind of lapsed verbal encounter, functioning more as a means of excluding nonmembers than as a support for sustained focused interaction among the participants.[41]

Persons who can sustain lapsed encounters with one another are in a position to avoid the problem of "safe supplies" during spoken encounters—the need to find a sufficient supply of inoffensive things to talk about during the period when an official state of talk prevails. Thus, in Shetland Isle, when three or four women were knitting together, one knitter would say a word, it would be allowed to rest for a minute or two, and then another knitter would provide an additional comment. In the same manner a family sitting around its kitchen fire would look into the flames and intersperse replies to statements with periods of observation of the fire. Shetland men used for the same purpose the lengthy pauses required for the proper management of their pipes.

To these comments on the structure of engagements I would like to add a brief remark on the information that encounters convey to the situation as a whole. In an earlier section, it was suggested that an individual divulges things about himself by his mere presence in a situation. In the same way, he gives off information about himself by virtue of the encounters in which others do or do not see him. Involvement in focused interaction therefore inevitably contributes to unfocused interaction conveying something to all who are present in the situation at large.

In public places in our society, what is conveyed by being in or out of encounters differs appreciably according to sex and the periods of the week. Morning and lunchtime are times when anyone can appear alone almost anywhere without this giving evidence of how the person is faring in the social world;

41. Being "with" someone at a given moment is to be distinguished from the party relationship of having "come with" someone to the occasion, the latter representing a preferential claim as to whom one will leave with, be loyal to, and the like.

dinner and other evening activities, however, provide unfavorable information about unaccompanied participants, especially damaging in the case of female participants. Weekend nights, and ceremonial occasions such as Thanksgiving, Christmas, and, especially, New Year's Eve, are given special weight in this connection, being times when an unengaged individual in a semipublic place may feel very much out of place.

It should be added, finally, that in so far as others judge the individual socially by the company he is seen in, for him to be brought into an engagement with another is to be placed in the position of being socially identified as the other is identified.

3. Accessibility

In every situation, those present will be obliged to retain some readiness for potential face engagements. (This readiness has already been suggested as one way in which situational presence is expressed.) There are many important reasons why the individual is usually obliged to respond to requests for face engagements. In the first place, he owes this to himself because often it will be through such communication that his own interests can be served, as when a stranger accosts him to tell him he has dropped something, or that the bridge is out. For similar reasons he owes this accessibility to others present, and to persons not present for whom those present may serve as a relay. (The need for this collective solidarity is heightened in urban living, which brings individuals of great social distance within range of one another.) Further, as previously suggested, participation in a face engagement can be a sign of social closeness and relatedness; when this opportunity to participate is proffered by another, it ought not to be refused, for to decline such a request is to reject someone who has committed himself to a sign of desiring contact. More than this, refusal of an offer implies that the refuser rejects the other's claim to membership in the gathering and the social occasion in which the gathering occurs. It is therefore uncommon for persons to deny these obligations to respond.

Although there are good reasons why an individual should keep himself available for face engagements, there are also good reasons for him to be cautious of this.

In allowing another to approach him for talk, the individual may find that he has been inveigled into a position to be attacked and assaulted physically. In societies where public safety is not firmly established, especially in places such as the desert, where the traveler is for long periods of time remote from any source of help, the danger that a face engagement may be a prelude to assault becomes appreciable, and extensive avoidance practices or greetings at a distance tend to be employed.[42] Here, of course, the "physical safety" component of civic order and the communication component overlap. But apart from this extreme, we should see that when an individual opens himself up to talk with another, he opens himself up to pleadings, commands, threats, insult, and false information. The mutual considerateness characteristic of face engagements reinforces these dangers, subjecting the individual to the possibility of having his sympathy and tactfulness exploited, and causing him to act against his own interests.

Further, words can act as a "relationship wedge"; that is, once an individual has extended to another enough consideration to hear him out for a moment, some kind of bond of mutual obligation is established, which the initiator can use in turn as a basis for still further claims; once this new extended bond is granted, grudgingly or willingly, still further claims for social or material indulgence can be made. Hence, in one important example, a man and a woman can start out as strangers and, if conditions are right, progress from an incidental encounter to matrimony. We need only trace back the history of many close relationships between adults to find that something was made of face engagements when it need not have been. Of

42. The case of desert contacts is vividly described in a short story by Paul Bowles, "The Delicate Prey," in *The Delicate Prey and Other Stories* (New York: Random House, 1950), pp. 277-289, esp. pp. 279-280.

course, persons usually form "suitable" relationships, not allowing casual encounters to be a wedge to something else. But
there is sufficient slippage in systems of conviviality segregation
to give mothers concern about their daughters and to provide
one of the basic romantic themes of light fiction.

I have suggested some reasons why individuals, at least in our
own society, are obliged to keep themselves available for face
engagements, and I have also suggested some of the dangers
persons open themselves up to in so doing. These two opposing
tendencies are reconciled in society, apparently, by a kind of
implicit contract or gentleman's agreement that persons sustain:
given the fact that the other will be under some obligation,
often unpleasant, to respond to overtures, potential initiators
are under obligation to stay their own desires. A person can
thus make himself available to others in the expectation that
they will restrain their calls on his availability and not make
him pay too great a price for his being accessible. Their right to
initiate contact is checked by their duty to take his point of
view and initiate contact with him only under circumstances
that he will easily see to be justified; in short, they must not
"abuse" their privileges.

This implicit communication contract (and the consequence
of breaking it) receive wide mythological representation, as in
our own "cry wolf" tale. Understandably, infractions of the
rule against undesired overture do cause some anxiety, for the
recipient must either accede to the request or demonstrate to
himself and the others present that his availability for face engagements was not part of his character but a false pose, to be
maintained only when no price was involved in maintaining it.

In noting the implicit contract that makes persons present
delicately accessible and inaccessible to each other, we can go
on to note a basic margin of appetite and distaste to be found
in social situations. The reasons why individuals are obliged to
restrain themselves from making encounter overtures provide
many of the reasons why they might want to do so. And the obligation to be properly accessible often covers a desire to be selec-
tively quite unavailable. Hence, many public and semipublic

places, such as cocktail lounges and club cars, acquire a special tone and temper, a special piquancy, that blurs the communication lines, giving each participant some desire to encroach where perhaps he does not have a right to go, and to keep from being engaged with others who perhaps have a right to engage him. Each individual, then, is not only involved in maintaining the basic communication contract, but is also likely to be involved in hopes, fears, and actions that bend the rules if they do not actually break them.

It has been suggested, then, that as a general rule the individual is obliged to make himself available for encounters even though he may have something to lose by entering them, and that he may well be ambivalent about this arrangement. Here mental patients provide a lesson in reverse, for they can show us the price that is paid for declining to make oneself available and force us to see that there are reasons why someone able to be accessible should be willing to pay the price of remaining inaccessible.

In brief, a patient who declines to respond to overtures is said to be "out of contact," and this state is often felt to be full evidence that he is very sick indeed, that he is, in fact, cut off from all contact with the world around him. In the case of some "organic" patients, this generalization from inaccessibility appears quite valid, as it does with certain "functionals." There are patients, for example, who, before admission, had progressively withdrawn from responding to such things as the telephone and doorbell, and, once in the hospital, decline all staff overtures for engagement, this being but one instance of a general withdrawal of concern for the life about them.

In the case of other patients, however, refusal to enter proffered engagements cannot be taken as a sign of unconcern for the gathering, but rather as a sign of alienation based on active feelings such as fear, hate, and contempt, each of which can be understandable in the circumstances, and each of which can allow the patient to show a nice regard for other situational proprieties.

Thus, there are patients who coldly stare through direct ef-

forts to bring them into a state of talk, declining all staff overtures, however seductive, teasing, or intensive, who will none
the less allow themselves face engagements carefully initiated
and terminated by themselves without the usual courtesies.
Still other patients who are out of contact to most persons on
the ward will engage in self-initiated encounters with a small
select number of others, by means of coded messages, foreign
language, whispering, or the exchange of written statements.
Some patients, unwilling to engage in spoken encounters with
anyone, will be ready to engage in other types of encounters,
such as dancing or card playing. Similarly, I knew a patient who
often blankly declined greetings extended him by fellow-
patients on the grounds, but who could be completely relied
upon not to miss a cue when performing the lead in a patient
dramatic production.

As might then be expected, a patient declining to conduct
himself properly in regard to face engagements might be well
conducted in regard to unfocused interaction.[43] One illustration was provided by a patient I observed, a young woman of
thirty-two, who at one point in her "illness" was ready to handle
her dress and deportment with all the structured modesty that
is required of her sex, while at the same time her language was
foul. During another phase of her illness, this patient, in the
company of a friendly nurse, enjoyed shopping trips to the
neighboring town, during which she and her keeper got wry
pleasure from the fact that the patient was "passing" as a "normal" person. Had anyone made an opening statement to the
patient, however, the masquerade would have been destroyed,
for this was a time when the patient was mute in all verbal
interaction or, at best, spoke with very great pressure.

A touching illustration of the same difference in capacity for

43. Manner books contain the same suggestion. See, for example, *Good Manners* (New York: L. M. Garrity and Co., 1929) , p. 31:

Many people whose "acting" manners are good have poor "talking" manners.
They may be gossipy or they may tell off-color stories; or say things that hurt
people's feelings, or they may chatter on so continuously that no one else can
get a word in "edgewise."

focused and unfocused interaction was provided at Central Hospital by patients who were fearful and anxious of their whole setting, but who none the less made elaborate efforts to show that they were still what they had been before coming to the hospital and that they were in poised, business-like control of the situation. One middle-aged man walked busily on the grounds with the morning newspaper folded under one arm and a rolled umbrella hooked over the other, wearing an expression of being late for an appointment. A young man, having carefully preserved his worn grey flannel suit, bustled similarly from one place he was not going to another. Yet both men stepped out of the path of any approaching staff person, and painfully turned their heads away whenever someone proffered an exchange or greeting of some kind, for both employed the tack of being mute with many of the persons whom they met. The management of a front of middle-class orientation in the situation, in these circumstances, was so precarious and difficult that (for these men) it apparently represented the day's major undertaking.[44] In other cases, of course, it is not fear that seems to account for the inaccessibility of otherwise properly mannered persons, but rather hostility: to acknowledge a staff overture is partly to acknowledge the legitimacy of the staff person making the overture, and if he is a serious worthy person then so must be his implied contention that the individual with whom he is initiating contact, namely, oneself, is a mental patient properly confined to a mental ward. To strengthen one's feeling that one is really sane, it may thus seem reasonable to disdain encounters in which the opposite will be assumed—even though this results in exactly the kind of conduct, namely, inaccessibility, that confirms the hospital's view that one is mentally ill.

A final point about accessibility should be mentioned. As pre-

44. Just as it is evident that the individual may comply with rules regarding unfocused interaction while failing to comply with regulations regarding focused interaction, so cases can be found of mental patients who dress in a spectacularly improper manner but who are none the less ready to be socially tractable as conversationalists. Here are two pieces of evidence in favor of distinguishing conceptually between focused and unfocused interaction.

viously suggested, conversational engagements are often carried out as involvements subordinated to some other business at hand, just as side involvements, such as smoking, are often carried out as activities subordinated to a conversational main involvement. The question arises as to the limits placed upon this coexistence in middle-class society. There are, for example, records of middle-class Navy personnel postponing a visit to the "head" until others have left so as not to have to defecate while being accessible to others for talk. I have also been told by a middle-class informant that she was always uneasy about painting her toenails while in the presence of her husband, since the painting involved too much attention to leave her sufficiently respectful of the talk.

4. Leave-taking Rights

Just as the individual is obliged not to exploit the accessibility of others (else they have to pay too large a price for their obligation to be accessible), so he is obliged to release those with whom he is engaged, should it appear, through conventional cues, that they desire to be released (else they have to pay too great a price for their tact in not openly taking leave of him). A reminder of these rules of leave-taking can be found in elementary school classrooms where leave-taking practices are still being learned, as, for example, when a teacher, having called a student to her desk in order to correct his exercise book, may have to turn him around and gently propel him back to his seat in order to terminate the interview.

The rights of departure owed the individual, and the rule of tactful leave-taking owed the remaining participants, can be in conflict with each other. This conflict is often resolved, in a way very characteristic of communication life, by persons active in different roles tacitly cooperating to ease leave-taking. Thus, business etiquette provides the following lesson:

on when to go—your exit cues are many. They range from clear-cut closing remarks, usually in the form of a "thank you for coming in," to a vacant and preoccupied stare. But in any case they should come from the interviewer. It should not be necessary for him to stand, abruptly; you should have been able to feel the good-bye in the air far enough in advance to gather up your gear, slide forward to the edge of your chair and launch into a thank-you speech of your own. Nor should it be necessary to ask that embarrassing question, "Am I taking too much of your time?"; if that thought crosses your mind, it's time to go.[45]

In fact, persons can become so accustomed to being helped out by the very person who creates the need for help, that when co-operation is not forthcoming they may find they have no way of handling the incident. Thus, some mental patients may characteristically hold a staff person in an encounter regardless of how many hints the latter provides that termination ought now to occur. As the staff person begins to walk away, the patient may follow along until the locked door is reached, and even then the patient may try to accompany him. At such times the staff person may have to hold back the patient forcibly, or precipitously tear himself away, demonstrating not merely that the patient is being left in the lurch, but also that the staff show of concern for the patient is, in some sense, only a show. Pitchmen and street stemmers initiate a similar process; they rely on the fact that the accosted person will be willing to agree to a purchase in order not to have to face being the sort of person who walks away from an encounter without being officially released.

45. *Esquire Etiquette, op. cit.,* p. 59.

CHAPTER 7

Acquaintanceship

In our society, as in others, there are institutions that pertain specifically to the privilege and duty of participating in face engagements. There is, first of all, the social relationship of "acquaintanceship." Its preconditions are satisfied when each of two individuals can personally identify the other by knowledge that distinguishes this other from everyone else, and when each acknowledges to the other that this state of mutual information exists. Once this information relationship has been established between two persons, it seems, with certain exceptions, to give rise to a social bondedness, placing both individuals on a new, typically nonterminable basis in regard to each other. Thereafter, when they come into the same social situation, they are likely to possess either a duty or a right regarding face engagement. (Should one individual forget the "face" of the other, the other need only establish the context of the original acquaintanceship-formation and he will receive engagement rights and often an apology as well.) Thus, the right to initiate face engagements is so important that it tends to get built into the relationship as one of its important ingredients.

We can begin to consider the institution of acquaintanceship by specifying two of the common-sense uses of the term "recognition." There is first what might be called *cognitive recogni-*

tion, the process by which one individual "places" or identifies another, linking the sight of him with a framework of information concerning him. The identification ritual at criminal "line-ups" is one clear example; to "recognize" a man whom one was supposed to meet by something he promised to carry or wear is another. Typically, cognitive recognition links the person recognized to information that refers exclusively to him, such as his name, or a specific configuration of statuses, or a unique personal biography—in brief, his "personal identity." Sometimes, however, cognitive recognition merely implies the placing of an individual in some general social category, but in a context where any member of the category can play a crucial role, as, for example, when pickpockets recognize a plainclothesman who is personally unknown to them, thereby, as the argot puts it, "making him on his merits."[1] Cognitive recognition, then, is the process through which we socially or personally identify the other.

Second, there is "social recognition," namely, the process of openly welcoming or at least accepting the initiation of an engagement, as when a greeting or smile is returned. Perhaps we ought to include here the according of a special role within an engagement, as when a chairman acknowledges and fulfills an individual's desire to be given the floor. Cognitive recognition is a private act that a concealed spy can engage in, but it is difficult to engage in it without expressing that one is doing so. Social recognition is a glance specifically functioning as a ceremonial gesture of contact with someone.

Now, as previously suggested, in order to carry out certain forms of social recognition it will be necessary for the participants to recognize each other cognitively, or affect having done so, or apologize for not doing so. As might be expected, then, it

1. D. W. Maurer, *Whiz Mob, Publication of the American Dialect Society No. 24,* 1955, pp. 140-141:

Both McCarthy and Wilkerson [two detectives] were reputed to be able to do that phenomenal act—*make a man on his merits,* that is, spot a criminal by his dress, manners, appearance, behavior, etc., even though he was unknown to them personally.

will be possible, when two persons meet who are not well known to each other, to distinguish two types of incipient expression that can touch the face: the expression of someone immediately anticipating a social recognition from another; and the expression of someone going through the rapid cognitive process of physically recognizing or "placing" someone. These two expressions, of course, often occur simultaneously, and properly so; at other times the social recognition expression may momentarily and embarrassingly precede the other expression. And sometimes, when the context makes it dangerous for one person to admit that he is acquainted with the other, we find the "placing" expression without the social one, as we also do when an individual happens upon a person whom he knows about but has not met.

One question to be asked of acquaintanceship is: how important a part of any relationship is it?

In general, acquaintanceship is an aspect of all social relationships built on mutual personal identification; relationships that differ greatly in degree and kind will equally share it. None the less, we can expect acquaintanceship to be a minor aspect of relationships. There are exceptions, however. Common sense designates by the phrase "mere acquaintance" a relationship in which the rights of social recognition form the principal substance of the relationship. Further, after persons have been "close" it is possible for their relationship to decay, stopping only at a point where they are "still on talking terms," or, after that (and with a discontinuous leap), at a point when they are "not talking," in either case conferring on mere engagement practices the power of characterizing the relationship.

The special force of the obligation to give social recognition to persons with whom one is acquainted—the obligation, that is, to be readily accessible to them—can be discovered in different ways. Most obviously, we find in middle-class society a great taboo against the "cut"—the practice of pointedly denying an encounter overture. Etiquette books contain many warnings against this communication practice:

As a general rule never *cut* anyone in the street. Even political and steamboat acquaintances should be noticed by the slightest movement in the world. If they presume to converse with you, or stop you to introduce their companion, it is then time to use your eye-glass, and say, "I never knew you."[2]

Mrs. Post provides a slightly more contemporary version:

It may be annoying to be passed by an "unseeing" acquaintance, but one should be careful not to confuse absent-minded unseeing-ness with alert and intentional slight.

The "Cut Direct"

For one person to look directly at another and not acknowledge the other's bow is such a breach of civility that only an unforgivable misdemeanor can warrant the rebuke. Nor without the gravest cause may a lady "cut" a gentleman. But there are no circumstances under which a gentleman may "cut" any woman who, even by courtesy, can be called a lady.

A "cut" is very different [from poor sight or a forgetful memory]. It is a direct stare of blank refusal, and is not only insulting to its victim but embarrassing to every witness. Happily it is practically unknown in polite society.[3]

From this rule it follows that when one person does not want to enter into a greeting engagement with another, he will usually act so that the other can believe (or at least take the line) that the slight was due to an unintended not-seeing of the overture; in turn, the person making the overture, if doubtful about his reception, will not press his greeting so obviously as to leave himself no social fiction should his overture be declined. And when it is known that one individual may feel obliged to cut a second, others and the pair themselves will usually be at pains to keep them from coming together, an avoidance relationship being thus established. Nor is this taboo against the cut a mat-

2. *The Laws of Etiquette,* by "A Gentleman" (Philadelphia: Carey, Lee and Blanchard, 1836), p. 62.
3. Emily Post, *Etiquette* (New York: Funk and Wagnalls, 1937), p. 30.

ter of official etiquette only. Even when two persons have great moral cause for mutual animosity they are likely to be willing to exchange a few civil words if brought together unavoidably. And even when they are not on talking terms, they may still feel an uncontrollable urge to exchange recognitional nods when brought together. This minimal courtesy has a special significance for us, for a failure to exchange this kind of greeting exposes such persons to the situation at large as two persons who are filled with hostility to each other, and not with the mood of the social occasion. To cut someone is thus to express lack of respect for the gathering at large, to display flagrant insensitivity to the minimal solidarity the gathering demands from all its participants.

Acquaintanceship, then, obliges individuals to proffer each other engagement, if only in the form of passing smiles. This custom shows once again how the communication rules of the community tend to cut through particular interests of the moment. But we should expect that there will be some accommodations, each, in its own way, throwing further light on communication regulations.

There are circumstances, for example, in which consideration for the other requires that one give to him the right to decide whether or not social recognition and a greeting will occur. Thus, where the context is one that reflects negatively upon a person in it (especially where this person is a female and is noticed to be present by a male acquaintance), the person with most to lose by being made to face up to being present may be given the right to determine whether or not an engagement will occur. Some writers on etiquette have felt that, since a gentleman can never know when a lady is in a context where she will be undesirous of having herself identified, the initiation should at all times come from the female:

> It is a mark of high breeding not to speak to a lady in the street, until you perceive that she has noticed you by an inclination of the head.[4]

4. *The Laws of Etiquette, op. cit.,* p. 60.

But other writers modify this stricture:

> Under formal circumstances a lady is supposed to bow to a gentle-
> man first; but people who know each other well bow spontane-
> ously without observing this etiquette.[5]

In some societies, it may be added, social recognition between
the sexes apparently may jeopardize the reputation of the female and, for this reason, be uniformly restricted. Hindu society provides an example:

> Outside of the household, relationships between the sexes are very
> limited indeed. Women wear long veils, and are expected to look
> demurely at the ground on the approach of a man. A corollary of
> the fierce restraint on meetings between young men and girls is
> that every slightest encounter is interpreted as leading inevitably
> to sexual intercourse.[6]

Rural Paraguay provides another example:

> A woman must be exceptionally circumspect at all times. She
> should always avoid the appearance of having a private conversa-
> tion with a man even on the street in broad daylight.[7]

Tact with respect to social recognition and face engagements is
of course not restricted to relations between the sexes, but is
found wherever one party to a recognitional engagement is considered to have extra rights or to be worth treating carefully.[8]

5. Emily Post, *Etiquette, op. cit.,* p. 29.
6. G. M. Carstairs, "Hinjra and Jiryan: Two Derivatives of Hindu Attitudes to
Sexuality," *British Journal of Medical Psychology,* 29 (1956) , 135-136.
7. E. R. and H. S. Service, *Tobati: A Paraguayan Town* (Chicago: University
of Chicago Press, 1954) , p. 207.
8. I cite a personal example from informal social life at a provincial British
university, circa 1949. When a junior staff person and a senior staff person who
were acquainted came into the staff common room at a time when few other persons were there, then the junior sometimes felt that sitting far away from the
senior was an act of unfriendliness, and sitting within easy chatting distance a
presumption, and so the junior would sometimes take up a chair on the boundary
between these two distances, placing the senior in the position of being able to
determine how much spoken interaction, if any, was to occur.

The assumption that an individual may purposely recognize an acquaintance, or cut him, or avoid recognition in various ways, may give an oversimplified view of matters. As already suggested, the process cannot that easily be deliberately controlled, and lack of control must be taken into consideration in deciding on strategies of action. A sense of proper recognition conduct seems to take deep hold of a person once he has learned it, so that a current view he might have as to an expedient line of activity may not be one that his spontaneous tendencies in the situation will allow him to follow. In deciding rationally on a current course of action, he may well have to try to suppress more automatic tendencies—or rather, what have become automatic tendencies for him. (This is a factor apparent throughout communication behavior.) If an individual avoids looking at another to whom his spontaneous attention is nevertheless drawn, his avoidance will have a special and self-conscious cast. In not looking at someone to whom one's attention is spontaneously drawn, one usually displays a movement to him that is self-consciously blocked; this becomes especially apparent when one anticipates entering a face engagement with him, but is not in a position, socially, to initiate the encounter oneself.

The physical character of many scenes of social interaction has a bearing on the discrepancy between what one intends to do and what one unconsciously begins to do. Often there will be present in the situation many barriers to visual and aural communication—these often being the bodies and activities of other people—which provide excuses, however thin, for the not-seer, and which can in turn be seized upon by the not-seen as excuses the other had. While making communication rules more elastic, such barriers multiply the occasions when one person is oriented to engagement with another but hesitates because he is not sure the other is available. An example from a novel may be cited:

As he [Rigault] entered the Rue Gustave-le-Bon he saw Maître

Marguet at the far end, walking on the opposite pavement. He
never encountered him without a twinge of anxiety. The fact was
that sometimes the lawyer recognised him, and returned his greeting or even anticipated it, and sometimes he passed by without
noticing him. The thing might be accidental, or it might be capri-
cious (he himself never failed to recognise the town's leading figures, some instinct warning him, even when his thoughts were
elsewhere, to raise a hand to his hat). Rigault kept his head carefully rigid, glancing furtively sideways to see what the other did.
The lawyer was walking with his eyes lowered, seeming very preoccupied. Deciding that the raising of his hat would probably go
unnoticed, Rigault resolved to begin this gesture only at the last
moment, which left him the possibility of completing it or abol-
ishing it by pretending to scratch his ear. But then a reasonless,
almost religious apprehension caused him to hurry his movements. They were still four paces removed from the orthodox,
level position when his hand went to his head. Maître Marguet,
on the opposite pavement, looked up and replied with an ample
gesture; and Rigault, instantly relaxed, felt a wave of well-being
pass through him. It was more than gratified vanity: it was the
sweetness of a response, the fulfilment of a social instinct.[9]

Once we see the role of acquaintanceship in social life, we are
led to ask how this relationship may develop between two individuals. Presumably, acquaintanceship can develop "informally," as when persons in the same office or factory come to
"know about" each other and gradually acknowledge this to
one another, so that knowing about becomes knowing. A special case of this is found among ritually profane persons such as
young children. Here it may be enough for each to know that
the other goes to the same school for acquaintanceship to be
automatically assumed.

Acquaintanceship may also come about informally through
joint participation in the same encounter, although differences
in status of the participants may here act as a restriction. This
may be illustrated from a report on a janitor's response to the

9. Marcel Aymé, *The Secret Stream,* trans. Norman Denny (New York: Harper
& Bros., 1953), p. 30.

way he was treated by a hospital physican, as recounted to a researcher by another janitor:

> Of course they're [the doctors] not all like that. Some of them wouldn't say hello if they tripped over you. Now you take Dr. Zeigler. He came down here once and asked Al to fix something that belonged to him, so Al dropped his work and went ahead and fixed this thing. Zeigler was nice as could be, stood around very friendly and chatted while Al fixed this thing. Well, Al says he met him up in the hall next day and the doctor walked right by him as if he had never laid eyes on him before. Al says he has met him lots of times since then and the doctor never lets on he recognizes him. Al said to me, "What do you think ails him?" I told him, "I don't know, Al, maybe some of these doctors think they are better than we are. Just don't pay any attention to him."[10]

The relationship of acquaintanceship may also develop "formally" in our society, as when two individuals are introduced, typically by a third party but sometimes, when conditions are right, by themselves. An introduction, even more than acquaintanceship that develops informally, ought, it is felt, to have a permanent effect, placing the introduced persons forever after in a special and accessible position in regard to each other. The difference is that, while informal acquaintanceship may spring up without the participants in fact "knowing" each other's name, formal acquaintanceship presumably involves an exchange of names and an obligation to be able thereafter to refer to the other by his name. Thus, with persons who have been formally introduced, or who have used names to each other on the basis of informal acquaintanceship, the offense of forgetting may take two distinct forms: not knowing that one ought to know a particular person (the greater of the sins); and knowing that one knows the person, but not being able to remember his name.

If acquaintanceship places individuals in a preferential com-

10. Interview material recorded by E. Lentz, "A Comparison of Medical and Surgical Floors" (New York State School of Industrial and Labor Relations, Cornell University, 1954).

munication relationship, or, rather, *is* a preferential communication relationship, then we can understand why some persons will avoid those places and occasions where troublesome introductions are likely to occur. More important, it can easily be appreciated that an introducer may feel an obligation to make sure that no harm resulting from the new relationship will come to those whose communication relation to each other he has altered. Since harm of this kind seems to flow from the poor to the affluent, the male to the female, the weak to the powerful, the introducer may feel obliged to check with the one who has the more to lose before effecting the introduction, and assume that the one who has something to gain will have no objection to the relationship.[11] Where the context is a close or continuing one, making it difficult for the persons introduced to employ the courtesy of foregoing their rights, the introducer will presumably have to take special care. As one etiquette book puts it:

You must never introduce people to each other in public places unless you are very certain that the introduction will be agreeable to both. You cannot commit a greater social blunder than to introduce to a notable person someone she does not care to know, especially on shipboard, in hotels, or in other very small, rather public communities where people are so closely thrown together that it is correspondingly difficult to avoid presuming acquaintances who have been given the wedge of an introduction.[12]

One of the complications in understanding the institution of

11. Here we find some striking cross-cultural similarities. Take, for example, J. M. Dixon, "Japanese Etiquette," *Transactions of the Asiatic Society of Japan,* 13 (1885), 1-20, p. 2:

Friends or acquaintances may not be introduced to one another unless it is known that the introduction will be agreeable to both parties. Suppose two persons, however, are of the same rank and social position, it is proper to accede to the request of one of them to be introduced, without previously asking the permission of the other. It is not in good form to introduce a person of lower rank to one of higher rank without receiving the express permission of the latter, but a request from one of higher rank to be presented to one of lower rank must be complied with instantly.

12. Emily Post, *Etiquette, op. cit.,* p. 16.

introduction in our society is our interpersonal deference system, because introduction is one of its ritual coins.[13] When "with" one person, a chance meeting with a second person requires the individual to introduce the two, except when contact with the newcomer clearly must be brief. Failure to introduce, in middle-class society, may be considered an open affront to one or both of those not introduced. Underlying this convention is the rule that, under proper circumstances, an individual has the right to introduce to each other any two persons with whom he is acquainted (a rule that can lead an individual to be put under pressure or under obligation to "arrange an introduction").

The issues raised by obligatory introductions are met in various ways, in addition to the basic one of limiting one's acquaintances to social equals, who will not be embarrassed by being introduced to one another, and to trustworthy persons who will not abuse introductions provided them. As Mrs. Post suggests, there is a middle-person etiquette:

> When two people—either friends or acquaintances—are walking together and they meet a third who stops to speak to one of them, the other walks slowly on and does not stand awkwardly by and wait for an introduction. If the third is asked by the one she knows, to join them, the sauntering friend is overtaken and an introduction made. The third, however, must not join them unless invited to do so.[14]

Further, introductions made at such times, and even fleetingly at large social occasions, are sometimes treated by both

13. The *forms* of introduction themselves are of course tied to the deference system, and differences in the relative rank of the persons introduced will be felt. Thus, "in polite society," the custom is to introduce the subordinate to the superordinate. Also, the naming employed may be asymmetrical, with one person being introduced, say, by first name, and the second by formal title. And whether symmetrical or asymmetrical, the naming couplet employed may be selected from varying places in the hierarchy of formality, from nicknames to civil titles. Finally, the right to initiate or modify a particular naming usage between two persons may be differentially allocated.

14. Emily Post, *Etiquette, op. cit.*, pp. 16-17.

introduced parties as "courtesy" introductions only, and are not drawn on when the individuals next find themselves in a similar situation unless, through preliminary signs, each signifies inclination to do so. Finally, where there is marked difference in the status of the unacquainted persons, a strategy may be employed to form a relationship of acquaintanceship without introduction:

> On occasions it happens that in talking to one person you want to include another in your conversation without making an introduction. For instance: suppose you are talking to a seedsman and a friend joins you in your garden. You greet your friend, and then include her by saying, "Mr. Smith is suggesting that I dig up these cannas and put in delphiniums." Whether your friend gives an opinion as to the change in color of your flower bed or not, she has been made part of your conversation.
>
> This same maneuver of evading an introduction is also resorted to when you are not sure that an acquaintance will be agreeable to one or both of those whom an accidental circumstance has brought together.[15]

The same "half-way" introduction has been employed in introducing servants to house guests.[16]

15. *Ibid.*, pp. 17-18.
16. *Ibid.*, p. 18.

CHAPTER 8

Engagements Among
the Unacquainted

ONE might say, as a general rule, that acquainted persons in a social situation require a reason not to enter into a face engagement with each other, while unacquainted persons require a reason to do so.[1] In these two rules, the same fundamental principle seems to be operative, namely, that the welfare of the individual ought not to be put in jeopardy through his capacity to open himself up for encounters. In the case of acquainted persons, a willingness to give social recognition saves the other from the affront of being overlooked; in the case of unacquainted persons, a willingness to refrain from soliciting encounters saves the other from being exploited by inopportune overtures and requests.

If the assumption is correct that a kind of tacit contract underlies communication conduct, then we must conclude that there are imaginable circumstances when *any* two unacquainted persons can properly join each other in some kind of face engagement—circumstances in which one person can approach another—since it will always be possible to imagine circumstances that would nullify the implied danger of contact.

1. There is here, apparently, a noticeable difference between the Anglo-American tradition and the Latin tradition, the latter being one where entrance into an encounter with strangers is apparently more broadly licensed. See the interesting description of the two systems of manners in Millicent Fenwick, *Vogue's Book of Etiquette* (New York: Simon and Schuster, 1948), pp. 117-118.

I should like now to consider some of these circumstances under which some kind of engagement among the unacquainted is permissible, and sometimes even obligatory, in our American middle-class society.[2]

1. Exposed Positions

Every social position can be seen as an arrangement which opens up the incumbent to engagement with certain categories of others. In some cases these others will be chiefly limited to persons with whom the individual is already acquainted or to whom he has just been introduced in the current engagement. In other positions, such as that of salesperson or receptionist, the individual will be obliged to hold himself ready to be approached by unacquainted others, providing this is in line of daily business. (This fact makes some persons enjoy performing the entailed role and others consider it as socially inferior.) We have here an important example of engagement among the unacquainted, and one that does not disturb social distances because there is a patent reason why properly mannered customers would desire to initiate such encounters.

There are social positions, however, that open up the incumbent to more than mere occupational-others. Thus, in cities, policemen, priests, and often corner newsstand vendors are approached by a wide variety of others seeking a wide variety of information and assistance, in part because it is believed to be clear that no one would seek to take advantage of these public figures. Policemen and priests are especially interesting, since they may be engaged by strangers merely initiating a greeting as opposed to a request for information.

Furthermore, there are broad statuses in our society, such as

2. It must be stressed that here, and in the communication arrangements yet to be considered, there is much variation from one society to another. For an illustrative comment, see the references to street behavior in India in N. C. Chaudhuri, *A Passage to England* (London: Macmillan, 1959), pp. 82-86.

that of old persons or the very young,[3] that sometimes seem to be considered so meager in sacred value that it may be thought their members have nothing to lose through face engagement, and hence can be engaged at will. None of these persons, it may be noted, has the kind of uniform that can be taken off; none can be off duty during part of the day. Here, then, *persons* are exposed, not merely incumbents; they are "open persons."

There is still another general circumstance that opens up an individual for face engagements; namely, that he can be out of role. Given the assumption that the interests of the individual ought not to be prejudiced by forcing him into contact, and given the fact that these interests of his will be expressed through his playing his serious roles, we can expect that when he is not engaged in his own roles there will then be less reason to be careful with him as regards communication; and this, in fact, is the case. Thus, when an individual is visibly intoxicated, or dressed in a costume, or engaged in an unserious sport, he may be accosted almost at will and joked with, presumably on the assumption that the self projected through these activities is one from which the individual can easily dissociate himself, and hence need not be jealous of or careful with. Similarly, when an individual finds himself in a momentarily peculiar physical position, as when he trips, slips, or in other ways acts in an awkward, unbecoming fashion, he lays himself open for light comment, for he will need a demonstration from others that they see this activity as one that does not prejudice his adult self, and it is in his own interest to allow them to initiate a

3. Children in some towns may even be approached at will for small favors. On the other hand, again as one might expect, in some difficult cities such as Chicago, adults initiating a face engagement with strange children may be suspected of improper designs and so in some cases will be careful not to engage children gratuitously, even in passing. When a child is "with" an adult, the improper possibilities of the contact can be ruled out, thus reestablishing the right of the strange adult. We can understand, then, why a male's comment to a child can be employed as a way of initiating contact with the woman accompanying the child. Dogs, of course, being even more profane than children, provide another classic bridging device to their masters.

joking contact with him for this purpose.[4] Thus, as might have been predicted, the first persons in America to drive Volkswagens laid themselves open to face engagements from all and sundry, since they did not seem to be seriously presenting themselves in the role of driver, at least as a driver of a serious car.[5]

I have considered in terms of the language of status and role some of the grounds on which the individual's usual right to be unmolested by overtures is set aside. There are still other times of license, but ones when the terminology of social role is not very suitable. Thus, if an individual is in patent need of help, and if this help is of little moment to the putative giver, then satisfying this "free need" provides a nonsuspect basis for initiating communication contact. For example, when an individual unknowingly drops something in the street, he momentarily becomes open for overtures, since anyone has a right to tell him what has happened. As current etiquette suggests:

> Women must thank all those, including strangers, who do them little services. For example, if a stranger, man or woman, opens a door for a woman, or picks up something she has dropped, a woman should not allow timidity or shyness to stop her from saying thank you in a pleasant impersonal way. If the stranger seems to be trying to start an unwelcome conversation, one can, still with politeness but with increasing firmness, refuse to converse. But it is more attractive to take for granted that the gesture was motivated by politeness only than it is immediately to suspect another motive.[6]

It should be added that in the past some writers have felt that the very threat of a lady being accosted in a public place, or

4. On Shetand Isle, the local laird was a figure of waning authority, but he still had some distance rights from the crofters; however, on the occasions when he fixed his roof or puttered around fixing a boat, he was felt, by the crofters, to be relatively open to banter.
5. See, for example, the report on a New York to Florida trip in 1955, "On the Florida Highroads in a Low Car," *The New York Times*, Sunday, January 30, 1955, by G. H. Glueck.
6. *Vogue's Book of Etiquette, op. cit.*, p. 35.

even being seen to be alone, is sometimes cause enough for a pure-minded stranger to beat others to the draw:

> If a lady is going to her carriage, or is alone in any public place where it is usual or would be convenient for ladies to be attended, you should offer her your arm and service, even if you don't know her. To do so in a private room, as in the case mentioned, might be thought a liberty.[7]

A more contemporary version of this courtesy is found in the tack occasionally taken by a man passing a strange woman at night on a narrow isolated walk: instead of conspicuously according the female civil inattention, the man may proffer a fleeting word to show that, unlike a would-be assailant, he is willing to be identified.

A final basis of exposure may be mentioned. An individual's actions can create a need in others that exposes them to engagement. For example, if the others have been bumped into or tripped over (or in other ways deprived of their right to unmolested passage) by him, he can claim the right to engage them in order to convey assistance, explanation, apology, and the like, the others' need for such redress presumably outweighing their reluctance to being engaged by a stranger. The same holds true for potential, as well as actual, offenses. In a train compartment, for example, individuals may be asked by a fellow-passenger if it is all right if he smokes, or if he opens (or closes) a window. As these opening engagements are patently in the interests of those whose comfort might be affected, the offense or injury the individual might create by his inclinations thus exposes fellow-passengers to solicitous inquiries in advance.

2. *Opening Positions*

Having considered some circumstances under which persons become available to unacquainted others, we can examine the

7. Anon., *The Canons of Good Breeding* (Philadelphia: Lee and Blanchard, 1839), p. 66.

other side of the question: when does the individual have the right to initiate overtures to those with whom he is unacquainted? Obviously, one answer is that he can do this when the other is in an exposed position. Another answer is that some of the persons who are defined as open tend also to be defined as "opening persons," as individuals who have a built-in license to accost others. Just as the intentions of those who accost them are not suspect, so, in some cases, their intentions in accosting others may not be suspect. Priests and nuns provide one kind of example; police, who presumably will be able to produce a legitimate reason for the engagement after initiating it, provide another. Those who have responsibility for managing, or for guarding the entrance to, social occasions provide still another example, since they are allowed, and often obliged, to initiate engagements of welcome with all who enter, whether acquainted with them or not. Shopkeepers, in those societies that define shops, more than we do, as the scene of a running social occasion, may often find themselves in the host's role, required to engage each entrant and leave-taker in a special salutation. Freya Stark provides an illustration from Arabia:

> In Kuwait you are still at leisure to notice what a charming thing good manners are.
> As you step into the ragged booths you will greet the owner with "Peace be upon you," and he and all who are within hearing will reply with no fanatic exclusion, but in full and friendly chorus to that most gracious of salutations, and will follow your departing steps with their "Fi aman Allah," the divine security. Their shops they treat as small reception-rooms where the visiting buyer is a guest—and sitting at coffee over their affairs will look with surprised but tolerant amusement at the rough Westerner who brushes by to examine saddle-bags or daggers, unconscious of the decent rules of behavior. . . .[8]

In our society, license to approach, like license to be approached, is taken (if not given) by individuals who for a period find themselves out of role. Here, license to initiate im-

---

8. Freya Stark, *Baghdad Sketches* (New York: Dutton, 1938) , p. 192.

proper contact is merely part of the syndrome of license associated with anonymity, in the sense that an individual projecting
an alien self is not fully responsible for the good conduct of that
self. (In the same way, when he trips or slips, he projects a self
from which he can dissociate his inner being.) Again we see a
connection between exposed positions and opening ones, for
the very alienation from his projected self that allows others
to treat this self as approachable and expendable allows him to
misbehave in its name. The falsely presented individual may,
in fact, have a special need to make and to elicit overtures; in
both cases he is able to transmit an appreciation that what he is
appearing as is not his true self.

Nor is it only when engagement is patently to the advantage
of the person approached that emergency engagement with
strangers occurs. In our society, as presumably in others, bonds
between unacquainted persons are felt to be strong enough to
support the satisfying of "free needs," even where the person
receiving the service is the one who initiates the encounter that
makes this possible. A patent unthreatening need appears to
provide a guarantee of the good intentions of the person who is
asking for assistance. Thus, in our society, an individual has a
right to initiate requests for the time of day, for a light, for
directions, and for coin change—although, given a choice in the
matter, the accoster[9] is under obligation to select the individual
present whom he is least likely to be able to exploit.

Similarly, if an individual finds himself in a position where
he badly needs his apologies or explanations to be accepted, he
then has some right to engage others. Liberty to apologize for
accidentally inconveniencing another is also a liberty to present
oneself in a proper light, even at the expense of communication
rules. Thus, to parallel an earlier example, a man walking

9. Mutual claims in regard to matters such as directions can be strong enough
to cause Southern whites to respond politely to direction requests from Negroes.
See, for example, J. H. Griffin, *Black Like Me* (Boston: Houghton Mifflin, 1961),
p. 85. Harvey Sacks has suggested to me that, in the case of directions, a small re-
payment is automatically involved, namely, the imputation, which could be positive, that the asked person looks like "a native of these parts."

around in the grass looking for a key he has dropped has a right to comment on his predicament to a lone passing stranger to demonstrate that he is not improperly involved in some occult activity. The same kind of license occurs when an individual feels he has been mistreated in some way by an unacquainted other, and initiates a complaint, threat, or caution. While defense of one's honor may work hardship upon the person against whom action is taken, the person who institutes such action is not suspect as far as communication rules are concerned.

3. Mutual Openness

I have considered some of the conditions in which an individual can properly become open for face engagement with those with whom he is unacquainted and some of the conditions in which he can initiate an encounter with strangers. I want now to consider circumstances under which unacquainted individuals can be mutually open to each other, each having the right to initiate and the duty to accept an encounter with the other.

An important basis of mutual accessibility resides in the element of informality and solidarity that seems to obtain between individuals who can recognize each other as being of the same special group, especially, apparently, if this group be one that is disadvantaged or ritually-profane. In American society, Negroes at bus stops often extend greetings to Negroes who are strangers to them, as do Orthodox Jews to one another, or men with beards who meet in "square" surroundings.[10] Sports car drivers on the road may do the same—especially when the car of each is of the same make, and a rare one. And, of course, when fellow-nationals meet in exotic lands they may feel obliged or privileged to initiate a state of talk.

Mutual accessibility also occurs when each of the two persons involved finds himself in a position that is at once exposed

10. The last example was suggested by David Sudnow.

and opening. As one student has already suggested, when two persons unintentionally touch each other in passing on the street, both may take on the guilty role, with consequent mutual license to initiate an encounter for purposes of apology.[11] Even when it is clear that only one of the parties is at fault, mutual openness can occur. The offender can treat himself as an opening person, needful of setting the record right about himself, while treating the other as one in need of receiving assurances, and hence place himself in an exposed position. At the same time the offended person can feel that he has the right to initiate demands for apology, or to confirm that no offense has been taken. Similarly, when two pedestrians must pass each other on a narrow walk, or when a pedestrian and motorist pair are in doubt about a joint line of action, a mutually initiated meeting of the eyes can be employed to subtly apportion sides of the walk, or to subtly assure right-of-way to the other, or to ratify and consolidate an allocation that has been communicated.

Another important basis for mutual accessibility arises from what might be called "open regions"—physically bounded places where "any" two persons, acquainted or not, have a right to initiate face engagement with each other for the purpose of extending salutations. Open regions differ according to whether the right is also felt as an obligation, according to the character of the face engagement that is permitted, according to whether or not introductions form part of the consequence of the encounter, and according to the categories of participants that are excluded. I would like to describe briefly some of the kinds of open regions.

In Anglo-American society there exists a kind of "nod line" that can be drawn at a particular point through a rank order of communities according to size. Any community below the line, and hence below a certain size, will subject its adults, whether acquainted or not, to mutual greetings;[12] any community above

11. J. Toby, "Some Variables in Role Conflict Analysis," *Social Forces*, 30 (1952), 325.

12. Where strangers owe each other passing greetings, we must study the resulting engagement in connection with the civil inattention that precedes and follows

the line will free all pairs of unacquainted persons from this obligation. (Where the line is drawn varies, of course, according to region.) In the case of communities that fall above the nod line, even persons who cognitively recognize each other to be neighbors, and know that this state of mutual information exists, may sometimes be careful to refrain from engaging each other.[13] Perhaps this is done on the theory that, once acquaintanceship is established between persons living near one another, it might become difficult to keep sufficient distance in the relationship.

Villages, towns, and rural places that fall below the nod line do not, of course, put absolutely everyone on nodding terms. Thus, in Shetland Isle, there was a general feeling that strange seamen who sounded and looked British were to be brought within the circle of humanity, but not those from foreign ports. The latter tended to be walked past and looked at as if they were not social objects but, rather, physical ones; they tended to be

---

it, both types of behavior being part of a single complex through which individuals in these places establish each other as safe persons to be near. An example, which incidentally suggests how serious this type of activity can become, can be cited from cowboy life on the American prairie:

When nearin' 'nother person on a trail, etiquette required that a man approach within speakin' distance and pass a word before changin' his course unless, for a very good reason, he was justified in such a change. The West held that ever' person had the right to find out the intent of all other persons 'bout 'im. Unwarranted violation of this was usually interpreted as a confession of guilt, or as a deliberate and flagrant insult.

When two men met, spoke, and passed on, it was a violation of the West's code for either to look back over his shoulder. Such an act was interpreted as an expression of distrust, as though one feared a shot in the back. If he stopped to talk 'long the trail, he dismounted and loosened the cinches to give his hoss's back some air. When greetin' a stranger on the trail, one was careful not to lift his hand if the stranger rode a skittish hoss. Some critters would bolt if a man lifted a hand near 'em. He merely nodded and said, "Howdy." If the stranger lit to cool his saddle, the other didn't stay mounted while carryin' on a conversation. The polite thing to do was dismount and talk with 'im face to face. This showed one wasn't lookin' for any advantage over the other.

(R. F. Adams, *The Old-Time Cowhand* [New York: The Macmillan Company, 1961], pp. 57-58.)

13. In the apt phrase reported in one housing study, such a neighbor does not "offer his eyes" to the other. See "Blueprint for Living Together," by L. Kuper, in L. Kuper, ed., *Living in Towns* (London: The Cresset Press, 1953), p. 61.

treated as "nonpersons." In spite of these limits, however, we can still speak of these rural settlements as "open regions," where coming into the region makes one accessible to anyone else in the vicinity.[14]

While rural and small town communities are perhaps the largest open regions, they are by no means the only ones. One instance, apparently, is the English sports field, as a report on the social life of American military personnel in Britain suggests:

> Some [American] airmen who have played golf at Davyhulme have been impressed with the friendliness of other players. "Why, they talked to us!" they say. The explanation that to the British a person's presence on a sports field is the equivalent of an introduction, and that one can talk to strangers then, is greeted with some disbelief. Other sports produce similarly friendly results—athletics, flying, and of course darts.[15]

In American society, bars,[16] cocktail lounges, and club cars tend to be defined as open places, at least as between men (and although women are not free to engage men, certainly an over-

14. In Shetland Isle some complications existed. There were three ecologically separated communities on the island and, therefore, some unacquainted residents. Males who were acquainted tended to exchange sociable statements when passing each other on the road. Males who were unacquainted but who identified each other as commoners and island residents exchanged very brief, two- or three-word highly patterned salutations; a Briton or local person of noncrofter status tended to be greeted with a different salutation. On the Shetland Islands in general, public solidarity extended past the point of offering greetings or satisfying free needs. When a male passed another male at some short-term task, help was often automatically given, whether the persons were acquainted or not.

15. "The Americans in Our Midst," *The Manchester Guardian Weekly*, August 5, 1954.

16. Persons sitting at the bar in a tavern are, by customary rule, in an especially open position relative to those sitting next to them, a rule that presumably can be the more consistently carried out because of another rule, which in general prohibits unaccompanied women from sitting at the bar. Accompanied women presumably have someone to talk to on one side whom they already know, which ordinarily limits the implication of being talked to by a stranger sitting on the other side. In any case, in those bars where unaccompanied women are allowed to sit at the bar, their decision to do so tends to be taken as a sign that, if they are not ready to begin a conversation with a strange man, they will at least not be affronted should a strange man attempt to begin one.

ture from a male to a female in these settings is not much of a social delict, this fact constituting one of the important attributes of these settings). Something similar can be said about vacation resorts and about other highly bounded settings:

> A ship may be compared to a country hotel. It is good manners to greet other passengers in a friendly fashion without, however, making presumptuous overtures. You speak to the people next to you in deck chairs, but you do not force conversation upon them. In general, as in a friend's house, the roof is the introduction, but this does not mean you are expected to do more than bow in greeting to fellow passengers as you encounter them during the day.[17]

And, as implied, social parties and gatherings in private homes bring into being open regions where participants have a right not only to engage anyone present but also to initiate face engagement with self-introductions, if the gathering is too large for the host or hostess to have already introduced them. As an early American etiquette manual puts it:

> If you meet any one whom you have never heard of before at the table of a gentleman, or in the drawing-room of a lady, you may converse with him with entire propriety. The form of "introduction" is nothing more than a statement by a mutual friend that two gentlemen are by rank and manners fit acquaintances for one another. All this may be presumed from the fact, that both meet at a respectable house. This is the theory of the matter. Custom, however, requires that you should take the earliest opportunity afterwards to be regularly presented to such an one.[18]

A contemporary source restates this theme:

> Nevertheless, it is still true that in a private house, or at any

17. A. Vanderbilt, *Amy Vanderbilt's Complete Book of Etiquette* (New York: Doubleday, 1958) , p. 637.

18. *The Laws of Etiquette*, by "A Gentleman" (Philadelphia: Carey, Lee and Blanchard, 1836) , p. 101.

party, a guest may speak to any other guest without an introduction of any kind.[19]

Another illustration of the open regions provided by convivial occasions is carnivals. During these costumed street celebrations, a roof and its rights is by social definition spread above the streets, bringing persons into contact—a contact facilitated by their being out of role.

The assumption of mutual regard and good will built into open regions guarantees a rationale for discounting the potential nefariousness of contact among the unacquainted, this being one basis for sociable accessibility. There are other bases. During occasions of recognized natural disaster, when individuals suddenly find themselves in a clearly similar predicament and suddenly become mutually dependent for information and help, ordinary communication constraints can break down.[20] Again, however, what is occurring in the situation guarantees that encounters aren't being initiated for what can be improperly gained by them. And to the extent that this is assured, contact prohibitions can be relaxed. (If the disaster is quite calamitous, everyone is likely to be forced out of role and hence into mutual accessibility.)

A final contingency that bears on mutual openness may be mentioned. Earlier in this report it was argued that the individual in our society has a right to receive civil inattention. It was also suggested that, when persons ratify each other for mutual participation in an encounter, the rule against looking fully at another is set aside. Typically, then, one person may legitimately begin to look fully at another a moment before he initiates an encounter, the legitimacy being imputed retroactively, after it is shown what the individual had been intending to do. If, then, persons find that they must stare at each other, they can try to cope with the matter by initiating a state of talk, the overture

---

19. *Vogue's Book of Etiquette, op. cit.,* p. 60.
20. A nice fictionalized illustration concerning a fire in a residential hotel is provided by Thomas Wolfe in *You Can't Go Home Again* (New York: Sun Dial Press, 1942) , Chap. 19, "Unscheduled Climax," esp. pp. 297-298.

being excusable (however embarrassing) because of what can be handled by means of it.

There are standard conditions under which the rule about not staring gives rise to these problems. When a few persons find themselves in a small space, as in a European railway compartment, or around the entrance of a store that is not yet quite open, civil inattention is hard to manage tactfully. To not stare requires looking very pointedly in other directions, which may make the whole issue more a matter of consciousness than it was meant to be, and may also express too vividly an incapacity or a distaste for engagement with those present.[21] A lengthy illustration may be taken from a very relevant essay by Cornelia Otis Skinner called "Where to Look:"

> Fortunately such where-to-look situations do not arise with any frequency. One which does, however, is the elevator one . . . both while in an elevator and while waiting for one. The act of waiting for an elevator brings out a suspicious streak in people. You arrive before the closed landing door and push a button. Another person comes along and after a glance of mutual appraisal, you both look quickly away and continue to wait, thinking the while uncharitable thoughts of one another. The new arrival suspecting you of not having pushed the button and you wondering if the new arrival is going to be a mistrusting old meanie and go give the button a second shove . . . an unspoken tension which is broken by one or the other of you walking over and doing just that. Then back to positions of waiting and the problem of where to look. To stare the other person in the eye seems forward and usually the eye doesn't warrant it. Shoes are convenient articles

21. In this connection, the plight of close-sitting diners in low-priced restaurants in the south of France is very usefully described by C. Lévi-Strauss in his *Les Structures Élémentaires de la Parenté*, Chap. 5, "Le Principe de Reciprocité" (Paris: Presses Universitaires de France, 1949), abridged and translated by Rose L. Coser and Grace Frazer, in L. Coser and B. Rosenberg, eds., *Sociological Theory* (New York: The Macmillan Company, 1959), pp. 88-91. Lévi-Strauss suggests an analysis of the "tensions" created by sitting opposite someone with whom one is not in a conversational relation, and describes the institutionalized solution: each diner pours the wine from his small table-bottle into the glass of the other, and with the exchange of these clearance signs, the table is open for conversation, the diners now being ratified coparticipants of a social encounter.

for scrutiny—your own or those of the other person—although if overdone, this may give the impression of incipient shoe fetichism.[22]

It [the where-to-look problem] continues even inside the elevator . . . especially in the crowded and claustrophobic boxes of the modern high buildings. Any mutual exchange of glances on the part of the occupants would add almost a touch of lewdness to such already over-cozy sardine formation. Some people gaze instead at the back of the operator's neck, others stare trance-like up at those little lights which flash the floors, as if safety of the trip were dependent upon such deep concentration.

A rather similar situation arises in a Pullman diner when one is obliged to sit opposite an unknown at a table for two. How to fill in the awkward wait between writing out "Luncheon #4 with coffee" and the arrival and serving of same? If one is not the type who, given the slightest provocation, bursts into friendly chit-chat with a stranger, the risk of getting conversationally involved with someone who is, brings out the furtive behavior of an escaped convict. Sometimes it becomes apparent that the other person feels the same way . . . a discovery which comes as a minor shock but no major solution. Two strangers sitting directly opposite each other at a distance of a foot and a half, and determined politely but firmly to avoid each other's eye, go in for a fascinating little game of "I don't spy." They re-read the menu, they fool with the cutlery, they inspect their own fingernails as if seeing them for the first time. Comes the inevitable moment when glances meet but they meet only to shoot instantly away and out the window for an intent view of the passing scene.[23]

It may be added that during such difficult times, if the individual decides against contact, he may well have to find some activity for himself in which he can become visibly immersed, so as

22. Cornelia Otis Skinner, "Where to Look," in *Bottoms Up!* (New York: Dodd, Mead, 1955) , pp. 29-30. All ellipsis dots are the author's.

23. *Ibid.*, pp. 30-31. The same kind of difficulty is mentioned by Hortense Calisher in "Night Riders of Northville," in *In the Absence of Angels* (Boston: Little, Brown, 1951), p. 121:

It can be awkward, drinking alone at a bar. Is the man behind it wholly a servitor at such times, or must recognition be made of the fact that two human beings are together in an otherwise empty room?

to provide the others present with a face-saving excuse for being unattended to. Here again we see the situational functions that newspapers and magazines play in our society, allowing us to carry around a screen that can be raised at any time to give ourselves or others an excuse for not initiating contact.

Airplane and long-distance bus travel have here underlined some interesting issues. Seatmates, while likely to be strangers, are not only physically too close to each other to make nonengagement comfortable, but are also fixed for a long period of time, so that conversation, once begun, may be difficult thereafter either to close or to sustain. In such cases, a strategy is to "thin out" the encounter by keeping it impersonal and by declining to exchange identifying names, thus guaranteeing that some kind of nonrecognition will be possible in the future. Amy Vanderbilt, in newspaper advice, illustrates this point:

> As for airplanes today, seatmates may not exchange a word in a trip across the continent. But plane conversation is in order if mutually desired and kept impersonal. As on trains, names need not be exchanged. And why should they? After all, it is relaxing to talk without identifying oneself.

Relationships with service personnel in our society, when talk is required, may be thinned out in the same way—a thinning, incidentally, that servers may attempt to counteract by asking the name of the customer and proffering their own.

4. Evasions and Infractions

We must now consider an important theme. Given the gains that can be obtained through the improper initiation of encounters, and given the penalty attached to engaging in these improprieties, it can be expected that persons will employ ruses to evade the rules and safely accomplish forbidden ends. Perhaps the gentlest of these designs is seen when an individual intentionally places himself in a position to facilitate overtures being made to him. The classic instance, of course, is that of the lady who drops her handkerchief so that a particular man will have a proper excuse for talking to her.[24] Mental patients provide instances of more resolute manipulation of the rules. One patient I observed over a three-month period did not so much break the rules as flagrantly misemploy available excuses for breaking them. She would ask persons—both ones she knew and ones she didn't—for minor favors, such as the time, in such a manner that the person approached would sometimes gradually realize that the favor was merely an excuse, and that in a certain way the asker was merely toying with the conventional conditions of contact. Or she would sometimes pester the kitchen staff for extra food, again with the implication of merely exploiting the bonds among persons that support the exchange of minor favors. Guards and attendants were also favorite targets of her engaging tendencies.

One of the most significant infractions of communication rules has to do with street accosting. There are, of course, some legal restrictions placed upon its varieties, upon begging, peddling, and pestering in public streets. But in the main, the force that keeps people in their communication place in our middle-class society seems to be the fear of being thought forward and pushy, or odd, the fear of forcing a relationship where none is desired—the fear, in the last analysis, of being rather patently rejected and even cut. But we know that there are many ways in which an individual can accept the fact that he is liable to this kind of disregard and is subject to this kind of risk, and go on

---

24. In a column by Ann Landers, the problem of a girl who wants to meet a boy who is interested but shy is handled in this way:

> Your problem is to force the man to talk to you first; that's the way he wants it. I can think of no better way than for you to drag off the bus with a heavy package almost as big as you are! It doesn't matter what—several dozen bricks in a large box, well wrapped, will do. Our hero's chivalrous instincts will not permit him to resist the picture of a maiden in distress. He'll be at your side asking to assist you. If he isn't, try dropping the package and/or twisting your ankle. When you get to your house, let him carry the package in, offer him refreshments and thank him.

from there to capitalize on the liberty his fall from grace brings to him. The liberties taken by the drunk and the costumed are mild instances of this. There are other examples we excuse less readily. Perhaps the classic type of improper opening person is he who makes a steady economic[25] and psychic living from this role. Here we find the street stemmer, the stall operator, and the panhandler, who accept the resentment of the community in order to buttonhole it into buying or giving something. The street prostitute is a special example; the eyes and smiles and sallies with which she approaches a man tell us precisely how all other women must be careful not to conduct themselves, lest it be assumed that liberties can be taken with them.

I think there is something to be learned from considering another type of communication exploiter, the homosexual. It is felt that such a person, when "cruising" for pickups, will utilize casual contacts involving innocuous requests or innocuous sociable comments as a cover. The special significance of this kind of exploitation of public solidarity has to do with its power to spoil casual contact between male heterosexuals. When the heterosexual is approached by an unacquainted male on what prove to be sexually improper grounds, he may suffer concern that his appearance has elicited this and that others present, identifying the accoster, will wrongly impute homosexuality to

25. There seems to be a growing tendency in Western societies to restrict these kinds of openings, if not in the city at large, then in all but a few streets. Current social control in London, for example, can be compared with conditions general throughout that city in earlier times:

> The crying of wares so well described in Lydgate's "London Lackpenny" was a necessary though frequently raucous art, which had to take the place of every type of modern advertisement, and could produce very satisfactory results when inflicted on a public that seldom knew the precise character and quality of the goods it wanted to buy. It was a common thing for traders who thought that they were making too little impression, to seize desirable customers by the sleeve and seek to detain them with argument, and the London cooks drew up an ordinance in 1475 because— . . . "divers persones of the saide Craft wᵗ their hands embrowed and fowled be accustumed to drawe and pluk other Folk as well gentilmen as other comon people by their slyves and clothes to bye of their vitailles whereby many debates and strives often tymes happen ayenst the peas."

(G. T. Salusbury, *Street Life in Medieval England* [Oxford: Pen-in-Hand, 1948], pp. 172-173.)

the accosted. More importantly, when he is innocently approached by a member of his own sex he may not be sure of the innocence, just as, when he innocently approaches another male, he may be unsure of the other's view of him. Hence casual solidarity among unacquainted males is threatened. A novelist provides an extreme example, namely, the predicament of a homosexual in a homosexual bar sincerely desiring a match:

> It was when I sat down by the entrance and took out my cigarettes that I realized I had no matches on me. There were no less than ten people, maybe fifteen, smoking around me, but in a place like this it was out of the question to ask for a light unless one knew somebody. The legitimate phrase, "Could you please give me a light?" was, in these surroundings, a recognized approach and a too obvious one at that. I walked up to the counter and bought a box of matches.[26]

Homosexuality, then, tends to do to the all-male (and to a degree to the all-female) world what has already been done to communication contacts between the sexes, except that, in the latter case, to be thought a desirable object may not in itself constitute much of an affront—indeed, it may constitute an expected compliment.

26. Rodney Garland, *The Heart in Exile* (New York: Lion Library Editions, 1956) , p. 47. As previously suggested, another set of quite spoiled relations can be found between Negroes and southern women with whom they are not acquainted. An illustration may be cited from Griffin, *op. cit.*, p. 22, where, as a Negro, he half rose to give a white lady his seat and was stared down:

> But my movement had attracted the white woman's attention. For an instant our eyes met. I felt sympathy for her, and thought I detected sympathy in her glance. The exchange blurred the barriers of race (so new to me) long enough for me to smile and vaguely indicate the empty seat beside me, letting her know she was welcome to accept it.
>
> Her blue eyes, so pale before, sharpened and she spat out, "What're you looking at me like *that* for?"
>
> I felt myself flush. Other white passengers craned to look at me. The silent onrush of hostility frightened me.
>
> "I'm sorry," I said, staring at my knees. "I'm not from here." The pattern of her skirt turned abruptly as she faced the front.
>
> "They're getting sassier every day," she said loudly. Another woman agreed and the two fell into conversation.

Just as homosexuals abuse the contact system in the society, so also do "sexual perverts," who rely on the right of adults to engage unknown youths and children, and exploit the contact thus made in a way which is considered unsportsmanlike.[27]

Of special interest here is some of the conduct classified under the psychiatric rubric of "exhibitionism." Whether the indictable act consists of words spoken, gestures conveyed, or acts performed, the communication structure of the event often consists of an individual initiating an engagement with a stranger of the opposite sex by means of the kind of message that would be proper only if they were on close and intimate terms. Apart from psychodynamic issues, exhibitionists often spectacularly subvert the protective social control that keeps individuals interpersonally distant even though they are physically close to each other. The assault here is not so much directly on an individual as on the system of rights and symbols the individual employs in expressing relatedness and unrelatedness to those about him. For example, there is the game played by a middle-aged female mental patient on a ward in a research hospital: on visitors' day she would wear only a bathrobe and slippers, proffer a male visitor appropriate small talk, and then, when very close to him and in a ratified state of talk with him, suddenly expose herself. At that moment the visitor would find himself trapped in an engagement that he could neither immediately escape from nor properly sustain.

It is necessary to add a comment concerning the relationship between exposed persons and illegitimately opening ones. Trou-

27. The unsettling of public trust, of mutual claims linking strangers, can also occur in other contexts. In times of internecine armed conflict, a very high level of distrust and anxiety may sometimes be found in public places. Take, for example, the comment by Lawrence Durrell on the period of the 1953-58 troubles in Cyprus in *Bitter Lemons* (New York: Dutton, 1959) , pp. 215-216:

> But the evil genius of terrorism is suspicion—the man who stops and asks for a light, a cart with a broken axle signalling for help, a forester standing alone among trees, three youths walking back to a village after sundown, a shepherd shouting something indistinctly heard by moonlight, the sudden pealing of a doorbell in the night. The slender chain of trust upon which all human relations are based is broken—and this the terrorist knows and sharpens his claws precisely here. . . .

ble makers who breach the communication line and systematically break the gentleman's agreement concerning communication often pay a price for their liberties. They come to be seen
as profane persons, as persons who have sacrificed for gain the
respect that is owed them. Once an individual has made this
sacrifice, there is little reason why others cannot approach him,
since, except for the fact that he may be contaminating, he
has no way to hold people off. A person who accosts others will
therefore often be a person whom others can accost at will, a
reciprocity that holds, it was suggested, for those who are denied
sacredness through no fault of their own, such as the very young
who do not yet have their quota of *mana,* and the old who have
lost theirs.

The openings I have cited, both legitimate and illegitimate,
initiate an official face engagement, even if only for a moment,
and support the contention that an individual is either all in or
all out of an encounter. But, of course, once this latter normative arrangement is firmly established, we can expect that certain kinds of advantage can be taken of it. For example, in
some Western communities there is the practice whereby a male
communicates regard for the attractiveness of a passing female
with whom he is unacquainted by whistling at her or greeting
her with some other expressive sign. What follows is up to her.
She can elect to act as if no relevant communication has occurred. Or she can elect to turn and ratify the comment by a
friendly or hostile comment, in either case creating a momentary face engagement. (Apparently the more impersonally appreciative the whistle, that is, the more it can be construed not
as a pickup, the more accepting the girl will be of it.[28]) But in

28. D. Larsen, "Do You Like to be Whistled At?" in the column "The Question
Man," *San Francisco Chronicle*, Monday, July 3, 1961, provides comments from
models at the House of Charm (San Francisco) suggesting that a whistle can be
received with good grace. One informant suggests:

Every woman who dresses well likes to be appreciated for her trouble. A wolf
whistle is rather a crude form of expression, but I suppose it is the equivalent
of being hissed at approvingly in Mexico or being pinched in Italy. A stranger
can't walk up and talk to a pretty girl, so he uses the U. S. whistle.

addition, she may smile visibly (so that the whistler knows his message has been appreciatively received) , and at the same time look straight ahead so as not to allow for the collapse of separateness and the formation of an engagement. This latter tack represents, in effect, a collusion of both individuals against the rules of communication—an unratified breach of communication barriers. The breach is a slight one, however, since the person whistled at has been on the move away from the whistler and will soon be out of range of engagement.[29]

5. Counter-Control

I have suggested that persons are kept from improperly approaching others by self-applied rules and by legal sanctions. But in addition to these means of social control there are other kinds, designed not so much to alter the offender's pattern of misbehavior as to allow a particular victim to escape from the

---

Another suggests:

It is nice to know you are whistleable. If I feel I deserve it I occasionally turn around and say thank you. A whistle is a compliment. Particularly if you know the man is just commenting on your beauty and not trying to embarrass you. If he is I put on my stony face and walk on.

And still another:

A long low whistle is a perk-me-up to a girl. It can add a smile to her face, a lilt to her step and put a twinkle in her eyes. It can do more for her than a new hat. Unpolished it may be, but it is a compliment. Part of the fun is that the whistler is often anonymous. You turn around and try to guess who.

29. On the same grounds we can understand why it is safe, and therefore not much of an offense, for an individual in a moving boat, train, or bus to proffer a greeting to a stranger who is stationary or moving in the other direction.

In our society, when a large number of men or boys or girls are together, one of their number seems likely to extend a greeting to a passing stranger. Presumably the threat of a two-person engagement developing is lessened by the numbers involved, and hence more easily tolerated. When the group is in uniform, and therefore to some extent out of role, even more license is likely to be taken, unless forbidden by the group's leader. When the members of such a group, in addition, are moving in a vehicle they are in no position to stop, and thereby moving away from the target of their sallies, even greater license seems to be taken and tolerated.

deprivation inflicted by the offense. I want to mention some of these techniques here, even though they, and some of the issues which follow, occur in regard to the acquainted as well as the unacquainted.

Some standard protective strategies are detailed in etiquette books:

> If one is approached on the street by a beggar and does not wish to give him money, any one of three courses may be followed: One may spare the beggar the embarrassment of a refusal by pretending not to notice his appeal; or one may refuse, saying, "No, I'm sorry"; or one may stop and offer help by suggesting a charitable organization to which the unfortunate can apply. A kind heart may extend this list even further, but the essential point is that if one is asked for charity, an apology must accompany a refusal. Quite apart from other considerations, any sign of anger or impatience is brutally ill-mannered.[30]

Another strategy is what might be called the "terminal squirm." Here, the unwilling recipient of the overture grudgingly turns his attention to the speaker, gives a noncommital reply, and then as quickly as possible turns away, taking for granted that the other will take this answer as a "signing out" cue. In our society, this technique is often employed by parents with their importuning children, and by mental hospital staff with importuning patients.

Given the fact that importuned persons attempt to avoid the importuners, we can expect that there will be an attempt on the part of importuners to counter this counter (and, in turn, an attempt on the part of the importuned to counter this counter to a counter) .

A counter to the strategy of acting as if no overture has been received is to inveigle an individual into an explosive demonstration that he is not in fact as little involved and affected by the entreaties as he appears to show. In everyday terms, this is sometimes called "getting a rise." Thus, children often play

---

30. *Vogue's Book of Etiquette, op. cit.,* p. 13.

games of making funny faces at one another to see who will win the contest between "straight face" and laugh-provoking gesture.[31] In mental hospitals, rise-getting seems to be a common pursuit, practiced by junior staff and by patients upon patients who insist on being mute, and by still other patients who make wonderfully humorous efforts to entice staff into communicative contact.

On a hospital ward studied by the writer, a middle-aged woman patient employed some expert techniques for getting others, against their wishes, into a state of talk. She would come progressively closer to the unwilling participant, increasing the loudness of her comments and the impropriety of their reference, as well as the grotesqueness of her facial grimaces, until a point was reached where the participant could no longer maintain the fiction of not being engaged, and would, in some way, respond. In addition to this technique of progressive profanation, she would employ antics, dancing, prancing, and jumping in the immediate presence of the recalcitrant participant, stopping only when she succeeded in getting the other involved. If these antics failed, she would sometimes employ the strategy of stopping abruptly and then looking into the eyes of the other in secret collusive derision of the self that had just behaved in a peculiar way. The other would then frequently find himself entering into this collusion, establishing communion with an individual who, apparently, had suddenly become sane. If this, too, failed, she would sometimes make offensive, abusive, or mimicking gestures at one individual, in a way that could barely be defined as behind his back, and then quickly turn to a second individual with a knowing, "I'm-just-trying-to-kid-this-fool" look; the person receiving this collusive look often allowed him-

31. The phenomenon of getting a rise or, reciprocally, rising, also occurs when the butt is already involved in a face engagement with the stimulator, in which case getting a rise will consist in forcing the butt suddenly to "flood out" and sharply increase his level of manifest seriousness, mirth, and the like. Sometimes the teaser employs a passing remark calculated to make the butt become suddenly affronted, only to perceive at the next moment the unserious intent. Sometimes the teasing or goading is continuous and mounting until successful, as in the game of "the dozens."

self to be trapped momentarily into a byplay, and thereby lost the game. Interestingly enough, she was able to combat the lack of civil inattention that nurses in the glassed-in nursing station accorded her—either by their pointed not-seeing of her or by their staring at her—by getting a rise from them even through the glass partition designed to protect them, and even at a time when they were making every effort to demonstrate that they would not be drawn into communication unless properly approached by a proper person.

PART FOUR

Accessible

Engagements

CHAPTER 9

Communication Boundaries

I HAVE suggested that the initiation of engagement among the acquainted and among the unacquainted is voluntarily regulated both by those who seek out communicative contact and by those who avoid it. Rules regarding leave-taking and disbandment of an encounter were also considered, although briefly. I want now to consider the regulations that apply to a face engagement once it has formed, but those regulations which apply only when there are bystanders in the situation, namely, persons present who are not ratified members of the engagement. Since this will involve a consideration of boundedness, I want to begin by reviewing the boundaries of social situations themselves.

1. Conventional Situational Closure

Whether an individual is allowed to enter a region, such as a room, or is excluded from it, he will often be required to show some kind of regard for the physical boundary around it, when there is one. Of course, theoretically it is possible for boundaries like thick walls to close the region off physically from outside communication; almost always, however, some communication across the boundary is physically possible. Social arrangements are therefore recognized that restrict such communication to a special part of the boundary, such as doors, and that lead persons inside and outside the region to act *as if* the barrier had cut off more communication than it does. The work walls do, they do in part because they are honored or socially recognized as communication barriers, giving rise, among properly conducted members of the community, to the possibility of "conventional situational closure" in the absence of actual physical closure.

A glimpse of these conventions can be obtained by noting a fact about socialization: children in our middle-class society are firmly taught that, while it is possible to address a friend by shouting through the walls, or to get his attention by tapping on the window, it is none the less not permissible, and that a desire to engage anyone in the region must be ratified by first knocking at the door as the formal means of making entry.

Windows themselves may provide an opportunity for partial participation in a situation and are typically associated with an understanding that such a possibility will not be exploited. Deviations from this rule can, of course, be found. In Shetland Isle, visiting Norwegian seamen, described by some islanders as "of the lowest type," would sometimes walk around cottages and peer directly into the windows. Dickens provides a similar illustration from the America of a century ago:

> After dinner we went down to the railroad again, and took our seats in the cars for Washington. Being rather early, those men and boys who happened to have nothing particular to do, and were curious in foreigners, came (according to custom) round the carriage in which I sat; let down all the windows; thrust in their heads and shoulders; hooked themselves on conveniently by their elbows; and fell to comparing notes on the subject of my personal appearance, with as much indifference as if I were a stuffed figure. I never gained so much uncompromising information with reference to my own nose and eyes, the various impressions wrought by my mouth and chin on different minds, and how my head looks when it is viewed from behind, as on these occasions.[1]

1. Charles Dickens, *American Notes* (Greenwich, Conn.: Premier Americana, Fawcett Publications, 1961), pp. 136-137.

In the many mental hospitals where the nurses' station is a glass-enclosed observation post, patients must be trained to keep from lingering around the windows and looking in on the life inside. (Interestingly enough, no hospital rule prohibits staff from looking out at a patient through these windows, thus maintaining an official form of eavesdropping.) The fashion of using "picture windows" for walls has, of course, introduced its own social strains, requiring great morale on both sides of the window to ensure conventional closure; there are many cartoon illustrations of consequent problems. It may be added (as the citation from Dickens suggests) that failure to recognize a region boundary is often associated with according to those who are improperly observed the status of nonpersons.

Where walls between two regions are known to be very thin, problems of reticence become pronounced.[2] Sometimes open recognition will be given to the communication possibilities, with persons talking through the wall almost as though they were all in the same social situation, as an analysis of a British semidetached housing development suggests:

> Developing our picture of neighbour linkage by ear from the comments of residents, we find that it is possible in these houses to entertain a neighbour's wife by playing her favorite records with the gramophone tuned to loud, or to mind her child or invite her to tea, all through the party wall.[3]

Here, of course, we see some of the special functions of sight: those on the other side of the party wall may not be present, or, if present, may not be attending, but it will be impossible to *see* that this is the case.

2. Accessible Engagements

When a face engagement exhausts the situation—all persons present being accredited participants in the encounter—the

2. *The Presentation of Self*, pp. 119-120.
3. L. Kuper, "Blueprint for Living Together," in L. Kuper, ed., *Living in Towns* (London: The Cresset Press, 1953), p. 14.

problem of maintaining orderly activity will be largely internal
to the encounter: the allocation of talking time (if the engagement is a spoken one) ; the maintenance of something innocuous to talk or act upon (this being describable as the problem
of "safe supplies"); the inhibition of hostility; and so forth.

When there are persons present who are not participants in
the engagement, we know that inevitably they will be in a position to learn something about the encounter's participants and
to be affected by how the encounter as a whole is conducted.
When a face engagement must be carried on in a situation containing bystanders, I will refer to it as *accessible*.

Whenever a face engagement is accessible to nonparticipants
there is a fully shared and an unshared participation. All persons in the gathering at large will be immersed in a common
pool of unfocused interaction, each person, by his mere presence, manner, and appearance, transmitting some information
about himself to everyone in the situation, and each person
present receiving like information from all the others present,
at least in so far as he is willing to make use of his receiving
opportunities. It is this possibility of widely available communication, and the regulations arising to control this communication, that transforms a mere physical region into the locus of a
sociologically relevant entity, the situation. But above and beyond this fully common participation, the ratified members of
a particular engagement will *in addition* be participating in interaction of the focused kind, where a message conveyed by one
person is meant to make a specific contribution to a matter at
hand, and is usually addressed to a particular recipient, while
the other members of the encounter, and only these others, are
meant to receive it too. Thus, there will be a fully shared basis
of unfocused interaction underlying one or more partially
shared bases of focused interaction.

The difference between participation in the unfocused interaction in the situation at large and participation in the focused
interaction in a face engagement is easy to sense but difficult to

follow out in detail. Questions such as choice of participants for the encounter or sound level of voices have relevance for the situation as a whole, because anyone in the situation will be (and will be considered to be) in a position to witness these aspects of the face engagement, which are the unfocused part of the communication flowing from it. But the specific meanings of *particular* statements appropriately conveyed within a face engagement will not be available to the situation at large, although, if a special effort at secrecy be made, this furtiveness, as a *general* aspect of what is going on, may in fact become quite widely perceivable and an important item in the unfocused interaction that is occurring. That part of the communication occurring in a face engagement that could not be conveyed through mediating channels is situational; but this situational aspect of the encounter becomes part of the unfocused communication in the situation at large only when some of the grosser improprieties, such as shouting, whispering, and broad physical gestures, occur.

In considering accessible engagements, it is convenient to take a vantage point within such an encounter, and to describe the issues from this point of view. The persons present in the gathering at large can then be divided up into participants and bystanders, depending on whether or not they are official members of the engagement in question; and the issues to be considered can be divided up into obligations owed the encounter and obligations owed the gathering at large (and behind the gathering, the social occasion of which it is an expression).

In order for the engagement to maintain its boundaries and integrity, and to avoid being engulfed by the gathering, both participant and bystander will have to regulate their conduct appropriately. And yet even while cooperating to maintain the privacy of the given encounter, both participant and bystander will be obligated to protect the gathering at large, demonstrating that in certain ways all those within the situation stand together, undivided by their differentiating participation.

3. Conventional Engagement Closure

By definition, an accessible engagement does not exhaust the situation; there is no situational closure, physical or conventional, to cut it off from nonparticipants. What we find instead is some obligation and some effort on the part of both participants and bystanders to act as if the engagement were physically cut off from the rest of the situation. In short, a "conventional engagement closure" is found. I want now to consider some of the elements of social organization this closure entails.

a. Bystanders extend a type of civil inattention, but one that is designed for encounters, not for individuals. Bystanders are obliged to refrain from exploiting the communication position in which they find themselves, and to give visible expression to the participants of the gathering that they are focusing their attention elsewhere—a courtesy of some complexity, since a too studied inattention to what one is in a position to overhear can easily spoil a show of inattention.[4]

Since there are many reasons why an individual might want to overhear the content of an engagement of which he is not a member, he may often simulate inattention, giving the impression that conventional closure has been obtained, while in fact he is furtively attending to the talk. How much of this eavesdropping actually does go on, and in what situations, is difficult to assess.

The expression of inattention and noninvolvement exhibited by those who are physically close to an encounter in which they are not participants can be observed in an extreme form at times when an individual could join the encounter (as far as its

4. Here I do not want to overstress rational intent in situational behavior. An individual is supposed to be entirely in or entirely out of an encounter. But even the individual who wants to follow this rule cannot completely control the expressed direction of his attention. If his attention is attracted to an accessible encounter, then his attempt to conceal the fact is likely to be visible both to those with whom he ought to be participating and to those whom he ought to be disattending.

participants are concerned) , but finds himself "psychologically" incapable of doing so. What can then result is a kind of conversational parasitism, often observable on mental hospital wards. For example, one psychotic young woman I observed would sit alongside her mother and look straight ahead while the latter was engaged in conversation with a nurse, maintaining what appeared to be civil inattention in regard to the neighboring engagement. But while attempting to keep her face composed like that of an uninvolved, uninterested bystander, she would keep up a running line of derisive comment on what was being said, uttering these loud stage whispers under great verbal pressure, from the side of her mouth. The psychological issue here, presumably, was that of "dissociation." But the direction of flow taken by the two dissociated lines of conduct—conversational participation and civil inattention—seemed entirely determined by the social organization of communication that is standard for social situations in our society. In a social situation, then, an individual may find himself torn apart, but torn apart on a standard rack that is articulated in a standard way.

There are circumstances in which it is difficult for participants to show tactful trust of bystanders and for bystanders to extend civil inattention; in brief, there are times when conventional closure is difficult to manage.

For one example of this we can return to small enclosed places like elevators, where individuals may be so closely brought together that no pretense of not hearing can possibly be maintained. At such times, in middle-class America at least, there seems to be a tendency for participants of an encounter to hold their communication in abeyance, with only an occasional word to stabilize their half-lapsed encounter. A similar kind of issue seems to arise in near-empty bars, as novelists have pointed out:

> We were alone in that bar, it was still the middle of the morning and the presence of the barman there was embarrassing. He could not help overhearing. In his white impassive coat he was a figure of reticent authority. But he probably realised this too, he was

nice enough to keep bobbing down behind the bar and shovelling about his glasses and his little trays of ice. So Harry ordered two more as it were from no-one, and soon these bobbed up.[5]

The cabdriver has something of the same kind of problem here as the bar man.[6] So too has the individual who is momentarily left to his own resources while a person to whom he has been talking answers a telephone call; physically close to the engaged other and patently unoccupied, he must yet somehow show civil inattention.[7]

Where civil inattention is physically difficult to manage, the scene is set for a special kind of dominance. In an elevator, for example, those in one of the engagements may continue fully engaged, forcing the others present to accept the role of non-persons. Similarly, when two unacquainted couples are required to share the same booth in a restaurant, and they elect to forego trying to maintain an inclusive face engagement, one couple may tacitly give way to the louder interaction of the other. In these situations, the submissive couple may attempt to show independence and civil inattention by beginning a talk of their own. But while it may appear convincing to the other couple, this weaker talk is not likely to convince its own participants, who, in carrying it·on, will be admitting to each other not only that they have been upstaged but that they are willing to try to pretend that they have not [8] It may be added that strength in these cases derives not from muscle, but, typically, from social class.

5. William Sansom, *The Face of Innocence* (New York: Harcourt, Brace & World, 1951) , p. 12.

6. F. Davis, "The Cabdriver and His Fare: Facets of a Fleeting Relationship," *American Journal of Sociology*, 65 (1959) , 160.

7. Similarly, in a three-person engagement, when a talker interrupts his talk to answer the phone, the two remaining persons may attempt a quiet, and often very limp, conversation.

8. In Britain, it is my impression that where one of the units present is of "good" speech, that is, received pronunciation, then it is this group that is likely to talk openly, as if the others could easily offer civil inattention and could easily stop their own conversation. This is one of the ways in which a visitor to Britain is struck by the startling vulgarity (according to American standards) of the British upper middle class.

b. Given the fact that participants and bystanders are required to help maintain the integrity of the encounter, and given the complicating fact that bystanders of this encounter may well be participants of another, we may expect some tacit cooperation in maintaining conventional closure. First, if bystanders are to desist in some way from exploiting their communication opportunities, then it will fall upon the participants to limit their actions and words to ones that will not be too hard to disattend. And this keeping down of the excitement level is, in fact, what is generally found. Interestingly enough, this tendency is matched by another that moves in the opposite direction, namely, acting in such a way as to show confidence in the willingness of bystanders not to exploit their situation. Thus, as already suggested, whispering or obvious use of code terms will often be thought impolite, in part because it casts a doubt on bystanders' willingness to be inattentive.

One consequence of the combination of these rules of conventional closure may be mentioned. It is a rule of conversation that participants show consideration for one another, by, for example, avoiding facts about which the other might be touchy, or by showing constraint in raising criticism, and so forth. Disparagement of persons not present, on the other hand, is usually quite acceptable, offering a basis of preferential solidarity for those in the encounter. In addition, the conversation may well involve business matters that an absent other cannot safely be made privy to. It follows, therefore, that the run of comments in a conversational encounter may have to be altered strategically when a relevantly excluded person approaches, lest the content of the talk put too much strain upon his willingness to offer civil inattention; when he approaches with the intention of entering the encounter, even more delicacy is required. The well-known example is that of the individual who comes into a room to find that conversation has suddenly stopped and that others present are seeking in a flustered way to find a new and tenable topic. Sometimes, as a relevantly excluded other approaches, a particular physical point is reached where the conversation can be altered without either letting the oncomer hear what would be embarrassing to him (or what would embarrass the speakers for him to hear) or giving him an impression that something embarrassing regarding him has been suppressed. This distance will, of course, vary with the social skill of the participants. Sometimes, too, a given room will have a special "safe region," from which vantage point any newcomer can be spied in time to safely alter the content of talk without showing that an alteration was necessary. In these circumstances we sometimes find skill-showing, where the talkers daringly and coolly continue their talk up to the very last moment for altering it safely.

c. The care that a bystander is obliged to exert for an accessible encounter extends past civil inattention to the question of how and when he can present himself for official participation. Even at social parties, where every encounter is supposed to be conducted in a fashion that makes it joinable by any guest, the entrant is expected to exert tact and, when cues suggest, not exercise his rights. When he does enter he is expected to accept the current topic and tone, thus minimizing the disruption he causes. Thus, early American etiquette suggests:

> If a lady and gentleman are conversing together at an evening party, it would be a rudeness in another person to go up and interrupt them by introducing a new topic of observation. If you are sure that there is nothing of a particular and private interest passing between them, you may *join* their conversation and strike into the current of their remarks; yet if you then find that they are so much engaged and entertained by the discussion that they were holding together, as to render the termination or change of its character unwelcome, you should withdraw. If, however, two persons are occupied with one another upon what you guess to be terms peculiarly delicate and particular, you should withhold yourself from their company.[9]

9. Anon., *The Canons of Good Breeding* (Philadelphia: Lee and Blanchard, 1839), p. 68.

Welcome or not, the entrant today is usually expected to knock at the door of the encounter before he enters, thus giving the encounter advance warning of his intention and the participants a moment to straighten their house for the newcomer.

d. One of the most interesting forms of cooperation in the maintenance of conventional closure is what might be called *spacing*:[10] the tendency for units of participation in the situation —either face engagements or unengaged individuals—to distribute themselves cooperatively in the available space so as physically to facilitate conventional closure. (Often this seems to involve a maximization of the sum of the squares of the physical distance among the various units.[11]) Of course, where the units of participation owe one another some expression of mutual trust and comradeship, full spacing may be specifically avoided.[12]

Spacing will of course ensure that "talk lines" are open, that is, that persons addressing one another in an encounter will have no physical obstruction to block the free exchange of glances. A

10. The term "individual distance" was apparently introduced by the ethnologist Hediger to describe the tendency of birds on a fence or railing to stay a particular distance from each other, the distance apparently varying with the species. He also employs the term "flight distance" to refer to the closeness with which an animal of a given species can be approached before taking flight. See H. Hediger, *Studies of the Psychology and Behavior of Captive Animals in Zoos and Circuses* (London: Butterworths Scientific Publications, 1955), pp. 40 ff. and 66. An interesting application of these and other ethnological concepts may be found in R. Sommer, "Studies in Personal Space," *Sociometry*, 22 (1959), 247-260.

11. In a useful paper, "The Anthropology of Manners," *Scientific American*, April, 1955, pp. 84-90, E. T. Hall cautions against cross-cultural generalizations on the matter of spacing:

> In the U.S. we distribute ourselves more evenly than many other people. We have strong feelings about touching and being crowded; in a streetcar, bus or elevator we draw ourselves in. Toward a person who relaxes and lets himself come into full contact with others in a crowded place we usually feel reactions that could not be printed on this page. It takes years for us to train our children not to crowd and lean on us. . . .
>
> In Latin America, where touching is more common and the basic units of space seem to be smaller, the wide automobiles made in the U.S. pose problems. People don't know where to sit.

12. A useful ethological analysis of types of mutual physical distance is provided by J. H. Crook, "The Basis of Flock Organisation in Birds," in W. H. Thorpe and O. L. Zangwill, eds., *Current Problems in Animal Behaviour* (Cambridge: Cambridge University Press, 1961), pp. 138 ff.

bystander finding himself interposed in such a line (in American society, at least) is likely to offer an apology and quickly shift his position.

While the phenomenon of spacing may be difficult to see because one takes it for granted, a tracing of it in reverse can be obtained by observing children and mental patients—those communication delinquents who sometimes play the game of "attack the encounter." On many wards, for example, a patient will follow a pair of talkers around the room until they have stopped moving, and then sidle right up to the edge of the encounter and lean into it. One adolescent patient I studied would intercept talk lines between two persons by waving her knitting needles in the way, or by swinging her upraised arms, or by thrusting her face into the face of one of the participants, or by sitting in his lap.

Along with physical spacing, we also find control of sound so that the various units in the situation can proceed with their business at hand without being jammed out of operation. In many cases this will mean restriction on the volume of sound, although, at occasions like social parties, where persons may be crowded close to others not in the same encounter, a general raising of voices may be found; this allows coparticipants to hear each other, but jams the opportunities of eavesdroppers. Here, too, accurately designed delicts can be observed, as when an adolescent mental patient, in a spirit of fun, places her face up against the face of someone engaged in talk with another at a distance, and then shouts so that he can neither hear nor be heard.

The requirement that visually open talk lines be maintained and that sound level not interfere with neighboring encounters, sets a limit to the distance over which spoken encounters can ordinarily be sustained. For example, should two persons carry on a conversation from one end of a crowded streetcar to the other, all the intervening passengers would have to remain out of the line of talk and modulate their own conversation so as not to jam the one being maintained over a distance. Such a conversation would necessarily also be fully available to everyone between the two speakers, and would therefore be likely to constitute an embarrassment, even were one of the speakers the conductor. Thus, engagements that must be carried on over such a populated distance are likely to be limited to the exchange of silent gestures, for these neither interfere with other encounters nor expose what is being conveyed. As might be expected, therefore, deaf and dumb persons who board a streetcar together and find themselves seated apart need not discontinue their exchange of messages, but are able to carry on conversation as long as sight lines are clear, their "talk" neither jamming the other talkers nor being accessible to them.

While physical spacing and sound control certainly have relevance to occasions such as social parties that are carried on within a relatively small physical region, they are perhaps even more important in public streets and roads and in semipublic regions. In Western society, the development of middle-class dominance is expressed in the rise of a relativly equalitarian use of public places. Even today, however, funerals, weddings, parades, and some other ceremonials are allowed to press their spirit momentarily upon the public at large. Technical units, such as ambulances, police cars, and fire engines cut through public traffic with an amount of sound not permitted to other units of traffic; and guests of a city may be given a motor escort. Some of these prerogatives, however, are but small remnants of practices that were once more general, such as the entourage and train associated with "clientage,"[13] which led a worthy to demonstrate his status by the cluster of dependent supporters that accompanied him through a town or a house of parliament, shouldering his way for him wherever he went. Nor are these rules uniform within Western society, as is suggested by the response of King Edward (of Britain) and his party during a 1906 visit to the Emperor of Germany:

13. For example, J. E. Neale, *The Elizabethan House of Commons* (New Haven, Conn.: Yale University Press, 1950) , pp. 24-26.

The Emperor had a standard attached to his motor and a trumpeter on the box who blew long bugle-calls at every corner. The inhabitants thus had no difficulty in making out where the Emperor was, and all the traffic cleared out of the way when they heard the trumpets blow. The King, however, detested what he called "theatrical methods" and drove about like anybody else.[14]

e. In terminating this discussion of conventional closure, I want to mention the kind of restructuring that can occur when a situation is transformed from one containing many encounters —a multifocused situation—to one that is exhausted by a single all-encompassing engagement. For example, at noontime on a ward of Central Hospital, when the attendant shouts, "Chow time!" he is addressing the whole place, and wherever the sound level of his voice reaches, the meanings of his words are meant to carry too. Similarly, at a small social party, the arrival of a couple may cause the hostess to interrupt the separateness of all the separate encounters in order to introduce the newcomers to the assembly. So also, at formal dinners, the moment the hostess indicates that the conversation will be "general," she opens up whatever is being said to all the guests. And, of course, whenever public speeches are given, the speaker's words, as well as the heat with which he speaks them, are meant to impinge on the situation at large. In all such cases, there is the understanding that the situation at large is properly open to the content of the words of an appropriate single speaker; he has, as we say, the floor.

The transformation of a multifocused situation into one that is exhausted by one face engagement is an interesting process to consider. At social parties we can observe a singer or guitar player make an effort to incorporate more and more of the room's population into his audience, until a point is reached where his singing officially exhausts the chamber, and the party is momentarily transformed into a performance.[15] At the same

14. Sir Frederick Ponsonby, *Recollections of Three Reigns* (New York: Dutton, 1952), p. 261.

15. I am here indebted to an unpublished paper by Robert Martinson on the transformation of informal engagements into performances.

time, as a particular encounter comes to include a larger and larger number of persons, side involvements increasingly occur in which a subordinate byplay is sustained, sometimes furtively, its volume and character modulated to allow the main show to prevail unchallenged as the dominating one.

In mental hospitals there is a special kind of "symptomatic" behavior that takes recognition of how the situation as a whole can be "talked to." Many patients talk to someone, present or not, in a voice loud enough for everyone in the situation to hear and be somewhat distracted. But those on the ward implicitly distinguish this kind of impropriety from that which occurs when a patient "addresses the situation," haranguing everyone present in a tone and direction of voice that suggests he is purposely breaching the barriers designed to render clusters of talkers and game players safe in their own focused interactions. (Interestingly, although the actual volume of sound may be greater in the case of a patient insufficiently modulating his contribution to a private conversation than in the case of a patient "addressing the situation," it is the latter that is likely to cause the greater disturbance.)[16]

16. Attacks on the situation should be compared with the attacks on encounters, previously mentioned, which children, mental patients, and other communication delinquents perform. Many middle-class parents in our society have experienced times when their child, forbidden to interrupt or even to enter a room where adults are talking, stealthily stalks the situation in self-conscious mimicry of stealthiness and stalking, resulting in much more disturbance to the gathering than his mere presence might entail.

CHAPTER 10

The Regulation of

Mutual-Involvement

1. Restrictions

EARLIER, in considering unfocused interaction, it was suggested that the individual is obliged to exhibit a margin of
control over all his involvements, especially involvement in his
own body. Now I want to consider restrictions on the way in
which individuals in an accessible encounter can properly give
themselves up to each other, that is, properly invest themselves
in mutual-involvements that are exposed to bystanders. This
will provide us with an opportunity to look not at what bystanders owe to an accessible encounter, but at what the participants
of the encounter owe to the gathering at large.

Anglo-American students of other cultures have long com-
mented on social differences in exposed mutual-involvements
permissible between selected categories, especially exposed involvements between the sexes. In some Latin countries, we are
told, public kissing on the lips "is considered an obscene act,"[1]
as it would be, apparently, in public places in the U.S.S.R. and
in many Eastern societies.

Within our own society there are instructive differences
among social occasions regarding permissible mutual-involve-

1. V. S. Pritchett, *The Spanish Temper* (New York: Knopf, 1954) , p. 170.

ment, few occasions being defined so as to prohibit all such activity and few being defined so as to allow the kind of mutual engrossment characteristic of love-making.[2] A couple necking or arguing on a business street might well be considered an affront in the situation—an obtrusion of private matters in places where a more public orientation is required. In parks and on beaches, however, these involvements are easily tolerated, and no street is so defined as to preclude modulated light talk between two individuals walking together. Book etiquette suggests that while it is permissible for persons at an ocean pier to kiss each other deeply, thereby withdrawing to an appreciable degree from other aspects of the situation, the same action by a suburban housewife meeting her husband at the 6:45 would be inappropriate; a lighter kiss is more in keeping with the situation.[3] Similarly, in our cities, the Howard Johnson type of restaurant may have a section reserved for families with young children, and in these locations a degree of family involvement

2. In some places in the world, peep shows are commercially organized which sell the opportunity to spy on performers engaged in sexual intercourse. Writers tend to take the position that this is a perversion of the sexual instinct. Few students, however, seem to have been concerned with the fact that what is also perverted in these arrangements is the regulation of exposed mutual-involvement; for presumably some of the excitement the voyeurs obtain from these shows derives from observing a pair of persons engaged in conduct that is ideally inappropriate in situations of more than two persons, and, in many of our subcultures, somewhat inappropriate even for two persons, hence conducted in the dark.

3. A news release provides a comparative illustration (San Francisco Chronicle, July 31, 1961; *Rome*):

A "kiss of delight" in broad daylight in a busy Roman piazza can land you in jail.

But "duty kisses"—the pecks on each cheek that male and female Italians give each other every time they meet—are still permitted.

A court case to determine what public kissing is permissible, ended this week after nearly a year in a sentence of two months in separate reformatories for an engaged couple.

The unfortunate lovers, Vittorio Grazini, 20, and his fiancee, Angelina Rossi, 22, had their fatal kiss last August at 6:30 in the afternoon.

The cop who arrested them claimed they had a "long kiss of delight" that was a menace to public morals. The judge agreed. Public kissing is against the law in Rome.

Adventurous Italian youngsters risk jail every evening to have long kisses of delight in the shadow of walls and monuments. But before the courageous Vittorio and Angelina tried it, nobody tested the law in a car parked in the middle of a crowd, and in sunshine. (Chicago Daily News)

in the discipline of children may be tolerated that might cause feelings of uneasiness in the other sections of the restaurant.

In those situations where all participants are obliged to sustain a main involvement not only in the same kind of activity but in the same encounter, byplays and other minor mutual-involvements are by definition an illegitimate withdrawal from the dominant engagement. But even where no single engagement continuously exhausts the situation, strict limits on mutual-involvement may be found. Thus, at church, where pious feelings may be obligatory, the enthusiasms of a greeting may have to be tactfully damped, and greetings that would ordinarily involve only a hand-wave may have to be suppressed completely. As one etiquette book suggests:

> The first point is that a church is not a social meeting place. Heads turned to look for friends in the congregation, merry nods and smiles, gay greetings, and a distracted restlessness are all out of place in church. If one happens to catch a friend's eye, certainly there is no reason to withhold a glance of recognition and a short subdued smile; but respect for the place and concentration on the ceremony should be the basis of all one's behavior.[4]

Should long-separated friends meet under these circumstances, it would be difficult indeed for them to do justice to their relationship without committing a situational impropriety. This dilemma, it may be noted, frequently arises at funerals, for at these unjoyous, highly organized occasions, there is a strong likelihood that persons will see each other after long separation and owe each other expansive greetings. Apparently, the very warm handshake provides a solution for this problem, allowing strict situational solemnity to be maintained in appearance, while in fact a shielded involvement is occurring whose depth and alienation from the occasion can be sensed only by the two participants.

Just as the involvement rules prevailing in some situations

4. Millicent Fenwick, *Vogue's Book of Etiquette* (New York: Simon and Schuster, 1948), p. 12.

can embarrass relationships, so certain relationships can effectively cause participants to feel that the gathering and the social occasion are threatened. When two persons are known to be intensely involved in their dealings with each other, their mere presence together in the same room can effectively suggest more mutual engrossment than is consistent with their other involvement obligations. In the past, consequently, we have been told that:

> It is in bad *ton* for a newly married couple, when going to an evening party, to enter the room together. Some older person, or some relative of hers, should take the bride in. It is in better taste that, on all occasions of appearing in public, the pair should not be exactly together. The recognition of that relation should as much as possible be confined to the fireside. It is not pleasant to see persons thrusting their mutual devotedness into the eye of society.[5]

Similarly, persons known to be having an affair can often bring some uneasiness to a gathering, even if this tension is successfully released through a joking, playful manner. Persons known to be at odds with each other can also suggest too much mutual-involvement, even though they manage never to come face-to-face during the social occasion to which they have both been inadvertently invited, or manage to cover with self-conscious nods such contact as cannot be avoided.

There will be attempts, then, to forestall unsuitable mutual-involvement. An everyday illustration is provided by the widespread current middle-class rule of etiquette that reminds husbands and wives to separate from each other at table and during

5. Anon., *The Canons of Good Breeding* (Philadelphia: Lee and Blanchard, 1839), pp. 87-88. On the other hand, it should be noted that in honeymoon resorts extensive mutual-involvement is exposed in the form of hand-holding and necking, as if a couple's new status gave them temporary parade rights, an extension of the right of their friends to blow car horns during the motor procession after the ceremony. The apparent contradiction is resolved when we appreciate that an involving relationship must either be strongly suppressed or be given some kind of public ratification, the couple, as a couple, taking the role of performers, at once oriented to each other and properly exposed to the audience.

small talk at social parties. Presumably the husband-wife pair would either have nothing to say to each other, in that case not expressing the spirit of the occasion, or have quite intimate things to say to each other, in that case affirming their world at home rather than the party itself.

2. Occasioned Mutual-Involvement

The restriction against exposed mutual-involvements can sometimes be seen not as a restriction against *any* mutual-involvement, but as a restriction against involvement that withdraws the participants from the gathering. Indeed, the individual may at times be obliged to open himself up for mutual-involvements, as implied in the rule of accessibility. But he must do this not merely on the grounds of prior relationship but on the basis of the present occasion. (Here we catch another glimmer of the trouble caused by newlyweds or those deeply engaged in courting, who, unlike persons whose relationship is more settled and seasoned, find it awkward to give up their mutual-involvement for the kind of courtesy involvement with a sequence of others that the social occasion often requires.) Thus we find a special kind of exemplary situational conduct when two persons with a long-standing, exclusive relationship manage to treat each other at a sociable gathering with courtesies owed on the basis simply of participation in the occasion; two bitter enemies show a similar regard for the occasion by being "civil." The same type of courtesy is exhibited by a teacher who addresses her child in class as though he were just another student, this being describable not merely as role segregation but also as a gesture of regard for the occasion.

Interestingly enough, in the natural history of some social parties, certain forms of fleeting sex play may be a sign that the spirit of the occasion has lifted everyone up with it, not that the party has collapsed into separate pieces. Indeed, should the sexual interaction occur between persons brought together only at and for the occasion, it may be a sign of the high degree to which participants have given themselves over to the gathering. The extreme of this, in fact—for example, the kind of sexual interaction said to occur at the annual Beaux Arts ball in Paris—can represent not a collapse of duties in regard to the situation, as might at first seem the case, but rather some kind of profane worship of them. Were husbands to engage their wives in this manner, the obligations to the occasion would indeed be threatened.

In noting the rule obliging individuals to sustain an occasioned mutual-involvement, we have perhaps a better means of accounting for our response to improper involvements than for predicting actual conduct, for these situational niceties are often ill-sustained. Resistance to the spirit of an occasion, as expressed in a refusal to sustain occasioned mutual-involvements, is apparently so useful a device for conveying so many things that someone in a gathering can usually be counted on to employ it. At public dances in the chief city of Shetland, for example, one could usually find a slightly resented handful of couples, solidly middle-class in social status, who withheld themselves from the plebeian pleasures sustained by second-generation crofters. This alienation was expressed by dancing in half-time to the vigorous music and sustaining quiet engrossing talk while doing so, conduct that was obtrusively out of mood with the prevailing ethos.

We see, then, that there will be times when the success of a social occasion such as a party is expressed through the success of the participants in finding congenial encounters in which to engross themselves. This engrossment provides proof that each person present is a desirable companion, and that each finds the social occasion significant enough to provide him with grounds for opening himself up to others. Given these assumptions, we can understand that a person caught for too long between encounters—caught "unengaged"—may cause anxiety to himself and the hostess, and that the latter may try to anchor him in a convenient port, which particular port being of only secondary significance. And we can also understand why an individual may feel that what he owes the gathering at large can at times override what he owes himself and his fellows in an encounter, providing us with additional evidence that the individual's engagement in a focused interaction is a fact available to all others in the situation, and hence a part of the unfocused interaction in the situation. Here we have the situational reason for one type of tact, namely, giving the appearance of being spontaneously involved in some occasioned encounter when in fact one is not. Mrs. Post can thus provide entertaining suggestions of how offense may be given in talk precisely in order that no offense will be given to the gathering at large and the social occasion.

> Even if you are placed next to some one with whom you have had a bitter quarrel, consideration for your hostess, who would be distressed if she knew you had been put in a disagreeable place, and further consideration for the rest of the table which is otherwise "blocked," exacts that you give no outward sign of your repugnance and that you make a pretense, at least for a little while, of talking together.
>
> At dinner once, Mrs. Toplofty, finding herself next to a man she quite openly despised, said to him with apparent placidity, "I shall not talk to you—because I don't care to. But for the sake of my hostess I shall say my multiplication table. Twice one are two, twice two are four—" and she continued on through the tables, making him alternate them with her. As soon as she politely could she turned again to her other companion.[6]

Another instance of the obligation to sustain an occasioned involvement with others may be cited from Shetland Isle. At a "progressive" whist of twenty tables during a social, the deep engrossment of a member of the gentry in his particular table of whist was likely to be taken as a sign of how thoroughly he was participating in the social occasion. By getting caught up in the spirit of one of the tables, he showed regard for the room as a whole. Had he disdained to invest himself thus, and insisted on wandering from one table to another, making gracious com-

6. Emily Post, *Etiquette* (New York: Funk and Wagnalls, 1937) , p. 273.

ments to players at all the tables in turn, he might well have tendered the common folk—the crofters—less of a compliment. (And yet if an ordinary crofter became so much involved in a particular hand of whist as to delay appreciably the finishing time for his table, this disregard for the necessity of shifting tables at the end of each game was likely to be considered an affront to the whole social occasion.)

If social occasions can be assessed according to their capacity to bring all participants into one occasioned encounter or another, then we can expect that rules will be found obliging those within any encounter to admit entrants. (This corresponds to the previously discussed obligation of the individual to make himself accessible, the difference being that while an individual may be inaccessible to others because of organic incapacity, this excuse is hardly available to encounters.)

There are many occasions, as on public streets, where those in an encounter need acknowledge few rights of others to enter. On the other hand, as already suggested, it is characteristic of occasions such as social parties that participants have a right not only to initiate face engagements but also to enter ones that are already in progress. Here participants, in order to demonstrate how thoroughly they have been lifted up and brought together by the party, may feel obliged to admit newcomers to their conversation easily. "Open" topics of conversation may thus be maintained in preparation for newcomers. A conversation that by its tone forbade the entrance of new members would be improper. Consequently, we can understand the strategy sometimes employed by those who would converse about intensely involving private matters in a public place: instead of huddling together in a furtive conspiratorial way, they affect a style of matter-of-fact openness.

3. Drift

I have suggested that those in an accessible encounter are obliged to keep their activity in tune with the ethos of the social

occasion, being obliged to exhibit within the situation a degree
of occasioned mood and involvement. But it was also implied
that each accessible encounter will properly carry its participants
some distance from the mood prevailing in the situation. Indeed, should this fail to occur, the social occasion may be blamed
for failing to provide a setting in which individuals can be
brought into face engagements and caught up spontaneously in
them. In the latter case, the encounter may have to draw on the
standard supplies of the social occasion for all of its sustenance.
Similarly, if an individual fails to let go of his concern about
the gathering as a whole or the progress of the occasion enough
to become caught up in a situated engagement, it may be felt he
has failed to give himself up to the social occasion. A nice
balance is thus required between keeping in step and stepping'
lively.

Of special interest in this connection is the phenomenon of
drift. Just as a social occasion as a whole is likely to manifest an
"involvement contour," carrying all of its encompassed encounters in a developing direction, so each particular encounter can
manifest dynamic properties of its own, not only generating a
world for its participants but carrying them further and further
into it. It is this movement or drift of individual encounters
away from the gathering at large and its social occasion that I
want to consider now.

Given the presence in a social situation of different face engagements—different clusters of persons engaged exclusively together in a talk, a game, or a joint task—how far may the
participants of any one of these little circles allow their mutual-
involvement to carry them from the other persons in the
situation?

The problem of drift can perhaps be seen most clearly in
those social occasions where a fairly high pitch of some kind of
affect is defined as appropriate. Thus, at a wedding it is not
proper for any cluster of individuals to become too serious or to
quarrel in any way; obviously this would be out of keeping.
Should a quarrel start, it must be quickly checked lest it carry

the encounter past the range of variation permitted. Similarly, in the case of funeral visits, knots of people not containing any of the immediately bereaved may begin a quiet chat, but find themselves getting gayer and gayer until their interaction becomes out of place and must be brought back to the sober tone of the surroundings. Drift, of course, occurs not only at ceremonials. Thus, in a surgery observed by the writer, the nurses scrubbing at the four scrub sinks just before the medical staff arrived would carry on the light sociable chatter that seemed fixed to the sink area. Sometimes, however, their talk would become louder and louder, more and more boisterous, until the head nurse of the ward would have to come into the scrub area and shush them.[7] So, too, there were moments when the anesthetist and his helper began a whispered conversation that carried them further and further away from the occasion, until a point was reached where the surgeon or the surgical nurse glanced up and across the barrier between operating field and anesthetic equipment with a look of amusement, wonderment, or disapproval, which was often followed by a "cutting back" of the drifting conversation.

In considering the tendency for accessible encounters to drift, we should not overlook other problems of affective movement. During occasions such as social parties, wakes, and other celebrations, a mood of hilarity or sadness or grimness may begin to develop, and soon may carry all participation units away from their emotional starting point. (Sometimes this developing contour of involvement may be assisted by means of pharmacological agencies such as alcohol.)

When all the encounters in a situation begin to drift at the same time in the same direction, they may together move past the point of propriety implicit in the social occasion. It is thus that an etiquette manual can warn that liquor at a christening should not be of the kind to turn it into a cocktail party.[8]

A second issue may be mentioned. When a social occasion has

7. This study is partly reported in "Role Distance," in *Encounters*.
8. *Vogue's Book of Etiquette, op. cit.,* p. 134.

taken hold of its participants, and the engagements occurring within it have together moved in a particular affective direction, a latecomer to the occasion may find himself out of step affectively with the prevailing mood and may have difficulty in catching up, in "getting with it." A sober person coming to a drunken gathering can have quite the same problem, and create the same offense, as a drunk person arriving at a still sober occasion. Wakes are of special interest here, because persons longest on the spot will have "worked through" some of their affective concern about the deceased, while at the same time they are likely to have been the "closest" to him and to be therefore held most responsible for giving a worthy show of grief. A latecomer may find a certain callousness among those present, which they may in turn be forced to conceal by a kind of recapitulation of the mourning process performed within the confines of the face engagement in which the latecomer is welcomed to the place of mourning.

4. Shielding

The difficulty of keeping in touch with the social occasion while at the same time becoming spontaneously involved in situated engagements is often reduced by the arts of concealment. Apparently one of the most significant involvement shields is that afforded by a conversational circle itself. In fact, there seem to be few conversational clusters in which control of facial and bodily expression is not employed to conceal either a deadness to the content of the encounter or an improper drift from the spirit of the occasion. A conversation occurring within a situation, then, is likely to present something of a collusion against the gathering at large; Mrs. Toplofty's multiplication tables, previously cited, are merely an extreme instance. And yet, of course, the very possibility that conversational content can be shielded from the gathering as a whole removes some of the threat that such smaller circles might have for the larger inclusive one if the drift or deadness were open and visible. We can thus appreciate why some "informal" sociable gatherings are deemed "successful" when each cluster carries away its participants to the point where they can barely conceal their departure.

The possibility of sustaining a concealed activity within conversations can become somewhat recognized and institutionalized, so that two different phases of a social occasion can simultaneously occur in the same place among the same participants, one phase being restricted to unfocused interaction and the other to matters that can be parceled out to conversations and concealed in them; one phase is likely, then, to be defined as dominant and the other subordinate. For example, in Shetland Isle it was obligatory for male neighbors and male extended kin to attend funerals dressed quite decorously in black, even to the point sometimes of wearing a black cap reserved only for such occasions. It was also obligatory for these male mourners to stand quietly and sedately outside of the cottage in which the deceased was laid out. But while thus standing, it was quite permissible to carry on entertaining conversational chats with one's fellow-mourners. To be sure, the sound level of these talks and the features of the talkers were respectfully modulated to fit funereal requirements, but the content of the talk went in another direction. In some cases it was even understood to be in bad taste to turn the topic from the ordinary pleasantries of neighborly talk to the deceased; attendance and funeral garb were what one owed the mourning family; sociable small talk was what one owed the others present.

The involvement shield provided by a conversation is somewhat portable, because the participants can together move about a room and take their talk with them. Perhaps the most important recently developed portable shield for encounters is the automobile. The protection provided by the back seat has already made social history, and use of the front seat in drive-in movies has become a kind of inadvertent outdoor shrine for paying homage to our society's use of shielding arrangements.

In this discussion I have treated mutual-involvement simply as one variety of situated involvement; the rules regulating situated involvements apply, in fact, with extra force. There are differences, however, between mutual-involvements and other kinds. For one thing, mutual-involvements improperly maintained by the individual necessarily involve others directly; further, of all objects of involvement, other individuals seem to be the most enticing and hence, in turn, the most in need of social control. But further issues are also to be found. An unengaged individual may easily exhibit the kind of involvement which gives others the impression that he is indeed in a pathological state; the same consequence, however, is rarely possible for persons improperly involved *together*. Except for the very marginal phenomenon of *folie à deux* (or *à trois, à quatre,* etc.), it seems to be assumed that as long as two individuals are in communication with each other—as long as they are joined in an encounter—whatever they are doing is not occult, however esoteric and opaque it may appear to be. This helps to explain why a person who is "with" another tends to feel free to engage in all kinds of antics, since he can assume his contact with the other will guarantee his sanity to bystanders.[9]

9. A parallel phenomenon has been observed in connection with the frame of reference by which criminality is imputed (as opposed to mental illness). Apparently there are depredations which can be interpreted as a game when committed by a group of youths, but which are viewed as crime when committed by a solitary offender.

CHAPTER 11

Uncontained Participation

PARTICIPATION in an accessible engagement not only directly exposes the individual to linguistic and expressive communication with the other participants in the encounter but also opens up the possibility that they will expressively communicate something about him to the bystanders. Seeking some degree of intimacy with potential fellow participants in the encounter, the individual can find himself spurned or otherwise mistreated in a way that is visible to bystanders. Given these potential exposures, we find regulations to safeguard the individual. These constraints appear in two-person engagements as considerateness for the other, and appear in larger engagements as expressions of loyalty to the encounter. In both cases we deal with a participant's obligation to stay within "his" engagement.

1. Diversion of Attention

One form of containment is found in the obligation of participants to withhold attention from matters occurring outside of the engagement. We can appreciate the operation of this norm by noting the various contexts in which the norm is not adhered to.

Quite momentary and minor disaffection constantly occurs, as when an individual turns away for a moment to see who has entered the situation, or to find a suitable chair, expressing by his manner and by the arts of shielding involvement that somehow his spirit is still attached to the engagement. Where individuals do not have to worry about each other's small slights because of a long-standing relation of familiarity and intimacy—as between some husbands and wives—one participant may hold the engagement together while the other scans the room in search of useful information. When a couple eats at what is for them a "good" restaurant, the member with his back to the assembled others may be annoyed to find his partner giving attention to the other tables instead of to the talk at hand.

Such disloyalty can of course become excessive, by middle-class standards, suggesting a demoralization (or at least an altered understanding) regarding what is ordinarily owed one's fellow participants. Hollywood restaurants provide good illustrations, apparently, as a treatment by Lillian Ross suggests:

> There was a stir in Dave Chasen's Restaurant in Beverly Hills when Dore Schary walked in. Chasen's is run by the former stage comedian whose name it bears, and it is popular with people in the motion-picture industry. . . . All the other patrons focussed their attention on Schary. They seemed to be looking around at everybody except the people they were with and with whom they were managing to carry on conversations.
>
> Schary was not a bit self-conscious. . . . He was almost the only man in Chasen's who was not at that moment looking around at someone other than the person he was talking to.[1]

More extreme forms of disloyalty are very commonly found among the mentally ill; it is often because of such delicts that persons are identified as mentally ill in the first place. For example, I observed a female psychotic, strongly attached to her mother and to her psychiatrist, who would, in the midst of a

1. Lillian Ross, *Picture* (New York: Holt, Rinehart & Winston, 1952) , pp. 19-20. See also pp. 22, 31, 51, 116.

conversation, allow all of her attention to be drained away by the sound of the ward door opening to admit the sound of familiar steps. At the approach of either her mother or her therapist, the patient's body would remain in the talk but her head and interest would turn elsewhere. After a few weeks, as she "recovered" from an "episode," this interaction indelicacy gradually disappeared until it was possible for either of these figures to walk by without causing the patient *visible* perturbation. Although these figures no doubt still drained away some of her attention, she was able or willing to disguise the fact. The same patient, while "in" a psychotic break, would play ping-pong with one person while allowing her attention to rest openly on a nearby foursome of her age-mates playing bridge. Gradually, as weeks went by and she "came out" of the psychotic break, she increasingly paid deference to her ping-pong game by according it her cognitive and visual attention, and increasingly during play she exhibited civil inattention to neighboring engagements.

2. Boundary Collusion

I want now to consider a special type of engagement disloyalty. During an encounter of three or more participants, it is possible for a subset of participants to form a byplay, a noninclusive engagement that is carried on simultaneously with the first but in a way carefully calculated not to interfere with it too openly. These byplays may be carried on relatively openly when they appear to be in the interests of the business at hand—as when a speaker quietly asks some questions of the chairman before turning to speak—or relatively furtively when byplay is patently not in the interests of the dominant interaction. This kind of disaffection seems especially common in large engagements where the presence of many loyal participants guarantees that the dominant engagement will be sustained. Disaffection is especially treacherous in clusters of three or four, where the participants remaining loyal may be in a numerical minority, subjected to pointed insult by the byplay of the others.[2]

In many instances, these subordinate byplays involve only members of the dominant encounter, and involve them in such a way as not to broadcast to the company at large—to the situation—that disloyalty is occurring. I do not propose to consider this phenomenon here, since it could just as well be considered solely in terms of the dynamics of the engagement itself.[3] Relevant, however, are those byplays that draw some of their membership from persons officially excluded from the dominant engagement, for here disloyalty is made visible to bystanders, and the doings of the betrayed engagement are "opened up," to at least some of the nonparticipants present.

An extreme form of disloyalty is found where an individual, in the process of being led into the role of the butt, is brought into an engagement maliciously, just so the instigator can be disloyal to the engagement that results. The perpetrator makes a pretense to the butt that he is treating him as a coparticipant, while at the same time openly using the interaction thus created as a source of amusement for himself and others. The model here, perhaps, is the kind of baiting of animals that people engage in at a zoo, where one individual interacts with an animal until the animal responds, and then uses the animal's response as a source of fun between himself and a second individual.

Open collusion is, of course, a phenomenon observed freqently in mental wards. A classic description is given by William Perfect, writing in 1787:

2. As might be expected, where an encounter must be sustained by persons unable to use their eyes to scan and monitor what is occurring, byplays employing physical acts become difficult to control and constitute a special threat to the integrity of the encounter. Thus, in a novel written on the blind by a blind novelist, Sidney Bigman, *Second Sight* (New York: David McKay Co., 1959), p. 50, we find a description of the consternation felt by one blind participant in an engagement of three men and one woman, when he hears rustling and suppressed giggling that does not seem to arise from what is being talked about by the full company at the time.

3. See *The Presentation of Self*, "Team Collusion," pp. 176-190, and "Fun in Games," in *Encounters*.

In the year 1776, the parish officers of Frindsbury applied to me for advice in the case of a maniacal patient confined in their workhouse. This unhappy object had been very desperate and had committed many acts of outrage and violence; was naturally of strong, muscular shape, and rendered much stronger by his present complaint. He had overpowered almost everyone before they could properly secure him, which was now effected in a very extraordinary manner. He was fastened to the floor by means of a staple and iron ring, which was tied to a pair of fetters about his legs, and he was hand-cuffed. The place of his confinement was a large lower room, occasionally made use of for a kitchen, and which opened into the street; there were wooden bars to the windows, through the spaces of which continual visitors were observing, pointing at, ridiculing, and irritating the poor maniac, who thus became a spectacle of public sport and amusement.[4]

Other illustrations of the same phenomenon can be cited from contemporary reports by sociology students of their work-experiences as psychiatric attendants:

A few attendants tease the patients in order to laugh at their bizarre reactions—such as a nip on the ear or a slap on the head to bring about a temper tantrum. This teasing sometimes becomes cruel, and does not seem to be restricted to trouble-makers among patients. This may be done to break the monotony, or may be due to psychological quirks in the few attendants who do it.[5]

Miss Kurt asked the attendant for a cigarette. The attendant replied, "say pretty please." Miss Kurt, on saying pretty please, was answered, "now say, 'hello, Miss Crandall' twice," pointing to the other attendant. Miss Kurt didn't answer. The attendant held a cigarette aloft and said again, "If you say 'hello Miss Crandall' twice you will get this cigarette." Miss Kurt did as requested.[6]

4. Quoted in A. Walk, "Some Aspects of the 'Moral Treatment' of the Insane up to 1854," *Journal of Mental Science,* 100 (1954), 811.

5. R. Willoughby, "The Attendant in the State Mental Hospital" (unpublished Master's thesis, Department of Sociology, University of Chicago, 1953), p. 90.

6. H. Taxel, "Authority Structure in a Mental Hospital Ward" (unpublished Master's thesis, Department of Sociology, University of Chicago, 1953), p. 68.

Similar interactions can be cited from Central Hospital. For example, an attendant would occasionally take a "pet" patient and dance with him or her while winking broadly[7] to the rest of the ward staff. The fun reached its climax at the point where the patient was released and the attendant turned back to participation with the rest of the now laughing staff. Similarly, a few patients would sometimes encircle a mute fellow patient who had taken the tack of obeying all commands. They would then address the mute patient, ordering him to do a series of increasingly self-profaning acts, until the circle was excited into laughter.

The same sort of treatment is often accorded young children in our society: the child is teased or prodded into responding to a question, and is then forsaken by the questioner who may turn to observing adults and to an engagement with them, the engagement focusing on the child as an unwitting source of amusement or pride for the adults.[8]

7. The wink is a classic device for establishing byplay in our society, but at the same time an item in our involvement idiom that seems to be passing into disuse, as lamented in the following paragraph from *Punch*, March 28, 1962, p. 505:

> . . . winking? No doubt it continues in private, in remote unexplored northern valleys, in old farces performed by tired touring companies; but as a major feature of the British Way of Life, it seems to have died out. The sly wink of the diplomat, often accompanied by the laying of a finger to the nose, the confiding wink of the comic, the jolly wink of the gay young curate boldly stretching the limits of the permissible at parochial parties, the meaning wink of the bookies' hanger-on, the insulting wink of the reveller at the unprotected female, the wink which, between financiers, is as good as a nod—they have all vanished from fiction and all but vanished from life, which has become, in consequence, less colourful and dangerous and much more prim.

8. Nor is it only to provide others with a captivating focus of attention that one individual may arouse another. In training a child to control his temper, or not to have any, the teaser may tease in the absence of a third person. The well-known instance is Balinese:

> Typically, the mother will start a small flirtation with the child, pulling its penis or otherwise stimulating it to interpersonal activity. This will excite the child, and for a few moments cumulative interaction will occur. Then just as the child, approaching some small climax, flings its arms round the mother's neck, her attention wanders. At this point the child will typically start an alternative cumulative interaction, building up towards temper tantrum. The mother will either play a spectator's role, enjoying the child's tantrum, or, if the child actually attacks her, will brush off his attack with no show of anger on her part.

(G. Bateson, "Bali: The Value System of a Steady State," in M. Fortes, ed., *Social Structure* [London: Clarendon Press, 1949], p. 39.)

Some extreme forms of engagement disloyalty are managed without the butt necessarily becoming aware of what is being done to him. The very obligation of the individual in a two-person encounter to tactfully support his fellow-participant in maintaining the illusion that both desire to be engaged together can itself lead to disaffection which is carefully concealed from the other, but sometimes from him alone. Thus, when one participant feels it is beneath him in some way to be publicly joined to the other in a special relationship of any kind, the disgruntled participant may secretly tease the other participant before the assembled company or communicate in other ways to them that the encounter is not one that should be taken seriously. At Shetland Isle dances I occasionally saw a girl maintain the right of any man to dance by accepting a request from a drunk or a deformed man, or a strange foreign seaman, but once in his arms convey by collusive gestures to the circle of people behind his back that the dance-engagement was a lark and that she was not to be judged by it. Cautionary tales in our own society tell of college or high school dances where a male, who may wish to be unburdened of the girl with whom he finds himself dancing, holds up a dollar bill behind her back as they pass the stag-line, a mute but raucous bribe for someone to "cut in." Of course, the possibility of this kind of sellout is one factor in social control, leading the individual to forego engagements in which his fellow-participants might not be loyal to him.

3. Scenes

It should be plain that failure of the participants in an engagement to contain their activity can not only lead to a betrayal of one or more of their numbers, but also cause the content and feeling generated in the engagement to flow over into the situation at large. At such times bystanders may become dislodged from their own involvements, making it very difficult for them to continue to extend civil inattention to the uncontained encounter.

An instance of this doubly offensive disloyalty is found during what are sometimes called "scenes." Here, an individual who is supposed to be enclosed in an engagement may make a deeply engrossing appeal to others outside it, even though the appeal bears on a specific issue generated within the original engagement. Thus, one pair of patients I studied would (according to nursing notes) travel on a bus under the guidance of a nurse, start an argument with each other, and soon "open up the encounter" to all the passengers, dragging them in on both sides of the altercation. A woman in a lower-class street who is struck by her male companion may similarly make a direct appeal to others for help, thereby forcibly embroiling them. The disturbed feelings created by such bursting of the bounds of the engagement give us a clear picture of exactly what the rules of public conduct operate to prevent. In the extreme, a scene can break down all conventional closure separating the various engagements and unengaged individuals in the situation, providing an instance of an exhaustive engagement where none had been expected or desired.

The fact that bystanders may desire or feel obliged to remain out of an accessible encounter allows for a special kind of half-scene, where persons in an encounter talk in a sufficiently loud and pointed fashion to be heard by an outsider, yet modulate their talk enough to give him a slight opportunity to disattend. Here the terms "grumbling" or "muttering," and "stage whisper," are sometimes used. Thus, two middle-aged ladies sitting at a drugstore counter waiting for their lunch sandwiches may, upon receiving them and finding the filling thin, ostentatiously lift up a piece of the bread and complain to each other in a tone of voice that the countergirl is half-meant to hear. (The countermeasure for this, as suggested, is for the person who is grumbled at to attempt directly to ratify the half-spoken comment as a message formally addressed to him, employing some such phrase as "Did you say something?")

In addition to "selling out" an encounter while he is yet a member of it, a participant can also leave it in such a way as to expose the feelings within the encounter to the situation at large. Those remaining in the encounter may not be given a chance to compose themselves during the leave-taking, and the leave-taker may decline to damp and muffle the particular affect generated in him as a participant of the engagement. Ordinarily, of course, a brief leave-taking ceremony functions to allow leave-taking without exposure.

One's expectation that a leave-taker will "cut back" to the tone and temper prevailing in the gathering at large becomes evident when an individual fails to discipline his leave-taking in this way. A special kind of momentary scene can be observed among children, opera stars, mental patients, and others who have the privilege of temperament, when they precipitously take leave of an engagement, stalking or flouncing out of it and often out of the situation, leaving a wave of affect marked materially by slammed doors and overturned chairs.

Yet it must also be said that the leave-taker is expected to show in the situation at large at least some marks of his recent participation, some lingering, albeit fading, signs of the animation the encounter inspired in him; should he not do so, he exposes the encounter as one that has failed to move him.[9]

It should be apparent that affective disorganization is particularly likely when the leave-taker leaves what was in the first place only a two-person engagement. In such cases the remaining person, having no others to whom to deflect his readied response, and left deeply involved in an encounter that no longer exists, finds himself in a poor position to cut back his own affect to that prevailing in the situation as a whole. This possibility can, of course, be exploited. For example, one patient I studied, who seemed to know exactly how to attack social arrangements at their joints, as it were, would—according to nursing notes—leave with a package from a store after paying the clerk all but one or two cents of the requested amount, thereby leaving him in a position neither to terminate his involvement in the encounter nor to sustain a role in it.

9. Suggested by Harvey Sacks.

4. Desertion

I have suggested that an individual can betray his encounter either by entering collusive byplays against it or by taking leave in a precipitous fashion. There is another possibility, however—one that is especially important for the kind of leave-taking that also terminates the engagement. Leave-taking, as already suggested, is a physical act well designed to express rejection of those taken leave of. In the case of two-person engagements, the person left is not only the person available as the target for this implication, but also finds himself perforce unengaged—and this state, during some social occasions, may be a threat not only to the unengaged individual but to those managing the occasion as well.

Perhaps the most familiar instance of this issue is found in the leave-taking considerateness associated with "getting stuck" at social parties. A girl at a party who is left without a dance or talk partner is left exposed as an undesired person (and, incidentally, exposes the party itself as an entity that cannot incorporate its members). Hence, there are often rules against a male dropping his partner, no matter how long he has been stuck with her, if this means she will be exposed to the gathering unengaged. In theory, in "society" the male must wait for the officially sanctioned means of release: delivery of the female to a desirable unit of participation, especially another male openly seeking her company.[10] Even then, however, the social task of the person released may not be at an end:

> If you are talking to a lady with the ordinary indifference of a common acquaintance, and are only waiting till some one else comes up, for an opportunity to leave her, you should not move the instant another arrives, for that would look as if your previous tarrying had been compulsory; but you should remain a few moments and then turn away.[11]

10. At public dances for the lower-middle and lower classes, a male's obligation to his current partner may extend only to walking her back to the female side of the hall; sauntering back with her, however, is more protective of the female than is walking with a rapid pace.

11. Anon., *The Canons of Good Breeding* (Philadelphia: Lee and Blanchard, 1839), pp. 68-69.

In the face of this difficult obligation, the withdrawer may devise strategies to reduce the potential offensiveness of his withdrawal. Currently, at informal parties, a person locked in an encounter may seize on a desire for a fresh drink as a reason for tactful leave-taking.

A more general tack is to rely on the tacit cooperation of the person who is being left; she must look for cues and hints and take them. An example is provided in book etiquette, again in regard to the protection a girl should give a boy who might get "stuck" with her at a dance. While he must be willing to dance a little longer than he might want, or even until officially released by another male, the female herself ought to come to his rescue after a while:

> The beginning of wisdom is to accept the fact that one has danced long enough with one partner and that he might like to change. A woman who clings for hours, pathetic though she may be, will not soon dance with that partner again. Failing that perfect refuge, a table and a group of friends, she should suggest leaving the floor quite quickly, as soon as getting stuck seems likely. The classic phrase for this is, "It's so hot—would you like a drink?" or, "Let's sit down for a bit." Once away from the floor, she and her partner should join a group of friends—better a group than a couple—unless a man comes up to speak to her, at which point her partner may slip away.[12]

The tactful work of the leave-taker and the left is sometimes facilitated by the person responsible for order in the occasion; this officer may provide diplomatic means of effecting other persons' tactful departures. Thus, the fact that a guest may use the punch bowl as a means of switching encounters can lead a wise hostess to arrange to have drinks and food out, but at a far table.[13] But, of course, the hostess's action may be even more direct: she may herself arrange to break into those conversa-

12. Millicent Fenwick, *Vogue's Book of Etiquette* (New York: Simon and Schuster, 1948), p. 79.
13. Suggested by Susan Irwin.

tional clusters in which she feels persons have been stuck. As one etiquette book suggests:

> Some of the tête-à-têtes will break up by themselves, if the guests have sense and experience enough to move around and handle themselves. But very often the intervention of the hostess will be needed. In fact, unless a tête-à-tête seems to be particularly animated and gay and the hostess is sure that both guests are enjoying themselves thoroughly, she should change the combinations from time to time.[14]

So, too, with partners who have been too long stuck with each other dancing. Here the hostess may ensure that there will be men present, often relatives of the house, who are willing to engage in "duty" dances and other emergency operations. The traditional role of the usher is a formalization of this function, giving to men whose sign of office is a white boutonnière the right and obligation to keep partners "circulating."[15]

14. *Vogue's Book of Etiquette, op. cit.,* p. 441.
15. Emily Post, *Etiquette* (New York: Funk and Wagnalls, 1937), pp. 322-323.

PART FIVE

Interpretations

CHAPTER 12

The Structure and Function
of Situational Proprieties

I HAVE suggested that the behavior of an individual while in a situation is guided by social values or norms concerning involvement. These rulings apply to the intensity of his involvements, their distribution among possible main and side activities, and, importantly, their tendency to bring him into an engagement with all, some, or none present. There will be then a patterned distribution or *allocation* of the individual's involvement. By taking the point of view of the situation as a whole, we can link the involvement allocation of each participant to that maintained by each of the other participants, piecing together in this way a pattern than can be described as the *structure of involvement in the situation*. (And just as we speak of *actual* allocations and structures of involvement, so we can consider matters from the normative point of view and speak of *prescribed* allocations and structures of involvement.) Since the shape and distribution of involvement nicely enfolds an aspect of everything that goes on within a situation, we can perhaps speak here of the structure of the situation. In any case, if we want to describe conduct on a back ward, or in a street market, a bridge game, an investiture, or a revivalistic church service, it would seem reasonable to employ the structure of involvement in these situations as one frame of reference.

Now let us briefly review the kinds of situational proprieties that have been described and the social functions that appear to be performed by them.

Rules about access to a bounded region, and the regard that is to be shown its boundaries, are patently rules of respect for the gathering itself. Regulations against external preoccupation, "occult" involvements, and certain forms of "away" ensure that the individual will not give himself up to matters that fall outside of the situation. Regulations against unoccasioned main involvements or overtaxing side involvements (especially when either of these represents an auto-involvement) seem to ensure that the individual will not become embroiled divisively in matters that incorporate only himself; regulations against intense mutual-involvement provide the same assurances about the conduct of a subset of those present. In short, interests that are larger or smaller than the ones sustainable by everyone in the gathering as a whole are curtailed; limits are put on those kinds of emigration of the self which can occur without leaving one's physical position. Being thus constrained to limit his involvements outside the situation as well as divisive ones within the situation, the individual perforce demonstrates that something of himself has been reserved for what remains, namely, the little system of regulated social life that is jointly and exclusively maintained by all those in the situation as a whole—the situation being that entity neatly matching the area within which the individual's regulation of involvement is perceptible. However, we know that the gathering and the joint life it currently sustains are merely an expression, a visible phase, of the social occasion within which the situation occurs. To engage in situational impropriety, then, is to draw improperly on what one owes the social occasion.

Similar implications emerge when we turn from those constraints that play upon choice of object of involvement to those that pertain to the way in which the individual handles himself. By sustaining a publicly oriented composition of his face and a suitable organization of the more material aspects of his personal appearance, the individual shows himself a person ready for social interaction in the situation. By inhibiting creature releases and keeping a check upon intense involvement, he ensures that he will be ready for any event that occurs within the situation, and that he is respectful of these possibilities. By keeping himself from going too far into a situated task, he is able to remain in readiness near the surface of the situation. Through all of these means, the individual shows that he is "in play" in the situation, alive to the gathering it contains, oriented in it, and ready and open for whatever interaction it may bring.

A similar picture presents itself when we look at some of the traffic regulations regarding accessible engagements, especially engagements during social occasions such as parties. Prohibitions against improper involvement with others are prohibitions against taking joint leave of the gathering and the encompassing social occasion. Often prohibitions regarding disloyalty to one's encounter are also prohibitions about intruding upon bystanders—persons presumably maintaining an appropriate regard for the social occasion. Rules obliging one to give oneself up to occasioned mutual-engagements, and rules against excluding deferential newcomers, are rules assuring that the occasion as a whole will provide the basis of involvement. By maintaining accessibility to all those present, one shows that the gathering is significant enough in itself to ensure that any participant, merely by virtue of his participation, has a right to obtain attention and an obligation to give attention to any other participant. Loyalty, damping, spacing, drift—these are all issues basic to the organization of both accessible engagements and the setting of bystanders in which they occur. These issues are difficult even to describe unless reference is made to their function as supports for the gathering as a whole and, behind this, the social occasion.

The constraints that apply to objects of involvement, to modes of managing one's involvements, and (through these) to the management of accessible engagements, seem together to provide evidence of the weight and reality of the "situation." Indeed, one might be inclined to summarize the whole matter by saying that the individual is obliged to demonstrate involvement *in* a situation through the modulation of his involvements *within* the situation. But this would be a loose way of talking. First, that which the individual owes is conveyed through appropriate modulation of situated involvements. What is thereby conveyed, however, is not "involvement," but rather a kind of respect and regard for that to which attachment and belongingness are owed. At the heart of it is a kind of concern that shows one to be a part of the thing for which one is concerned. Second, a situation, as defined in this study, is merely an environment of communication possibilities, and not the sort of thing to which one can become attached. The little society involved is that of the gathering in the situation, and the little social system found therein is made up from conduct performed in accordance with the norms of situational propriety. Finally, what is owed the gathering is owed the social occasion in which it occurs, the joint social life sustained by the gathering being an embodiment of the occasion itself.

Situational proprieties, then, give body to the joint social life sustained by a gathering, and transform the gathering itself from a mere aggregate of persons present into something akin to a little social group, a social reality in its own right. Behind this social function we can see still further ones.

When a situation comes into being, mutual accessibility of body signs is not the only contingency faced by those who are present. As already suggested, each person becomes a potential victim or aggressor in the potential occurrence of violent interpersonal actions, such as physical or sexual assault, blocking of the way, and so forth. Further, each person present is in a position to accost or be accosted by the others for the purpose of initiating a state of talk—a joint conversational engagement. And this, too, has its own dangers, for when persons are joined in this way they can command and plead with each other, insult or compliment each other, inform and misinform each other, or be seen (by others) as being on close terms, and the like. Further, when an engagement is sustained in the presence of bystanders, the participants open themselves up to being listened in on and interfered with, just as the bystanders become vulnerable to undesired distractions.

Although these various dangers of being in the presence of others are perhaps not frequently realized, especially in middle-class society, the possibility of their occurrence is always there. And it is through body signs that persons present signify to each other that they can be trusted not to exploit these threatening possibilities. Only when these signs are received may the individual feel secure enough to forget about defending himself, secure enough to give himself up to the merely-situated aspects of his involvements. Aside, then, from the disrespect an individual shows to a gathering by conducting himself improperly, such improprieties can also cause the others present to fear for their physical and social inviolability, whether rightly or not.

And here, incidentally, is one reason for arguing that social situations and the gatherings occuring therein are worth studying, even apart from the social occasion that incorporates them. Ordinarily, situations are thought to be so closely enmeshed in a particular on-going institutional setting, and these settings to be so very different one from another, that excision of situations and their gatherings for separate study might seem questionable. However, it is only in situations that individuals can be physically assaulted, accosted by requests for talk, or drawn away from conversations and other involvements by the antics of bystanders. It is in situations that these accessibilities will have to be faced and dealt with. And in facing these accessibilities and dealing with them, a common and distinctive character is given to the social life sustained in situations, regardless of the uniqueness of the larger span of social life in which each gathering is embedded and of which each is an expression.

CHAPTER 13

Tightness
and Looseness

AN ATTEMPT has been made to describe some of the regulations that govern involvements sustained *within* a situation and lead to a display of respect and regard *for* the gathering in the situation. Also, it has been implicitly claimed that each of these regulations is a generic structural feature of gatherings (when gatherings are taken as a natural class of social units), the evidence deriving not only from the variety of means by which adherence to the regulation is manifest, but also from the great variety of situations in which the regulation applies.

In some cases a continuum was claimed regarding a given regulation. I cited, at one extreme, situations in which the regulation barely constrained the participants to display their respect for the gathering, and, at the other extreme, situations in which much of this particular kind of situational respect was required. It should now be apparent that situations can be found that could have been used as illustrations of one extreme for many aspects of involvement. An example in our own society is a park on a summer Saturday afternoon. Here an individual can exhibit reduced situational "presence" by visibly loosening his tie and taking off his shoes, by dozing off, by wearing torn or rumpled clothing, by showing lessened concern about concealing belches. Here, too, he may permissibly allow for little margin of disinvolvement, throwing himself rather completely into roles such as that of third-baseman or fielder. Just as with the handling of self, so also with objects of involvement: in the park he can engage intensely in exposed mutual-involvements by quarreling, love-making (to a degree), or shouting to a friend coming up the path; he can immerse himself in auto-involvement as he cleans out the wax from his ear, eats chicken from a basket, or massages the muscle of his leg; he can loll in apparent disengagement, go into a brown study, and even exercise less than usual care about not appearing to be engaged in occult matters.

Conversely, some social situations, such as those occurring during a ceremonial investiture, are scenes in which few, if any, of these situationally unoriented activities are allowed. Here, each person present may be obliged to show constant orientation to the gathering as a whole and constant devotion to the spirit of the occasion, as expressed through all the avenues suggested.

It would seem, then, that there may be one over-all continuum or axis along which the social life in situations varies, depending on how disciplined the individual is obliged to be in connection with the several ways in which respect for the gathering and its social occasion can be expressed. Hence, for example, we may properly suspect that if the management of a restaurant or the host of a social party makes a chess set available to those present, allowing two players and a circle of followers to go into a kind of joint fugue, then other kinds of situational license are also likely to be allowed.

In daily speech, the terms "formality" and "informality" are sometimes used to refer to this central axis of situational regulation. And these terms might be so used here, providing we bear in mind that these terms tend to stress unduly the kind of clothing that is worn, the degree to which the sequence of acts in a social occasion is codified in advance and heavily enjoined, and the range of activities that is permitted. The terms "tight" and "loose" might be more descriptive and give more equal weight to each of the several ways in which devotion to a social occasion may be exhibited. In any case, once this summarizing continuum is defined, we must be careful to avoid the common-sense tendency to "explain" or account for particular aspects of the pattern by reference to the pattern as a whole. At worst such explanations are tautological; at best they merely shift the point that is to be explained—the shift being from the particular item to the pattern of which it is a part.

What has been said earlier about each of the modes of regulating involvement presumably could now be repeated about the over-all dimension of tightness-looseness. This, in fact, would merely be another way of talking about involvement structure.

For example, the same kind of social setting in different communities will be differently defined as regards tightness. Thus, public streets in Paris seem to be more loosely defined than those in Britain or America. On many Parisian streets one can eat from a loaf of bread while walking to or from work, become heatedly involved in peripatetic conversations, engage in a full-course meal at an open café table, expect not to show surprise at oddly costumed persons, and so forth. In Anglo-American society one would have to look to summer resorts to find a similar degree of looseness. (In any case, Americans tend to find France and summer resorts relaxing for the same reason: many public gatherings seem to demand less attachment and respect, allowing one an easier depth of either private or interpersonal concerns.) Similarly, in many Anglo-American communities a teacher will be expected to remain thoroughly oriented in and to the situation during school hours, while in a rural community in Southern Italy we learn that:

> It is not uncommon for a teacher to come late to class and to spend the morning smoking a cigarette and looking idly out the window.[1]

1. E. C. Banfield, *The Moral Basis of a Backward Society*, unpublished manuscript, p. V-7.

Our university students are expected to show considerable "respect" for the main focus of lecture-room attention, causing one writer to comment as follows on their Indian counterparts:

> The lecture halls attended by Indian undergraduates and aspirants for the M.A. and LL.B. are often scenes of disorder—not always the organized rampageousness which attracts the worried attention of the President of the Republic, the Prime Minister, Governors and Chief Ministers of States, journalists, the University Grants Commission, Vice-Chancellors, Gandhian social workers, *et al.*—but the random individual disorder of shuffling feet, audible conversation, note-passing, and gestures of fearful bravado.[2]

Contrasts can also be made between somewhat similar gatherings within the same nation and even within a section of a nation. Thus, in many geographical regions in America, a continuum can be traced regarding the formality of dress required of men who patronize public eateries. There are still establishments that require dinner jackets. Those next in line insist at least on ties and jackets, and may keep a supply of ties handy to accommodate would-be customers who turn up informally attired. At summer resorts in the same geographical regions, one can find establishments whose posted house-rules demand that T-shirts be worn in addition to swimming trunks, these establishments thereby distinguishing themselves from those final seats of beach informality in our society where eating, drinking, and dancing are allowed even to barefoot men in swimming trunks. Incidentally, it might be noted here that societies seem to have their own limits regarding tightness and looseness and that these limits seem to change over time. In spite of some recent efforts to bring pomp back into American life, the most formal of evening clothes are becoming more and more rarely used, and decorations such as jewelled tiaras can properly be worn these days at almost no occasion.

Any social establishment is itself likely to provide instructive

2. E. Shils, "Indian Students," *Encounter*, 17 (September, 1961), 13.

variation in tightness or formality requirements, according to place and time. In Central Hospital, for example, attendants claimed that they need wear their ties and "look smart," that is, situationally oriented, only when on that half of the campus that contained the administration building. On the night-shift, when doctors and nurses were absent, attendants would administer medication without bothering to take their cigarettes from their mouths, and tended to slouch more while sitting or standing.[3]

The ward system, which forms a central aspect of the social structure in mental hospitals, can also be delineated in terms of involvement rules—the "bad" wards being ones where tight situational orientation is little demanded; the "good" or convalescent wards being ones where many more exhibitions of respect for the gathering are required.[4] The communal institutions of Central Hospital were themselves differently defined as regards tightness. In the large 300-man refectory, which fed the men on a 900-patient chronic men's service, eating with one's hat on was not forbidden; the place had something of the atmosphere of a train depot. However, at the Red Cross House (containing a large sitting room-dancehall), the staff felt that patients should have some "respect" for the place, and act in it as they would in their homes. Posted signs, collective bawlings-out, and other injunctions established that no hats, no spitting, no refuse on the floor, and no "horsing around" were to be permitted.[5]

3. Night-shift laxity has been reported in several studies. See, for example, S. M. Lipset, M. Trow, and J. Coleman, *Union Democracy* (New York: The Free Press of Glencoe, 1956), p. 139.

4. Conversely, the "good" wards are ones where other kinds of privileges are available, and the "bad" ones are places where these are not. When staff use these labels they often mean to refer to differences in situational propriety; patients, on the other hand, tend to have in mind the merely-situated component of privileges on the ward. The same term, then, will designate the same ward but will tend to connote different things to the two status levels. It may be added that, in general, mental hospitals seem to operate on the basis of a privilege quota: the patient who requires situational license must sacrifice the merely-situated component of privilege, and to the degree that he desires the latter, he must be ready to "behave himself."

5. When we see that some of these controlling factors inhere in the behavior

Just as there are differences between situations in regard to the tightness of conduct occurring therein, so, of course, there are differences between different roles, each of these differences being maintained across several different situations. At one extreme we have the mental patient on a chronic ward who has not yet decided to try to get out by good behavior. He may feel that he has earned and paid for the right to act loosely and that he might as well exercise it. He thus plays the role of an "involvement freak," and, as already suggested, shares with children, old people, hoboes, and bohemians the special license and expectation of being frequently remiss in situational obligations. At the other extreme are high ecclesiastical and military officers who carry their solemnity in their uniform, and prefer gatherings that are tight enough to be saluted.

Here, incidentally, one finds a very pervasive difference between middle- and lower-class males in American society. Those who work without a tie, in clothes they do not have to worry about keeping clean, are persons who can afford to touch and be touched by the physical environment around them. The "informality" of their dress is one part of a complex, the whole of which is the understanding that these persons need not maintain a tight orientation in public social situations. While waiting for a bus or talking to a friend on the street, they can slouch, lean against a building, or squat on any substitute for a seat, and thus express a looseness of orientation to the gathering as such, which is consistent with the role that has been accorded them.[6] That their clothing allows this is as much effect as cause of their situational orientation. (A limiting case is the person, such as a chimney sweep or miner, who can soil the environment around him and will therefore have a special basis for circum-

---

setting, we can more readily understand why some mental patients may improve greatly merely by being brought down to a "better" ward; but we cannot as easily determine how much new human material a setting can incorporate without losing its customary involvement structure.

6. Good photographs illustrating this kind of use of the environment may be seen in J. Ruesch and W. Kees, *Nonverbal Communication: Notes on the Visual Perception of Human Relations* (Berkeley: University of California Press, 1956), pp. 53, 58, and 70.

spection.) Middle-class people in public places, on the other hand, have more obligation to keep relatively erect and stiff, relatively ready to respond interactively. And, again, the fact that their clothing and cleanliness patterns are incompatible with too great a familiarity with the physical environment of the street would seem to be as much effect as cause of their level of orientational discipline. Persons tightly attired can, of course, express meager concern for the gathering, but they are perhaps more likely than those informally dressed to do this by means of relatively subtle cues.

Since the very old and the very young have special license as regards involvement rulings, we might ask whether, in American society at least, the sexes are differently defined in this regard. Some evidence suggests that women, in general, are more tightly defined than men. There is at least a popular belief that the female toilet takes longer than the male, and that therefore more is entailed in making a female presentable than in making a male presentable. So, too, a man who appears on a public street with his hair tousled, his tie loosened, and a cigarette dangling from his lips seems to be less of an affront to public decorum than is a woman similarly disarrayed.[7] And yet, of course, women are sometimes defined as creatures who are not expected to be full-fledged participants in public meetings, and so can sometimes engage in somewhat taxing side involvements such as knitting, in recognition that they have not been deeply

7. The possibility that women are more tightly defined than men has received some incidental consideration in the literature on drinking. E. Lemert, *Social Pathology* (New York: McGraw-Hill, 1951), p. 353, suggests:

Drunkenness in a woman has a much higher visibility than that in a man, which can be traced to the symbolic qualities of drinking and drunkenness in women in the past, when drinking customarily symbolized the bawd and the harlot. The lack of a long experience with drinking on the part of women in America may explain the greater loss of control they show in their tippling. Another possibility to be counted is that women are more likely to be badly maladjusted when they first turn to excessive drinking, and as a result their overt behavior becomes more flagrantly disorganized. The high-pitched and shrill laughter of the drunken woman often brands her behavior more quickly for what it is than in a man. Women are supposed to be neater, cleaner, and more fastidious about their dress than the opposite sex, so that disarray brought by drunkenness also demarcates their condition more sharply.

drawn into the occasioned main involvement. Similarly, there are coming to be more semipublic situations where a young woman may half-daringly slip her shoes off, while a man in the same settings cannot; but perhaps this is merely a sign that the female's tightness of orientation is more than shoe-deep, and that a foot sheathed only in nylon is already almost presentable enough for safe public display.

To speak of the general level of tightness or looseness built into a role is to imply a social rigidity: that is, the individual may be unable from the start to fit into certain social gatherings, finding that some are defined too loosely and others too tightly. Correspondingly, the individual will tend to exhibit alienation from those gatherings for which his role causes him to be unsuitably involved, and even be led to exhibit this kind of alienation at times when he does not want to.

In this context it is worth considering the relation of work and clothing to the problem of fitting into gatherings. Some clothing, like that worn by deep-sea divers or firemen, is inextricably geared to the task at hand. These personal fronts can hardly serve in nonoccupational situations, nor can the possessor, unless he changes clothes. Even during the coffee-break he will be showing a certain kind of devotion to the job. In the case of white-collar tasks, however, work clothes transcend the work place and enable the worker to merge into gatherings occurring off the job. Correspondingly, when he is on the job, there will be parts of himself that he need not submerge into work, and this in fact provides him with one basis for self-possession and dignity. Those who must wear a uniform at work, and who cannot leave it in the locker room when they leave the premises, are likely to feel that they are under special constraint to give much of themselves to work and to carry this contribution to any nonwork situation in which they happen to find themselves. In the army, of course, this may be quite explicitly stressed by admonitions to respect one's uniform. We find, then, that persons often feel unfairly restricted in uniform; they carp about not being able to melt easily into loose gatherings that happen to occur, and they feel their autonomy is threatened.[8]

In general, of course, the individual tends to avoid gatherings where more commitment will be demanded than he is in a position to give at the time, the implication being that enough concern for the occasion would be too much for him. Thus, we read in etiquette books that after a death in the family one should not go to dinners of more than eight persons, or to fashionable restaurants, the opera, the theater, or the races. The implication is that in all of these settings participants are expected to maintain a somewhat festive spirit and give themselves up rather extensively to the occasioned involvement; and since a properly downcast person will not be in a position to "come out of himself" this far, he should not go at all.[9] He may even feel at times (as when someone close to him has just died) that he *should not* be able to handle a particular set of situational requirements, and hence may feel obliged to avoid a particular gathering even though he is really prepared for it.

I want to consider now the possibility that within the same situation different classes of participants may have different over-all involvement obligations or be obliged to convey the same level of orientation through different components of the involvement idiom. (As was earlier suggested, it may indeed be difficult to determine which of these factors—obligation, or idiom—is operative in a particular case.) In general hospitals in our society, for example, it is acceptable for patients to ride the elevator in their bathrobes; secretaries in the organization do not have a right to the equivalent of such looseness. Female doctors in such settings may show their appropriate regard for the setting by wearing no nail polish, relatively unstylish clothes, relatively informal hair-do, and medium-heeled shoes, and by keeping quite busy; secretaries, less able to show respect

8. As will be later argued, some individuals may, of course, desire to maintain a pervasive alienation from their society at large, and seek membership in uniformed quasi-military groups partly in order to ensure that they will always be a little out of place.

9. Millicent Fenwick, *Vogue's Book of Etiquette* (New York: Simon and Schuster, 1948), pp. 154-155.

through the deeply serious handling of their main involvement, may show it by using a relatively stylish personal front. Something similar is found at social occasions where guests may be allowed a considerable range of posture and dress, so long as they allow the occasion to animate them; at the same time the guests are reminded that the gathering as such is weighty, by the presence of servants whose clothing and manner are frozen into a rigid and continuous devotion to the occasion as a whole. Similarly, an onlooker at a wedding procession may have a right to chew gum, flick lint from his jacket, blow his nose discreetly, or converse momentarily with his neighbor; but the groom walking down the aisle would be very much out of place were he to indulge in these subordinate involvements.

We usually think of tight occasions as ones in which the participants have many onerous situational obligations, and of loose occasions as ones relatively free of these constraints. But this is only partly so. One individual's right to be lax in his orientation to the gathering implies a duty on the part of the others present to accept this laxity without taking corrective action. Thus, on some chronic male wards at Central Hospital, patients had an understanding with attendants that it was permissible to sleep on the floor, drool, hallucinate, and spit into paper cups; an extremely loose, informal definition of the setting prevailed, which provided one of the few comforts known to this way of life. But, in one such setting, I observed that when a patient urinated against a hot steam radiator to save himself the trouble of going to the toilet, fellow patients sitting in the cloud of evaporating urine seemed to appreciate that they had tacitly agreed to forego the right to respond with anything but a slight frown or ironic smile to what was happening around them. Similarly, I have seen patients watch passively, from a few feet away, a young male psychotic rape an old, defenseless mute man, the event occurring in a part of the dayroom that was momentarily outside the view of the attendant. The bystanders seemed to express the fact that, while disapproving glances were safe, any interference would have brought them further into situational social reality than was comfortable. In any case, there appears to be a significant interdependence: toleration of intense auto- and mutual-involvements seems to be functionally correlated with the practice and norm of disattending to many immediate stimuli. Long-term mental patients sometimes provide a fine display of this functional linkage through their wonderfully cultivated capacity to play two- and four-person card games right in the middle of what is in fact bedlam. Clearly there is here a suggestion that the inaccessibility of the regressed patient is part of a larger communication system, and that his "undistractability" is something whole tables of bridge can possess.

Tightly defined occasions can, of course, have their own compensations. An example is the army parade square, a region where extreme situational orientation can be found. Here it can be the rule that no statement is to be made by an officer to a subordinate that is not addressed in an impersonal way and with sufficient volume to make it a public utterance, as in the shout, "Smarten up, that man in the rear"; in response to which the person thus addressed may be obliged to be silent, or, if an answer is demanded, to limit all statements drastically and, as already suggested, speak while looking straight ahead, excluding himself from almost all mutual-involvement and ensuring that even his glance remains situational. Yet, here, the person on parade can feel that his mind has been left wonderfully free to wander. Contrariwise, the looseness of some cocktail parties may require of the guest that he keep very much on his toes mentally. Further, in those situations where the individual is required to show much respect for the gathering as a whole, he may be excused from any kind of deep involvement with individuals who are next to him. On the other hand, in those situations where no holds are barred, the interpersonal wrestling that may occur can be extremely strenuous and taxing. Here we have, of course, the traditional argument that is advanced in support of the ritualization of sociable occasions, of which a good statement by Elizabeth Bowen may be quoted at length:

Behaviour—social behaviour—is partly an art, partly instinct. In what is called our freer modern life, manners have come to count for a good deal less, which makes sheer manner count for a good deal more. Now that it is less vital to be correct, it becomes far more important to be acceptable. In fact, the decline of manners in the grand and fixed sense has made behaviour infinitely more difficult. A perpetual, forced recourse to instinct (the art element being discredited) gives our friends a harassed, unstable air. There is no longer the safety of a prescribed world, of which the thousand-and-one rules could be learnt, in which one could steer one's way instructed and safe. The world, even the great world, can have, in an age of manners, held no more terrors than does the Hyde Park Corner traffic, with its apparent complexity, for the unassuming driver who has passed his test. For each of the occasions of society, one of the thousand-and-one rules you have learnt fitted. You knew what to do, and did it. Society went like clockwork.[10]

Outside the set observances, which become instinctive, which cost little, which have the value of art, one might be free to *be*, but not bound to exhibit, oneself. There were far more "personalities" in the ages of manners. But so-called free, or intelligent, society imposes a constant tax on all the powers. There is no guide here. To please, even to conform to what is expected, one must constantly draw on a private natural genius, meant for one's own pleasure or for the intimacies of love. Exhaustion, a sense of spentness and deflation, follows in many people the unconventional supper, the *longueurs* of the free-and-easy week-end. You can go wrong at any point, and by going wrong drag up a host of agonies: here too much is involved. Manners were a protection; they also stabilized one. How much more gladly would one observe ritual than be put through a series of daunting hoops.[11]

In this study it has so far been assumed that the involvement rulings governing conduct within a particular situation remain constant for the duration of the situation and that, therefore,

10. Elizabeth Bowen, *Collected Impressions* (London: Longmans Green, 1950), p. 67.
11. *Ibid.*, p. 69.

the over-all tendency to tightness or looseness within the situation is something that can be neatly assessed, at least in theory. However, as has already been suggested, when we look beyond a social situation to the social occasion of which it is a part, important cycles of change are found in involvement rulings, especially, apparently, when the occasion is formal or tightly defined. Thus, an occasion may begin with a period of muttering and milling, move on to the formal official proceedings, and then terminate in another loosely defined period, exhibiting in this way a standard type of involvement contour.[12] Correspondingly, the occasion may start with a multifocused situation, move on to official proceedings which exhaust the situation, and terminate in a multifocused arrangement once again. A situation, then, may be the scene of a routine cycle of changes regarding approved tightness or looseness, with the result that a picture at any one point in time is likely to provide a misleading view of the whole.

Given the general level of tightness (or looseness) established in a situation, and the orderly changes prescribed in this regard, it is worth noting that the normative stability found in the situation may be due to the presence of guardians who informally or formally have the special job of keeping "order." Thus, we read of the *silentiarius,* the Roman slave whose job it was to regulate the noise level maintained by other slaves.[13] In our day, chaperones, referees, nursery-school teachers, judges, police, ward attendants, and ushers are among those who perform this function.

I want now to re-emphasize that when one thinks in terms of the looseness or tightness of situational orientation, and in terms of the dimensions and idiom through which this is exhibited, one has a means of passing a little beyond the rationalistic dicta by which we ordinarily account for our major explicit situational rulings.

12. An analyzed illustration is given in K. L. Pike, *Language in Relation to a Unified Theory of the Structure of Human Behavior* (Glendale, California: Summer Institute of Linguistics, 1954), Part 1, "Criteria for Closure," pp. 33-34.

13. H. Nicolson, *Good Behaviour* (London: Constable, 1955), p. 64.

Take, for example, our jumbled attitudes and rationalizations regarding body exposure. Instead of considering the amount or the parts of the body exposed, it might be more profitable to examine the *orientational* implications of exposure. The relative undress of a bathing suit is part of the whole looseness complex—which includes the way in which one handles one's voice and eyes as well as one's body—and it is this whole complex that is tolerated and even encouraged on the beach. (Why this complex should here be approved still remains a question, of course, but a slightly different one.) The relative undress of décolletage at balls may be appropriate for the opposite reason. The exposure of this much of the self would seem in part to be an appreciative acknowledgment that the participants are so tightly in step with the occasion as a whole, and so trustful of the good conduct of their socially homogeneous circle, that they can withstand this much temptation to undue mutual-involvement without giving in to it. (An extreme, here, is perhaps found in the morals-ruling in London, which permits nudes to appear on the stage providing they do not move while the curtain is up. Presumably the rigidity of their pose is such a strong mark of devotion and assimilation to the occasion as a whole that the license of nudity can be afforded them.[14]) Yet in almost any public situation in our society, a woman dressed only in an underslip, although completely covered by it, would be greatly out of place; for such attire implies that the wearer has not yet put on her situational costume, whatever it is to be, and is not in a position to honor her situational commitments, whatever they may be. Nudity in a nudist colony or a doctor's office, or on the posing platform in an art class, is manageable because here it is the garb that shows proper regard for the demands of the occasion. Logic would force one to claim that a woman's appearance in a slip on these occasions would be a gaffe; and, in fact, arrangements are sometimes made so that those who will properly appear nude will not first appear half-

14. A description of this practice is given by Hortense Calisher, "Bowlers and Bumbershoots at a Piccadilly Peepshow," *The Reporter,* October 4, 1956, pp. 33-36.

clothed and out of role. By the same logic one can understand how a model can appear half-clothed at a fashion show of under-clothing, for this is the way she shows appropriate involvement within the situation, albeit in a special performer role. Thus, apparently, the formality of a dress-modeling establishment (and hence its "tone," the desirability of its street location, and the like) can be indicated by the care that models take not to wander around the floor, after a showing, in the slips they have shown.[15]

Exposure of self in situational déshabille may be condoned, of course, in the household, at least within certain limits. The point here is that certain close relationships may be defined as ones that give the related persons the license to let occasions decay when these persons are alone in each other's presence. Hence, when a visitor to the house accidentally witnesses a resident of the house in disarray, a minor relationship crisis occurs, which is due to the momentary but embarrassing implication that the witness is in a relationship to the observed that would warrant the lapsing of situational niceties between them.

Clothing conduct during crises and disasters can be similarly analyzed. At a hotel fire, guests in undress are tolerated, not, perhaps, because eyes are turned to more important things, but because participants are allowed to be so deeply immersed in the crisis that their undress can be taken as a sign of appropriate engrossment, and the undress of others felt as an insufficient stimulus, under the circumstances, to induce inappropriate mutual-involvement. When the fire is brought under control, and the crisis abates, when in fact the occasion is such that alienation from it is a more possible thing, undress once again becomes a threat to situational orientation, and survivors begin to become sheepish about their lack of clothing.

The argument here is that any state of dress is proper or improper only in terms of what other evidence is available concerning the individual's allocation of involvement and hence his orientation to the social occasion and its gatherings. Since

15. Suggested by Eleanor Carroll.

dress carries much of the burden of expressing orientation within the situation, we can understand why such apparently petty matters of "mere" etiquette should be of concern. But given that this is the major reason why dress is important, we can expect and predict much variation in what will be defined as allowable dress. A male college student who enters the classroom in need of a shave and in trunks, or a female who enters with her hair in curlers, is nakedly showing lack of attachment to the behavior setting; but when an exam is being held, and all students in the exam hall are engrossed quite deeply in school work, having studied devotedly for the previous two weeks, then there is already sufficient sign of involvement in schooling, and thus the informalities of appearance I have mentioned may well be permitted, no longer being symbols of alienation. Similarly, an accountant or lawyer, with a downtown office, who attended to his clients dressed in an old sweater and no jacket would be considered to be disoriented in business situations and to the business world itself; the same man working overtime on Saturday afternoon can afford such laxness, however, because his mere presence in the office at an off hour is sign enough of regard for the work world.

Just as with nudity and dress, so involvement analysis can make some kind of sense out of our varied responses to noise and noise-making. The ruling against undue noise is sometimes seen as a rational response to the obligation to "show consideration" for those in the vicinity, in this case those who might be disturbed by the sheer physical effect of the sound. Yet in actuality, large amounts of noise (from a purely physical point of view) are often tolerated. What is an affront to the gathering, however, is overinvolvement in some situated task. Noise, in short, becomes an offense only when it exhibits overinvolvement—not, in the last analysis, because it is noisy. For example, in a large commercial office filled with typists, any worker whose machine makes a little more noise than the machines of others may be felt to be acting improperly, not because this little increment of sound makes things much worse, but because it betokens an inordinate concentration or an inordinate careless-ness about soundproofing. Here we can understand, too, that when a youth finds himself in the mental hospital because he played a phonograph too loudly in the YMCA, it may not have been merely that his inconsiderateness offended the officials, but rather that they did not know what world the boy inhabited if he could fill it so full with so much music.

If asked, the individual might say that he limits the noise that he makes out of considerateness for others present. How-ever, in showing this considerateness he is showing cognizance of persons by virtue of their presence in the situation, and in showing this he demonstrates that he is open to the gathering and respectful of it. It is a demonstration of his committed "presence" in the situation that the others may want of the individual, even more than the substantive value of the consid-erateness itself. Hence it is understandable that persons present may tolerate a great deal of noise from an individual, providing he makes a general apology in advance for the necessity of mak-ing it. The apology shows that he is alive to those in the situa-tion and hence to the gathering itself, and provides an effective substitute for the evidence of considerateness that quietness usually provides. It should also be understandable that silence, coming from a person in a situation where participants are obliged to be busily engaged in tasks or talk, can itself be a noisy thing, loudly expressing that the individual is not prop-erly involved and not attuned to the gathering; this silent kind of noise can distract attention, just as the loud kind can.

The same argument can be repeated in regard to exposed mutual-involvements. Again the noise emerging from them is noisy to the extent that it expresses unoccasioned involvements. Thus, two persons in a movie theater, quietly talking together about something entirely unconnected with the evening's enter-tainment, may thereby exhibit an unoccasioned mutual-involve-ment, and by doing so cause more resentment than those who make much more physical sound but do so in expressing their approbation or disapprobation of what is being seen.

In general, then, when we find that places such as parks can become the scene of robbery, refuse dumping, sexual solicitations, loitering (on the part of drunks, bums, and ambulatory psychotics), we must understand this collapse of public order not merely in terms of the fact that it may be possible to avoid the police in these places; we must understand that the involvement structure institutionalized in very loosely defined behavioral settings reduces appreciably the degree to which these nefarious acts are improper. A park may be the place that maximizes the acceptability of these acts and hence minimizes the price of being caught performing them.

CHAPTER 14

The Symptomatic Significance
of Situational Improprieties

CONTRARY to an assumption that some sociologists make, there seems to be little doubt that improper behavior in one situation can sometimes tell us a great deal about the offender's reception in other situations. In any given society, different situations will be the scene of many of the same normative assumptions regarding conduct and of the same situational rulings. An individual who is remiss in one way in one situation, then, can be remiss in this same way whenever he shows his face to man. Thus, a person with senile deterioration who drools spoils his participation in all his situations in the same way and for the same reason. A person who is hard of hearing or who is near-blind will not be able to maintain the communication niceties that have here been considered at length; he will be forced to be all thumbs in all his situations.[1] Thus, improper conduct in one situation can bespeak a general disenfranchisement in face-to-face interaction. Such conduct need not arise from a psychopathological condition; presumably it can, however, give rise to one through the response the individual may make to his excommunication. Some offenses, then, tell us about the price the

1. For examples of the consequences of these communication incapacities, see F. Warfield, *Cotton in My Ears* (New York: Viking, 1948) , and R. Criddle, *Love is not Blind* (New York: Norton, 1953) .

offender must pay for his offensiveness, and the price he may pay for his price.

Granting the occurrence of widely relevant offensiveness, the general procedure in this study has been to try to learn what this offensiveness costs the gathering in which it occurs, rather than what it means to and about the offender in the first place. In this section, however, let us return to the more traditional theme: when an individual intentionally or unintentionally conducts himself in a way that others consider situationally improper, and shows thereby that he is either alienated from, or an alien to, the gathering, what other information can this provide them about his current condition—apart from what his impropriety tells them about his likely fate?

The meaning that offended persons impute to an offensive act is partly determined by whether they feel the act was intentional or unintentional. However, the complexity and ambiguity of this dichotomy, and the shifting but intimate relevance of its bearing, prevent any simple discussion of the actual or imputed meaning of situational offenses.[2] In actual use, the dichotomy does not so much refer to a physiological factor of volition or control accountable by reference to the distinction between striped and smooth muscles, the cerebrospinal and the autonomic nervous systems, but rather to the kind of responsibility that is placed upon the individual for an undesired act.[3] The undesired acts in themselves need not be characteristically voluntary or involuntary from the physiological point of view. For example, to fail to appear at a social party because of one's disapproval of the host is considered to be an intentional act; the

2. Helpful comments on this issue may be found in G. Ryle, *The Concept of Mind* (London: Hutchinson's University Library, 1949), "The Distinction between Voluntary and Involuntary," pp. 69-74; and H. L. A. Hart, "The Ascription of Responsibility and Rights," Chap. 8, in A. G. N. Flew, ed., *Logic and Language (First Series)* (Oxford: Blackwell, 1955), pp. 145-166. See also J. L. Austin, *Philosophical Papers*, Chap. 6, "A Plea for Excuses" (Oxford: Clarendon Press, 1961).

3. There are, of course, other common-sense uses of the dichotomy—for example, in characterizing a very desirable task performance, the question being whether or not the individual can execute it again.

same failure due to the sudden death of a kinsman may be considered a fully warranted, excusable reason for staying away. In the first case we speak of the individual staying away voluntarily, in the second case, involuntarily.

Of any situationally offensive act and of any offender the following questions can be asked, taking the point of view of the others present: Does the actor have the capacity and training to appreciate the meaning of his offense, and if so, does he in fact appreciate its meaning? Is the act within the physical control of the actor, and if so, would he be willing to change his conduct if he were apprised of its meaning and given the opportunity to do so? Does the actor have extenuating reasons, external to the participants in the situation, for committing the offense?

These factors, in various combinations, provide so many concrete possibilities that little implication can be drawn from the mere presence or absence of one sense or another of intentionality. A few of the more familiar combinations of factors may be cited.

There is a class of offenses sometimes called acts of malice or spite. These often imply arrogance, disdain, and deep hostility, as when a middle-class person yawns directly before others in a slow and elaborate manner. Maliciously offensive acts give the following impression: they are easily controllable; their significance can be and is appreciated by the offender; the offender would not modify his conduct at the time even if given a second chance, and seems to have no reason for the act other than what he can convey by it to those he offends. Quite similar to malicious offenses are "contingent" ones, which have the same qualities as spiteful acts except that the offender has reasons for his act outside of the occasion and its participants. Here we have the individual who inconsiderately laughs out loud over something he is reading, not out of malice, but because he is genuinely amused. The more "legitimate" the offender's reasons, of course, the more these contingent offenses are viewed as fully excusable, and the less intentionality is imputed to them.

Malicious acts represent some kind of extreme of intentionality. At the other extreme, that of complete unintentionality, is the delict of the individual perceived as having an organic brain injury: his offense is not controllable by him, sometimes he cannot and hence does not appreciate its significance, and he may not be amenable to correction. Somewhere in between these extremes is the individual who offends because he is accustomed to a different idiom and structure of involvement from the ones sanctioned by those in the situation. His offensive act is one he controls; he might be willing to alter his conduct if he appreciated its current significance, and of such appreciation he is fully capable. There is also the case of the withdrawn individual who could, if he wished, withdraw from his withdrawal, and who, in that sense, controls his act. He may not appreciate the significance of his act for others, since he has no interest in discovering it, although presumably he could discover it if he wanted to; and he is not currently amenable to changing his conduct.

Then, of course, there is the individual who is too preoccupied, too nervous, or too self-conscious to fit in, the basis of his uneasiness being one that others consider temporary, natural, and understandable. Such an individual can appreciate the difficulty he is causing and may well do so; indeed, he may actively desire to correct his conduct but be unable to do so at the moment. The creature release known as a "tic" is an example, this misconduct sometimes evoking pity and contempt for the tiqueur's incapacity to sustain the image that his other means of self-control claim for him. A similar instance is the individual whose repertoire of clothing provides dress that is either too formal or too informal for the occasion he must attend, thus forcing him to be out of place. Finally, there is the individual who accidentally and uncharacteristically intrudes upon a situation in which he cannot fit, thereby committing an offense he wishes he had not committed and would have been fully capable of avoiding had he known in advance what was to happen.

Note that in all these examples the witnesses would be just in conceiving of the offender as someone who was alienated from the gathering and its rulings, although there is some realization that in no two cases are the bases for alienation the same.

Because the significance of an offense is dependent on whether or not the act was intentional, and because so many different kinds of intentionality and unintentionality exist, we can see that an offense *as such* tells us very little about the offender. All those who exhibit alienation from a gathering may share nothing but their alienation. With this understanding, then, one can proceed carefully to try to list some of the things that a situational impropriety can tell us about the person who commits it, aside from the fact that he is in some sense alienated from the gathering. What this amounts to is an isolation of the types of social unit, other than social occasions, that can be the objects of alienation.

1. Community

It is a fact that the individual's relationship to gatherings and social occasions sometimes tells us something about his relationships to broader units of social life. Thus, on Shetland Isle, the few men who did not bother to shave regularly were also the ones who refused to keep a tidy front yard, even in cases where their holdings were where visitors to the island would see the untidiness. The same individuals also declined to support the local socials in any regular way, and one of them sometimes worked on Sunday,[4] thus showing civic as well as situational insensitivity. Similarly, in a study of urban British lower-class ceremonial life, it is reported that members of the community defined "respectability" in terms of not borrowing money, not applying for unemployment assistance, and not making free with the neighbor's front door, and that this civic decorum was reflected in situational proprieties also:

One of the outstanding characteristics of the respectable people is that they are "particular," which implies that they try hard to

4. I would like to repeat that symbolic significance is involved here, and that therefore occasions could be found when Sunday work was permissible. Thus, the charitable job of helping a needy short-handed neighbor bring in his crop was quite permissible on Sunday, for in such a context Sunday labor became an expression of regard for the community, and a gesture of respect, not alienation.

maintain their standards in spite of adversities and difficulties. . . . While unemployment or other adversity enforces a limitation of expenditure, this does not, among the respectable, result in the complete abandonment of standards, for, as they say, "it's not how *much* you get, but what you *do* with it that matters."

The notion of "being particular" applies especially to children and to cleanliness. In hard times before the war, the children might have had to wear cast-off clothing, but at least, the women insisted, it was clean. "Every child is rough and ready some part of the day, but you *can* be particular." In another context, one informant who was commenting on the poor condition of her house, pointed out that she had at least tried to "cover up," by putting a newspaper over the fireplace and a curtain over the gap where the cupboard door should have been. "But the rough ones," she said, "don't even care about covering things up. You can't help having a poor or a broken-down house, but you can help keeping it looking nice."[5]

And certainly this tie-in between situational and other deviations is found among mental "prepatients"; an individual who ruminates all day on the sofa often turns out to be one who also offends by, for example, not keeping appointments or not bothering to put air in his car tires.

Further, as has already been discussed, an institutional role having its primary locus in one place may require the performer to carry marks of his membership wherever he goes, thereby setting him apart from the public at large, though often through no fault of his own. T. H. Pear provides examples of this in a discussion of the status symbolism of personal front:

A more serious question was debated; though, according to the newspaper accounts, obliquely, when a high-level conference in London discussed at considerable length, whether clergymen of the Church of England should wear laymen's clothing publicly at any time except when playing lawn-tennis or other approved games. Here is an example of the belief, held tacitly by many people, and recently stated in the case of an R.A.F. officer, that

5. M. Broady, "The Organisation of Coronation Street Parties," *Sociological Review*, 4 (1956) , 227.

holders of offices ought to be regarded as never off duty: that a publicly assigned role overshadows all others. There are echoes of this in the assumption in some schools, implied rather than stated, that a schoolboy outside the school premises, not wearing his school cap, is—or is about to be—up to no good. In the Army, "other ranks," but not officers, have "walking-out" dress; the implication that a pretty nurse-maid awaits the soldier is delightfully Victorian and West-end. The "civvies" of some National Service "other ranks" are carefully censored by the authorities, who justify it with understandable rationalisations about "Teddyboys."[6]

Where the individual employs such insignia not because of institutional regulation but because of personal election, the link between civic and situational alienation would seem to be especially evident. The insignia then become a kind of proclamation of distance from the ordinary course of social life, and of some sort of skewing of relationship to the public at large. Note, for instance, the self-imposed uniform worn by members of erupting social movements, such as the early European fascist groups. Something similar is seen among sailors who express their life-experience solidarity and their alienation from land society by placing a tattoo between themselves and the appearance-proprieties of the host culture.[7] Something of the same effect is obtained by college students and beatniks (and their fellow-travelers) who express distance from the employed adult population by a full beard,[8] or a two-day growth, and by bedraggled clothes. And although the dress pattern of young, male, urban Negro drug users may not be collegiate, this attire, too, seems to be linked to the maintenance of expressed distance.[9]

6. T. H. Pear, *Personality, Appearance and Speech* (London: Allen and Unwin, 1957) , p. 58.

7. See S. M. Ferguson-Rayport, R. M. Griffith, and E. W. Straus, "The Psychiatric Significance of Tattoos," *Psychiatric Quarterly,* 29 (1955) , 112-131.

8. A good description of the alienation implications of a beard can be found in L. Lipton, *The Holy Barbarians* (New York: Messner, 1959) , pp. 25-26.

9. See, for example, H. Finestone, "Cats, Kicks, and Color," *Social Problems,* 5 (1957) , 3.

The tabooed creature releases that usually provide evidence of insufficient situational presence seem to provide a favorite idiom for expressing some kind of disregard for broad elements of conventional society, pointing to the voluntary elaborations that can be made of acts that are supposedly involuntary. College students, for example, sometimes compete with each other in belching prowess, conveying something about their relation to the adult world in doing so. Preadolescent boys have a special game built around flatulence, which manages both to penalize the offender and to bypass civilian standards at the same time.

2. Social Establishments

Situational improprieties may also be employed as a means of expressing resentment that the offender may feel toward something more circumscribed than a class or a community, for example, the social establishment or institution in which he finds himself. Here, the "milieu" approach to institutional psychiatry has provided us with much data, as illustrated by the following statements:

> It would appear from the utilization of the unconventional incontinent response in the aforementioned situations that this response is a symbolic and obscure gesture on the part of the patients who have difficulty in expressing themselves at all or in expressing themselves clearly and directly. They utilize this response as a form of communication to convey the "unsatisfactory" character of their surrounding social milieu and their participation in it and the fact that certain important requirements are not being fulfilled.[10]

It should be noted here, however, that more careful examination of the nature and meaning of patients' acts indicated that much

10. M. S. Schwartz, "Social Interaction of a Disturbed Ward of a Hospital" (unpublished Ph.D. dissertation, Department of Sociology, University of Chicago, 1951) , p. 199. See also M. S. Schwartz and A. H. Stanton, "A Social Psychological Study of Incontinence," *Psychiatry*, 13 (1950) , 399-416.

of the grossly disturbed and disturbing behavior was more a manner of participating in an excessively restrictive and depriving hospital environment than an inherent part of psychotic illness. Most emotional outbursts appeared to be temporary, impulsive reactions of fear, anger, or overactivity, and were essentially self-limited when not aggravated by intervention of personnel.[11]

In mental hospitals, one of the most dramatic instances of establishment alienation is provided by the patient who is appropriately oriented in the situation in all visible ways while calmly doing a single thing that sets him quite outside the present reality. If deviant use of the involvement idiom provides a means of symbolizing alienation from the situation, these isolated incongruities seem to provide symbols of symbols—a kind of gesture or proclamation of alienation. Thus, at Central Hospital I have observed an otherwise well-demeaned (albeit mute) youth walking down the ward halls with a reasonably thoughtful look on his face and two pipes in his mouth; another conducted himself with similar nicety while chewing toothpaste; another, with soap on his shaved head; another, while smilingly walking backwards with a neatly folded towel on her head; another, with a ball of paper screwed into his right eye as a monocle; another, with a foot-long strip of woven newspaper dangling from his pocket. One patient would graciously accept tobacco for his pipe and then pop the offering into his mouth with a continued artful gesture of gratefulness for the smoke; another would quietly enter the cafeteria and eat his meals peacefully, departing when told to, and manage all this compliant behavior with a dinner-roll balanced on his head. Still another patient would act as if he were approaching a member of the staff for purposes of intelligent conversation, and would then mutter something in an affected English accent while showing that he had a cigarette butt stuck into his ear. And frequently patients would lie on benches in an ordinary relaxed

11. M. Greenblatt, R. H. York, and E. L. Brown, *From Custodial to Therapeutic Patient Care in Mental Hospitals* (New York: Russell Sage Foundation, 1955), p. 257.

manner while keeping a few fingers or an arm extended and stiff, showing that they were not giving in to actual relaxation. Sometimes these proclamations were made with a sly look on the patient's face, so that it appeared that he was more than ordinarily aware of the implications of his acts and was performing them with these implications in mind.

As already suggested, this situational self-sabotage often seems to represent one statement in an equation of defense. It seems that the patient sometimes feels that life on the ward is so degrading, so unjust, and so inhuman that the only self-respecting response is to treat ward life as if it were contemptibly beyond reality and beyond seriousness. This is done (it appears) by projecting a self that is correspondingly crazy and, as far as the actor is concerned, patently not his real self. Thereby the patient demonstrates, at least to himself, that his true self is not to be judged by its current setting and has not been subjugated or contaminated by it. On the same grounds, he implies that the conduct that was responsible for getting him into the hospital is equally not a valid representation of his real self. In short, the patient may pointedly act crazy in the hospital to make it clear to all decent people that he is obviously sane. This would account for the very knowing looks that such patients sometimes give sympathetic outsiders, which often seem to imply, "It's a ridiculous hideous world here, isn't it?"

The aim, then, of some of these bizarre acts is, no doubt, to demonstrate some kind of distance and insulation from the setting, and behind this, alienation from the establishment. And the means consist of communications about the allocation of one's involvement.

There is another type of attack on the establishment that might be mentioned; it is more clear cut, involving less of self-destructiveness and more of nose-thumbing. Again Central Hospital provides examples, as seen when a patient pushes back his chair and, one nostril at a time, methodically blows out mucus in a wide arc, or spits in the same parabolic manner, or flicks a lighted butt halfway across the dayroom while keeping a disdainful look on his face.[12] In effect, if not by intent, these "malicious" offenses are all gestures of contempt for the gathering and for the social organization in which it is housed.

While proclamations of alienation and gestures of situational contempt are certainly means by which the individual places some unapproved distance between himself and the establishment in which he finds himself, there is still the paradoxical fact that these acts may be symptomatic of deep concern about the establishment. For these are strategies by which the individual resolves the conflict between his presence in the gathering, and the reasons he has for showing alienation from it. If such solutions to the conflict were not found, the individual might well be forced to do something even more drastically improper.[13] The individual, in other words, is bothering to do something about his situational obligations, even though he is intentionally doing what is felt to be wrong. When an individual displays his alienation from a gathering by leafing through a magazine or pouring a drink when he should be listening to the talkers, the offensive act is at least keeping him from leaving the room entirely. There is a sense, then, in which those who actively dispute the proprieties governing a gathering show the gathering (and hence the encompassing establishment) more respect than do those who give no attention to it at all. It might be added that one underestimated difference between those who actively resist the demands in situations and those who fit in, is that resisters are likely to become consciously aware of social gatherings as an area of life in their own right, whereas conventional persons often maintain the rules consistently enough to remain unaware of the situational obligations their conduct sustains.

A further basis for alienation from the gathering is illustrated by those who seem so fearful of what is likely to happen to them,

12. To be classed here is the interesting side involvement reported in the newspapers in 1958—that of a well-known bridegroom who kept a cigarette in his mouth during the marriage ceremony.

13. Since funeral and wedding groups can be quite alienated from everyday society, their license to disrupt public order can be seen, perhaps, as a similar type of "working through."

and so anxious about what the situation may bring, that they cannot properly immerse themselves within the situation—they cannot give themselves up to the gathering appropriately. This occurs, of course, in any circle of persons at moments of social embarrassment. Extreme examples have already been cited in regard to mental patients who have difficulty in containing themselves in a legitimate main involvement; other instances of this kind can be given. Thus, a paranoid patient may be so distrustful of the setting as to carry on a hallucinatory conversation by whispering behind his hand, not trusting himself to speak openly even to someone not there. One patient observed had apparently felt at ease during the last eight years only when crouched in the deep-walled doorways leading from the sleeping rooms into the dayroom. When the ward was getting its daily mopping, the patient would scuttle from one doorway to the next, staying ahead of the cleaners but not trusting himself to the dayroom situation as such. Another patient would constantly attempt to withdraw from the situation by anxiously hiding her nose and eyes behind her hand. These patients gave the impression that something dangerous, like a plague or a small Balkan war, was going on in the dayroom. While the fears of these patients seem unrealistic, their responses nevertheless tell us something about what would happen if their concern were well founded. And this, in turn, tells us something about the kind of trustful relation one must have to those present if one is to sustain ordinary situational proprieties.

3. Social Relationships

In social establishments, as has already been suggested, a particular member may serve as guardian of situational order, being obliged to see that all present maintain a suitable allocation of involvement. A school teacher, for example, may interpret her pupils' noise and byplay as forms of impermissible involvement which challenge her dominance in the classroom. She may be called upon to bring to her classroom with a crack of the ruler the kind of order that a judge brings to his court by means of the gavel, and in her own way will be able to hold the unruly in contempt of court.

In such cases, certain kinds of involvement that are prohibited in the establishment may be presented as acts of interpersonal defiance and be understood as such. Sometimes such affronts are means of testing the limits, to determine how far the guardian can be pressed; sometimes, apparently, the offender may act in this way to see if the guardian will be true to him whatever he does.

The use of situational improprieties as a way of doing something about one's relation to an official in the situation is merely one illustration of the more general fact that situational niceties and offenses are constantly used as a reflection of some kind on one's relation to specific other individuals who are present.[14] This can be seen in the link in our society between the deference system and the involvement system, between degree of required interpersonal respect, on the one hand, and degree of tightness of conduct on the other. At home with his family, a lower-middle-class American may lounge in a chair, polish his eyeglasses with his shirt-tail, treat his children as if in many ways they were not really present, pick his nose, and be flatulent— the last, perhaps, only if his wife is not present. The same man in the same setting, but with his employer present, might be the very model of tight middle-class decorum.

Hence, when an individual wishes to show hostility to someone before whom he would ordinarily conduct himself tightly, extreme expressions of looseness become an available means. T. E. Lawrence, writing of life in an R.A.F. training depot, provides an illustration:

14. The study of the significance of minor bodily movements for the relationship of those present in a situation has been stimulated recently by Birdwhistell's work on "kinesics." Sociometry has been significant here, too. Again the most delicate data no doubt come from observations made by therapists concerning their interaction with patients.

... and so hot are our bellies that you will not wait three minutes in this hut of fifty-four men without hearing a loud spirtle
of wind from someone. "The cry of an imprisoned   ," they call
it: our surest humour, which may break the tension even of an
Armistice two minutes. The very sergeants shake with laughter
when one leaps out roundly: for farts are not punishable like any
other retort.[15]

Other, less institutionalized, variations on the same theme have
been recorded.[16] It should be added that if the relationship is
already one where informal looseness is appropriate, something
implying social distance can be expressed by reasserting tight
proprieties.

These aggressive devices are especially apt when the offender
and the victim cannot leave the scene (for whatever psychological or social reasons), for these devices allow the offender to remain in the situation with the target of his offense. That the
offender incidentally offends all others who enter the situation
is a price he must pay for his choice of weapon—and is sometimes connected with his eventual commitment to a mental
hospital. Correspondingly, if the individual chooses to use situational proprieties as a means of showing regard for a specific person, then, as was suggested earlier in connection with perfume,
others present will have to be allowed to share in this, too. In
any case, it is understandable that a standard mechanism in the
organization of involvement is found in the "by-your-leave" interchange whereby permission for relaxations is asked of and
given by, or proffered by and acknowledged to, the individual
present to whom marks of deference are due. In this way the
actor can partially disentangle the involvement structure from
the deference system.

Here, incidentally, is a pertinent type of dominance. The individual in the situation to whom the tightest conduct is owed
(as opposed to those to whom loose conduct is appropriate)

15. T. E. Lawrence, *The Mint* (London: Jonathan Cape, 1955), p. 38.
16. Some are reported in the brief note by A. S. Lorand, "Aggression and
Flatus," *International Journal of Psycho-Analysis*, 12 (1931), 368.

tends to "govern" the gathering regardless of the extent to which he is outnumbered by persons present who are on symmetrically familiar terms with one another and could act loosely were he not present. Thus, for example, the change men manifest in their conduct when women are present is not much influenced by how many women are present; often, one will do. Similarly, at Shetland Isle socials, after the games and presentations of awards had been run through, and the dance had begun, *all* the adult gentry tended to leave. Apparently they felt that, if even one should remain, his presence might cause the whole occasion to keep time to too slow a tune. This kind of dominance seems to be at the base of our understanding about what can be accomplished by the presence of one chaperone.

In situations where only two persons are present, situational proprieties are likely to carry a particularly heavy load of relationship information, especially, perhaps, in the handling of side involvements.[17] Thus, prostitutes have been said to demonstrate disregard for their clients by smoking or doing their nails during the transaction of business, and men have been reported to counter this move by leaving their hats on during the engagement.

The relationship between situational improprieties and the offender's emotional involvement in particular witnesses is, of course, something about which psychiatrists of the Sullivanian persuasion have given us much information. Some psychiatrists, in fact, would see this as the central problem in a consideration of improprieties.[18] A very important example that fits this analysis is the domestic behavioral disorganization that often characterizes an individual just before his family finds it necessary to commit him. While the difficulty he is having may well be caused by his relation to his spouse or parents, the expressions largely available to him, if he is not to desert the home, involve

17. See *Encounters,* p. 40.
18. For an example of the psychiatric analysis of improprieties, see S. Feldman, *Mannerisms of Speech and Gestures in Everyday Life* (New York: International Universities Press, 1959), esp. Part 2, "Gestures and Other Nonverbal Expressions."

the rejection of domestic situational duties. It is open to him to become, in the language of case histories, slovenly, lazy, unclean, preoccupied, inattentive, careless, vulgar, sleepless or too sleepy, unconcerned with the tidy care of the children, and so forth. The "recovery" of some of these offenders, when they find themselves in a hospital setting, is sometimes due, of course, not to the security and therapy claimed for these institutions, but to the fact, which psychiatrists themselves often point out, that the special targets for the offense are no longer present.

4. Engagements

It need only be noted that improprieties can, of course, occur because the individual is alienated, or wants to appear alienated, from an on-going engagement. Examples can be found during group psychotherapy sessions in mental hospitals, where patients, coerced to participate, may pointedly read magazines or play solitaire.[19]

I have suggested that a situational impropriety can convey to its witnesses, justifiably or not, that the actor is alienated not so much from the gathering as from his community, or his establishment, or his intimates, or his conversation. However, we must be quite clear that, no matter how distant or broad the target of an offense, the idiom in this case is first of all a means of expressing alienation from or attachment to the gathering that is present. Anything else the individual thus conveys, however much it constitutes the crucial implication of his act, must be superimposed upon these original situational meanings. Whatever the social unit to which the individual is concerned to indicate his relationship, many of the signs he must rely on will be written entirely in a situational language. Because of this tendency for the situational idiom to be made a convenience of

19. See, for example, H. A. Wilmer, *Social Psychiatry in Action* (Springfield, Ill.: Charles C Thomas, 1958), p. 262 ff. Wilmer's book, like some others on group psychotherapy, provides very useful material on the structure and dynamics of large-number engagements.

and pressed into service as the language of relationship, it is at once more and less important than we might at first perceive.

We can now come to the conclusions and to the point where the sociologist might find cause to nibble at the psychiatric hand that feeds him data. For while psychiatry forcibly directs our attention to situational improprieties, there appear to be ways in which psychiatry embodies and rationalizes lay attitudes toward this aspect of conduct, instead of carrying us beyond these conceptions.

At present, the psychiatrist who carries an appreciable load of diagnostic and commitment work in an office or hospital tends to give weight to his own spontaneous response to the conduct of the individual to whom he is giving a diagnostic interview, and it is largely in terms of this response that the psychiatrist decides whether the behavior of the subject is appropriate or inappropriate in the situation. If the behavior is inappropriate, he decides whether it is to be placed in one of the nonsymptomatic classes of situational impropriety,[20] or whether it betokens mental illness. In this, of course, he is acting somewhat like a layman, however expert his analysis of the psychodynamic implications of a particular impropriety, because while everyone in the society also makes these distinctions, there is no great consensus, especially in regard to the milder offenses, as to how the distinctions should be applied. In brief, it can be argued that the distinction between symptomatic and nonsymptomatic impropriety is a thoroughly ingrained mode of thinking in our society, leading us to divide up any set of improprieties in this twofold way regardless of the goodness of the fit or even its relevance.

20. Some of the grounds already suggested for nonsymptomatic impropriety are: accidents (defining these as inappropriate behavior which the actor could and would have avoided had he known in advance that he was to act thusly); temporary emotional states involving tiredness, nervousness, inebriation, and the like; understandable preoccupation, as when an expectant father cannot submerge himself properly in a situation; organic but not mental conditions, as when a deaf person cannot orient himself properly in a situation; or circumstantial conditions, as when an individual is unfamiliar with the ritual idiom of the persons he finds himself amongst.

This dichotomizing tendency is, of course, heavily reinforced by our institutional arrangements, for, after all, an individual who conducts himself improperly must either be placed in a mental hospital or not placed in a mental hospital, and in either case an appropriate rationale must be provided, since the differential consequences for the offender and his kin are very great.

Like everyone else, the psychiatrist is apt to interpret some conduct as improper merely because he is not familiar with the involvement idiom and the involvement rulings of the culture of the group from which the patient comes. It is possible to observe, for example, a male, lower-middle-class, middle-aged, Jewish, refugee psychiatrist make confident detailed judgments about the symptomatic significance of the affective tone of a female, lower-class, adolescent, Negro patient—an interesting achievement, since there are not many engagements in which both of these persons could find the immediate presence or the conduct of the other a natural, easeful thing. Similarly, those who know a mental patient slightly, and see him only during fleeting encounters, are likely to interpret one set of acts as symptomatic of his mental disorder, while those who have lived with him are likely to pass by these acts and focus upon others.[21] So, also, acts that appear to be signs of mental disorder to an outsider, such as the sight of mental patients lying on the floor or taking food from a neighbor's plate, can become normatively natural when, having become familiar with the behavior setting, one learns that the floor is used because the benches are hard or of insufficient number, and that, since no one owns the food, and there is sometimes enough of it, one might as well pick it from the neighbors' plates as stand in line for more. And from psychiatrists themselves one learns that the most regressive "primitive" kind of act can sometimes eventually be "understood" in such a way that its bizarre "meaningless" quality recedes and its pathetic human quality becomes evident.

21. A treatment of these issues may be found in C. G. Schwartz, "Perspectives on Deviance—Wives' Definitions of Their Husbands' Mental Illness," *Psychiatry*, 20 (1957), 275-291.

But it can be claimed that all of these questions are merely qualifications, and that the basic position of layman and psychiatrist is still sound: it can be argued that the important thing about some improprieties is not that the rules have been broken, but that the offender elected, or had cause, to do so odd a thing as to break these particular rules. There is concern when an individual responds to an unpleasant event by falling into a catatonic stupor, but obviously our concern (it is claimed) is and should be for what has happened to the mind of the offender, not for what has happened to the gathering in which the stupor occurs. It can also be claimed that the more grievously the individual offends the prevailing rulings, the more profoundly is his underlying personality damaged and the more profoundly is he sick, although this claim is more the operating assumption of administrative and office psychiatry than it is the avowed doctrine of Freudian psychodynamics. A good example here is the person with Huntington's chorea, whose gradual social deterioration is claimed to reflect an irreversible gradual loss in basic organic capacity for being a human being.

No doubt there is much truth in this position, but none the less a supplementary, if not alternative, sociological argument should be introduced alongside it.

A particular gathering, as a gathering, may have hardly any significance at all. (The several individuals who make up the gathering will, of course, have human significance in their own right.) Taken together, however, gatherings have great significance, for it is through these comings together that much of our social life is organized. Additional concern for the rules governing behavior in social situations derives from the fact that infractions may be taken as a sign that the offender cannot be trusted to refrain from exploiting his position in the situation for purposes of assault, interference, or accosting, even though the original infraction itself may be felt to be harmless. Hence, those who practice a particular involvement idiom are likely to sense that their rules for participating in gatherings are crucial for society's well-being—that these rules are natural, inviolable, and fundamentally right. And these persons will need some means of defending themselves against the doubts that are cast on these rules by persons who break them. The greater the infringement, the greater will be the need for this compensative defense.

One way of correcting situational offenses is to look upon the offender as someone who is unnatural, who is not quite a human being, for then the offense becomes a reflection on him and not on what he has offended. To the degree that the broken rule is important for the organization of gatherings, to that extent and in that measure there will be a need to treat its infraction as a profound indictment of the self or being of the offender. Current psychiatric diagnosis and treatment—in practice, although not according to some psychological theories—offer this way out, although the offender is accused of psychological sickness, not of witlessness or possession by the devil. Here, apparently, the relatively small number of organic cases that in fact support this view can be used as the basis of a not too conscious model.[22]

Psychiatrists seem little to suspect that they assume and support a kind of prearranged harmony that is almost too good to be true. For what can be more pleasing to one's sense that all is right with the world than to be given scientific evidence that the kind of bad behavior we cannot explain by our other methods is simply due to the sickness of the person who so behaves, and that, naturally, the worse he behaves, the sicker he is? Whatever psychiatry does, then, for the offender—and this varies greatly—it functions additionally to protect the sanctity of the social occasion and the sentiments of the participants. This is an important service. We *need* to think that situational offenders are sick; sometimes, of course, it may be demonstrable that they really are sick, but even then this demonstrability may not be the reason for our thinking them so.

If the position is taken that many nonorganic "functional"

22. See E. Goffman, "The Medical Model and Mental Hospitalization," *Asylums* (New York: Doubleday Anchor, 1961), esp. pp. 351-352.

forms of mental disorder are not forms of sickness at all, but a class of situational offenses that is punished and neutralized by the imputation of illness, then certain difficulties in the lay-psychiatric perspective can be resolved.

One of these difficulties is that the manner of a patient classified as "regressed" seems without fail to give us the impression that he is utterly and irrevocably different from ordinary human beings—a feeling, incidentally, that sociologists are familiar with from their studies of castes and social classes. This view is associated with the lay-psychiatric assumption that an appropriate level of animation and situational orientation is the natural human state, and that a catatonic-like stillness must be caused by something specific, or at least constitute something specific that must be explained. Thus when the patient "comes out of it," as he usually does, there is really no very satisfactory way to integrate our present image of him with the past one. Nor can we explain how it is possible for some patients who seem quite out of contact suddenly to give someone a too-knowing wink or express a feeling that is a little too meaningful to be discounted. These discrepancies might be handled sociologically by assuming that the patient had never "gone into" anything in the first place, and that, therefore, there was nothing for him to come out of. It might be claimed that once an individual releases himself from respect for social gatherings, for whichever of the multitude of possible reasons, then immobility (or, for that matter, motor excitement) becomes a convenient stance, and that what really needs explaining is our normative level of appropriate animation—even though there are only rare exceptions to its maintenance. Of course we need to know what it is that places an individual outside the claims of a gathering, and certainly such alienation is sometimes a symptom of a deep disturbance in the personality; but our attitude to the situational proprieties that we ourselves religiously sustain makes us bad students of impropriety. We can agree with the lay-psychiatric approach that the human personality has an organic base and ordinarily cannot be expected to undergo fundamental change very quickly, but then we must look elsewhere for an explanation of sudden changes in the patient's "condition." And when we do look elsewhere we find that what can and does change utterly and at a moment's notice is the propriety of his situational conduct and his choice of strategies for expressing his relation to those about him. Both the latter changes may, of course, come slowly, but every normal human being has the capacity at a moment's notice to dynamite the proprieties in a situation.

A further illustration of the difficulties of the lay-psychiatric approach may be cited. As has been previously suggested, the notion that "functional mental disorders" are instances of sickness similar in certain ways to the sickness exhibited by a paretic is partly based on the fact that in many cases it is extremely difficult to discover from behavior alone whether an individual patient is suffering from an organic or functional psychosis. The assumption seems to be that the misbehavior of organically diseased patients is thoroughly symptomatic, and that if functionals exhibit these behaviors, too, it can at least be said of them that they are conducting themselves symptomatically. How a psychogenically-based disorder can give rise to a whole pattern of behavior similar to that seen in organic cases is not explained. But in terms of the sociology of situations, surely this happy coincidence between organic and functional behavioral symptoms is only to be expected. Whatever the diverse grounds —social or organic—of deviance, there is usually only one set of situational rules that apply within a given situation. And it is just these rules that must be broken if eventful deviation is to be perceived, whether this deviation is called a symptom or not. Take, for example, the form of possession called "weré" of the Shango cult in Trinidad:

> Finally, a form of possession known as "weré" occurs with some frequency. Individuals in this state are considered "messengers of the powers." Weré possession is a half-way state between full possession and normal behavior, and a high degree of consciousness is retained. It is marked by disobeying ceremonial regulations by such acts as smoking, swearing, or mocking sacred places

by spitting on the *tombs* of the powers. The behavior becomes extremely childish; the possessed may speak with a marked lisp, wet or soil himself, and use vulgar language and gestures. He is treated tolerantly by onlookers, as one might treat a naughty but loved child. One person in this state maintained that he had just landed from "New York Thity" and that his plane was parked outside the gate. He cordially invited all available females to examine the inside of the plane with him (evoking gales of hysterical laughter from all present) .[23]

It is possible to view this kind of conduct as a form of transitory psychosis, but the more we learn about the qualifications required for engaging in this behavior, and the community position of those so qualified, the more we appreciate that the same vocabulary of improprieties must be relied upon regardless of the reasons and meaning of deviation. (This lesson, of course, has been taught by Freudian psychiatrists themselves, in their theory if not in their practice, in connection with the notion that a psychotic symptom can be a defense, and can be altered radically without changing the underlying psychopathology, while at the same time similar symptoms may be exhibited by persons of quite dissimilar psychopathology.)

Here, paradoxically, the comparative approach has perhaps done us some disservice. Psychiatrists visiting foreign countries often find the culture utterly strange and the language very difficult to understand. But often, too, they find the behavior of local mental patients perfectly familiar; once they are on a native back ward the visitors find themselves at home. Since they similarly find themselves in a familiar territory when looking in on a foreign operating room or observing a native case of measles, the tendency is to assume that what mental patients have is a medical kind of culture-free disorder. Here, however, the possibility might be entertained that some of the same rules of situational propriety may be basic to social gatherings in many different cultures. To the degree that there are these cross-

23. W. and F. Mischel, "Psychological Aspects of Spirit Possession," *American Anthropologist,* 60 (1958) , 252-253.

cultural uniformities, there are internationally recognized improprieties, and psychiatrists are in fact at home anywhere in the world.

A final example of the utility of the situational view may be suggested. In mental hospitals, we usually find that behavior is tolerated which would cause witnesses great anxiety on the outside. In fact, patients are often employed within the hospital community in the most exacting of tasks for persons of their socio-economic status, even while exhibiting the most garish situational improprieties. This functioning is called "a good hospital adjustment," and the apparent capacity of these patients tend to be attributed to the "protectiveness" of the hospital environment, an explanation that allows everyone to go on thinking of the patient as sick. Upon examination, however, we find that a basic way in which social life on the inside differs from that on the outside is that insiders are persons whose threat to the situational order has been beautifully met by according them the status, with its accompanying incarceration and stigmatization, of hospitalized mental patients. There is no need to sanction negatively each infraction because the very setting in which these infractions occur is, in itself, a continuous negative sanction. The infraction is something that has been paid for in advance. What was dangerously offensive to the public weal on the outside is an unimportant thing on the inside. The patients who actually come to like the hospital life may do so partly for this very reason. Being thoroughly accused of insanity, they need not fear the profound humiliation and embarrassment which often follows when this accusation is made by previously unsuspecting people.

A situational analysis, then, suggests some alternatives to the psychiatric view, but in so doing points up the social functions of the medical model. Psychiatry and mental hospitalization in part can serve as the therapy that our society gives to its threatened proprieties. But this is, alas, a costly cure, one part of which is grimly borne by the state, and one part by the offender.

There remains at least one serious question. Granted that

symptoms of mental disorder are often instances of situational impropriety, it cannot be because of this (it is argued) that psychiatry is concerned, because there are other situational offenses and situational licenses with which it is not concerned. Insolence, contempt, indifference, presumption—all are qualities expressed through situational impropriety, and yet it is appreciated that persons expressing these qualities need not be sick. Similarly, men at conventions may indulge in all kinds of antics; but no one would automatically claim that such persons were insane. So, too, there have been notable aristocratic eccentrics who have affronted many proprieties and in spite of this escaped the charge of insanity. "Given the situation," one would say, all of these antics are understandable and perfectly consistent with mental health.

A problem here is the term "situation," for in this context it has a special meaning. The situation's gathering, as used in this report, is affronted in many of these cases. But the social circumstances of the offender are such as to render him immune to penalization. Whether we deal with one offender or with a group of them indulging jointly in the same offensive practice is not the issue; the question is whether the offender is in a position to prevent action being taken against him. Many people commit situational offenses. Society, indeed, might get hopelessly clogged without such deviation. A mental symptom, however, is a situational offense that the offender does not get away with; he is in a position neither to force others to accept the affront nor to convince them that other explanatory grounds ought to be accepted.

Situational requirements are of a moral character: the individual is obliged to maintain them; he is expected to desire to do so; and if he fails, some kind of public cognizance is taken of his failure. But once this character of situational obligations is granted, we must see that a study of them leads off in many different directions. We may expect to find many different motives for complying with them, many different reasons for breaking them, many different ways of concealing or excusing infractions, many different ways of dealing with offenders. We may also expect to find that rules maintained or broken before one audience will not be handled in the same way by the same person when he is before another audience. And, of course, we find that an involvement ruling upheld in one community will not be honored in the next. One theme of this study, then, is that a moral rule is not something that can be used as a means of dichotomizing the world into upholders and offenders. Indeed, the more comparative information we gather about a moral rule, the less easy it becomes to make statements about an individual who breaks it. Certainly we should hesitate to accept without further evidence the common-sense and psychiatric view that there is a unique class of situational offenses that requires the student to shift from the social plane to a special one bearing on the profoundest aspects of the personality.

If, then, we see inmates of mental hospitals as individuals who infringe involvement rules, and if we obtain a more sophisticated view of these rules, it will be possible to question somewhat the hard-earned conception that inmates necessarily are "sick persons." Even a loosely defined social gathering is still a tight little room; there are more doors leading out of it and more psychologically normal reasons for stepping through them than are dreamt of by those who are always loyal to situational society.

CHAPTER 15

Conclusions

THIS study has been concerned with behavior in public places, specifically that aspect of public order pertaining to the conduct of individuals by virtue of their presence among others. Only a segment of this conduct was considered. Regulations governing physical violence were hardly discussed, nor were those regulations pertaining to claims for substantial assistance that individuals in some societies can make upon strangers who are present. Moreover, I gave attention to only a few of the "circles of the self" which persons present draw around themselves, and for which the individual is obliged to show various forms of respect. Consideration was restricted to the regulation of communicative acts, both expressive and linguistic, and especially to acts whose significance extended beyond conversation-like circles to the situation at large. To be sure, the regulation of communication conduct is not all there is to public order, but certainly this regulation is important enough to consider on its own, with concepts tailored to its particular demands. A special concern was to show that the symptomatology of the "mentally ill" may sometimes have more to do with the structure of public order than with the nature of disordered minds.

In this report, three basic social units were employed, all three of which were interaction entities. One was a *face engage-*

ment or encounter, consisting of a circle, typically conversational, where a single focus of visual and cognitive attention is ratified as mutually binding on participants. Another was a *social occasion,* consisting of the wider social-psychological unit that provides the frame of reference in terms of which engagements occur. The third, and the only one treated in any detail, was a *social gathering.* At the beginning this was defined as the full set of persons mutually present to one another during any one continuous period of time, their presence staking out a *social situation;* namely, an environment of monitoring possibilities anywhere within which an entrant would become a participant in the gathering stationed therein. Near the end of the study the concept of the "gathering" began to take on added meaning. By virtue of being in a social situation that is itself lodged within a social occasion, individuals modify their conduct in many normatively guided ways. The persons present to one another are thus transformed from a mere aggregate into a little society, a little group, a little deposit of social organization. Similarly, the modifications in their behavior which they suffer by virtue of finding themselves in a particular social situation— their enactment of situational proprieties—constitute, when taken together, a little social system. It may be added that when the term "social situation" is used in everyday life, it sometimes refers not to an environment of communication possibilities, but either to this little social system, this little social reality, that the persons present come to sustain, or to the subjectively meaningful transactions that they feel are occurring at the moment amongst them.

May I repeat: when in the presence of others, the individual is guided by a special set of rules, which have here been called situational proprieties. Upon examination, these rules prove to govern the allocation of the individual's involvement within the situation, as expressed through a conventionalized idiom of behavioral cues. This allocation entails appropriate handling of matters we can discern as occasioned main involvements, "aways," occult involvements, auto-involvements, mutual-involvements, margin of disinvolvement, and so forth. Through the governance of these rulings the individual finds that some of his capacity for involvement is reserved for the gathering as a whole (and behind this, its social occasion), as opposed to matters of concern to only a portion of those present or to those not present. This obligatory phrasing of involvement represents a kind of dutiful attachment to the gathering, a kind of belonging to it. The individual will find, then, that every participation in a social situation will represent one sense of what is meant by personal attachment. Starting with situational proprieties, we have ended up with the problem of attachment.

In the sociological study of different species of human organization, such as political movements, professional bodies, local communities, or families, it has proved very useful to put the question of appropriate personal attachment: in what ways is the member obliged to give himself up to the organization, and in what ways is he expected to hold himself off from it? This question helps us to see that the individual is known by the social bonds that hold him, and that through these bonds he is held to something that is a social entity with a boundary and a life substance of its own. In looking at behavior in social situations one finds that the same key question helps us to bring together and understand many of the scattered details of things we know about interactional activity. There is reason, then, to view a social gathering as a little society, one that gives body to a social occasion, and to view the niceties of social conduct as the institutionalized bonds that tie us to the gathering. There is reason to move from an interactional point of view to one that derives from the study of basic social structures. A social gathering may be only a filmy pinpoint of social organization, but however minuscule it is, there is reason to examine it sociologically. When we see the gathering as something that must embody the social occasion in which it occurs, we have some added reasons for giving it weight.

The broad conceptions that sociology brings to the study of human organization can be used, then, in thinking about occasions, gatherings, and encounters. Even the special coordinates employed in small-scale institutional analysis can be used—the language of role, position, status symbol, social relationship, formal and informal organization. A propriety that regulates the conduct of an individual can often be seen as regulating the conduct of an incumbent of a given position in a given organization. It might seem, then, that in order to talk about situational proprieties all that was needed was to add to the traditional list of role-expectations that inhere in given positions. And sometimes this was done, as for example in reference to such special institutionalized obligations as that of "keeping order."

However, when we try to study involvement obligations closely, a more basic kind of conceptual adjustment seems to be required. Face-to-face interaction takes place in its own kind of units, in what have here been called engagements, gatherings, and social occasions. A social establishment can be seen as a system of these units, just as it can be seen as a system of roles. But though an individual's organizational position will formally and informally influence his involvement obligations during interactions that occur within the organization, there need be no one-to-one relation between his place outside the interaction and his place within it. Persons who differ little in status within an organization may find themselves with quite different interaction obligations at a given moment; those with quite different statuses within the organization may find themselves currently cast in the same interaction role. Further, while it is true that conduct obligations vary from role to role within an organization, it is just as true that these obligations vary from one set of persons-present-to-one-another-in-roles-in-given-places to other such sets. And for some of these obligations the set of role-takers-in-interaction is a more natural unit than the individual role itself. Some rules of conduct can best be studied by looking at the conduct of the Chairman of the Board; but there are other rules that can best be studied by looking at Board meetings themselves. The study of situational obligations is different from the study of social role obligations.

Of course, as suggested, the individual may employ situational improprieties (and also proprieties) to say something about his relationship to a community, a social establishment, a kinship network, a two-person bond, and any other unit of social organization one might care to mention. And whatever his intent, those in his presence are likely to make interpretations of this kind about his conduct. In fact, whenever the individual comes into the immediate presence of a representative of a social organization of any kind, or into the witnessed presence of any symbol of the organization, he can hardly help but communicate something about his relationship to this organization. However, the idiom mainly available to him for expressing this relationship is, in the first instance, an idiom designed to express attachment to or alienation from social gatherings, and behind these, the social occasions within whose compass they occur. A man who attends a social party with a two-day growth of beard may be seen (and sometimes correctly) as being alienated from his wife, or his host, or his social circle, or the profession to which the male guests belong, or the community at large. But these are superimposed meanings, for in the first instance his impropriety pertains to the social occasion, and to the rulings designed to regulate conduct in social situations that occur within the occasion. Whether the intended target of his offensive act is but one of the persons present or, at the other extreme, the wider community incorporating many persons who are absent, it is all those present, and only those present, who are the *immediate* recipients of the offense. And while they may be prepared to understand sympathetically that the offense was not intended for the gathering which they together constitute, this understanding is not automatic, but depends, rather, on special information and a special effort at interpretation.

Finally, it should be said that although the individual is in a position to show attachment to (and alienation from) the gathering in which he finds himself, and although attachment is a very standard sociological theme, still, in the case of social occasions, this attachment is of a very special kind. Gatherings are things going on at the moment, from moment to moment, and thus evidence of one's attachment must be immediate and continuous. Further, this attachment does not involve the committing of such things as one's financial resources or promises to work in the future, but rather one's attention, interest, and orientation—in short, one's capacity for involvement.

Given, then, an interaction frame of reference that is related to institutional analysis but analytically distinct from it, the main lines of interaction analysis can be laid out. We look within an act for the involvement it seems to express; we look to the involvement for the regulations by which it is bound; and we look to these regulations as a sign of what is owed to the gathering and its social occasion as realities in their own right.

In concluding, then, it should be admitted that the merely-situated aspect of activity in a situation may often be much more important and substantial than the situational aspect. And it is true that the component of activity that is intimately regulated by involvement obligations is often picayune and petty. Yet it is out of these unpromising materials that the gossamer reality of social occasions is built. We find that our little inhibitions are carefully tied into a network, that the waste products of our serious activities are worked into a pattern, and that this network and this pattern are made to carry important social functions. Surely this is a credit to the thoroughness with which our lives are pressed into the service of society.

It seems typical of this use which society makes of its members that persons who neglect to show signs of respect for gatherings are often said to have no "pride" or to lack "self-respect." Here the implication is that an individual's capacity and willingness to sustain situational proprieties are so crucial to one's fundamental judgments of him that, should he decline to conduct himself properly, one must conclude that he is going against what he surely must feel to be his true self.

It has been argued, then, that what the individual thinks of as the niceties of social conduct are in fact rules for guiding him in his attachment to and detachment from social gatherings, the niceties themselves providing him the idiom for manifesting this. He often follows these rules with very little thought, paying what he feels is but a small tribute to convention. But should he be caught acting improperly, or catch others doing so, the embarrassment can be surprisingly deep. He may rationalize this response by reference to such things as the invidious class implications of uncouth acts (as when he becomes angered at someone for chewing gum too loudly, or for sniffling). But underlying this is the feeling that the other has not properly given himself up to the gathering, and, beyond the gathering itself, the social occasion. More than to any family or club, more than to any class or sex, more than to any nation, the individual belongs to gatherings, and he had best show that he is a member in good standing. The ultimate penalty for breaking the rules is harsh. Just as we fill our jails with those who transgress the legal order, so we partly fill our asylums with those who act unsuitably—the first kind of institution being used to protect our lives and property; the second, to protect our gatherings and occasions.